Essential law for information professionals

THIRD EDITION

Paul Pedley

facet publishing

Published by Facet Publishing,
7 Ridgmount Street, London WC1E 7AE
www.facetpublishing.co.uk

Facet Publishing is wholly owned by CILIP: the
Chartered Institute of Library and Information
Professionals.

First published 2003
Second edition 2006
This third edition 2011

344.41092
PED

Text printed on FSC accredited material.

British Library Cataloguing in Publication Data
A catalogue record for this book is available from
the British Library.

ISBN 978-1-85604-769-2

Typeset in 10/13 pt Aldine 401 and Humanist
521 by Flagholme Publishing Services.
Printed and made in Great Britain by CPIGroup
(UK) Ltd, Croydon CR0 4YY.

Dedication

This book is dedicated to the memory of Justin Arundale. During what was then The Library Association's Members' Day 2001, Justin approached me about jointly authoring a book on essential law for information professionals, and so this was his idea. I would very much like to record my thanks to him for his help, advice and encouragement during the initial planning stages. But before he had a chance to contribute to the book, Justin died (on 12 September 2002). As a result, I missed the opportunity that we would otherwise have had of being able to continue the exchange of ideas and thoughts about a topic that both of us had found to be so interesting.

Contents

Disclaimer

Paul Pedley is not a lawyer and is not able to give legal advice. The contents of this book are intended to raise awareness of key legal issues affecting information professionals, but the book does not constitute legal advice and should not be relied upon in that way.

Copyright notice

List of figures and tables

Copyright

Table

Box

Legal deposit

Breach of confidence

Patents, trade marks and design right

Contracts and licensing agreements

Data protection

Privacy

Freedom of information

The Information Commissioner

Human rights

The reuse of public sector information

Cybercrime and computer misuse

Disability discrimination

Other legal issues relevant to librarians

Table of statutes, etc.

Acts of Parliament

Statutory Instruments

International treaties and conventions

European directives

European regulations

European decisions

COM DOCS

Table of cases

NB Where the page number is shown in **bold**, this indicates that there is a case summary displayed in a text box.

Abbreviations

AA	Automobile Association
AC	Appeal Cases
ACTA	Anti-Counterfeiting Trade Agreement
ALCS	Authors' Licensing and Collecting Society
All ER	All England Law Reports
ALPSP	Association of Learned and Professional Society Publishers
API	Application Programming Interface
APPSI	Advisory Panel on Public Sector Information
ARROW	Accessible Registries of Rights Information and Orphan Works towards Europeana
ASA	Advertising Standards Authority
ASIST	American Society for Information Science and Technology
BAILII	British and Irish Legal Information Institute
BBC	British Broadcasting Corporation
BL	British Library
BNP	British National Party
CACD	Court of Appeal, Criminal Division
CAP	Committee of Advertising Practice
CAUCE	Coalition Against Unsolicited Commercial E-mail
CCTV	Closed-Circuit Television
CDPA	Copyright Designs and Patents Act 1988
Ch.	Chancery Division
CILIP	Chartered Institute of Library and Information Professionals
CIPD	Chartered Institute of Personnel and Development
CIQM	Centre for Information Quality Management
CLA	Copyright Licensing Agency
CMA	Computer Misuse Act
CPS	Crown Prosecution Service
CPU	Central Processing Unit
DACS	Design and Artists Copyright Society
DCMS	Department for Culture Media and Sport
DEA	Digital Economy Act 2010
DoS	Denial-of-Service
DPA	Data Protection Act 1998
DPP	Director of Public Prosecutions
DRM	Digital Rights Management

EBLIDA	European Bureau of Library, Information and Documentation Associations
EBLR	Electronic Business Law Reports
EC	European Commission
ECDR	European Copyright and Design Reports
ECHR	European Convention on Human Rights
ECJ	European Court of Justice
ECR	European Court Reports
EEA	European Economic Area
EEC	European Economic Community
EIIA	European Information Industry Association
EIPR	European Intellectual Property Review
EIR	Environmental Information Regulations 2004
EIRENE	European Information Researchers Network
EMLR	Entertainment and Media Law Reports
ERO	Electoral Registration Officer
EU	European Union
EuroCAUCE	European Coalition Against Unsolicited Commercial E-mail
EWCA	England and Wales Court of Appeal
EWHC	England and Wales High Court
Fam.	Family Division
FAQs	frequently asked questions
FOB	Firms Out of Business
FOIA	Freedom of Information Act 2000
FOI(S)A	Freedom of Information (Scotland) Act 2002
FRA	European Union Agency for Fundamental Rights
FSA	Financial Services Authority
FSR	Fleet Street Reports
GATS	General Agreement on Trade in Services
GATT	General Agreement on Tariffs and Trade
GCHQ	Government Communications Headquarters
HaaS	Hardware as a Service
HCA	High Court of Australia
HMG	Her Majesty's Government
HMSO	Her Majesty's Stationery Office (now incorporated into The National Archives)
HRA	Human Rights Act 1998
HREOC	(Australia's) Human Rights and Equal Opportunities Commission
IaaS	Infrastructure as a Service
ICANN	Internet Corporation for Assigned Names and Numbers
ICO	Information Commissioner's Office

ICOLC	International Coalition of Library Consortia
IEHC	High Court of Ireland decisions
IFLA	International Federation of Library Associations
INPADOC	International Patent Documentation Center
INSPIRE	Infrastructure for Spatial Information in the European Community
IP	Internet Protocol
IPO	Intellectual Property Office
IPR	Intellectual Property Rights
ISP	Internet Service Provider
JISC	Joint Information Systems Committee
LACA	Libraries and Archives Copyright Alliance
LDLA	Legal Deposit Libraries Act 2003
LGR	Local Government Reports
LISU	Library and Information Statistics Unit
Mac & G	Macnaghten & Gordon's Chancery Reports
MILE	Metadata Image Library Exploration
MLA	Museums Libraries and Archives Council
MPA	Music Publishers Association
MPAA	Motion Picture Association of America
MSP	Member of the Scottish Parliament
NA	Narcotics Anonymous
NESLI	National Electronic Site Licence Initiative
NHS	National Health Service
NLA	Newspaper Licensing Agency
OECD	Organization for Economic Co-operation and Development
OFT	Office of Fair Trading
OHIM	Office for Harmonization of the Internal Market
OPAC	Online Public Access Catalogue
OPSI	Office for Public Sector Information (now incorporated into The National Archives)
OS	Ordnance Survey
PA	Publishers Association
PACE	Police and Criminal Evidence Act 1984
PCA	Press Clippings Agency
PCC	Patents County Court
PFI	Private Finance Initiative
PII	Professional Indemnity Insurance
PLS	Publishers Licensing Society
PRCA	Public Relations Consultants Association
PSIH	Public Sector Information Holders
QB	Queen's Bench Division

RCD	Registered Community Design
RFID	Radio Frequency Identification
RIPA	Regulation of Investigatory Powers Act 2000
RNIB	Royal National Institute of Blind People
RPC	Reports of Patent Cases
RUSA	Reference and User Services Association
SaaS	Software as a Service
SCIP	Strategic and Competitive Intelligence Professionals
SIS	Secret Intelligence Service
SMS	Short Message Service
SSID	Service Set Identifier
TLR	Times Law Reports
TPS	Telephone Preference Service
TRIPS	Trade Related Aspects of Intellectual Property Rights
TSO	The Stationery Office
UCC	Universal Copyright Convention
UCTA	Unfair Contract Terms Act 1977
UDRP	Uniform Domain-Name Dispute-Resolution Policy
UKHL	United Kingdom House of Lords
UKOP	United Kingdom Official Publications (a product published by TSO)
UKSC	United Kingdom Supreme Court
UNESCO	United Nations Educational, Scientific and Cultural Organization
URL	Uniform Resource Locator
USPTO	The United States Patent and Trademark Office
VAT	Value Added Tax
WATCH	Writers Artists and Their Copyright Holders
WIPO	World Intellectual Property Organization
WPA	Wi-Fi Protected Access
WTO	World Trade Organization

Glossary of terms

'Acquis communautaire'/copyright acquis – The body of EU law (or Community legislation).

Civil law – There are several different meanings for the phrase 'civil law'. Civil law – in contrast to criminal law – deals with disputes between individuals or organizations. The state's role is simply to provide the means by which they can be resolved.

  The phrase is also used in the context of the legal system, contrasting the civil law with the common law system. The civil law system is used by most of Continental Europe and parts of Latin America, and in this system the law is written down in statutes in a very logical and organized (codified) way across all the subject areas. In such systems, precedent (reference to previous judicial decisions) is not normally recognized as a source of law, although it can be used as a supplementary source.

Common law – English law is called common law because it aims to be the same, whichever court made the decision. It is based on the principle of deciding cases by precedent, rather than to written statutes drafted by legislative bodies.

Computer misuse – Can refer to a wide range of activities including accessing inappropriate material on the internet (such as pornographic material), inappropriate use of e-mail, hacking, spreading viruses, fraud, theft, copyright abuse, or the use of a computer to harass others.

Contract – A contract is an agreement between two or more parties. It creates a legally binding obligation upon the parties involved. It is a promise, or set of promises, which the law will enforce.

Criminal law – The branch of law that defines crimes and fixes punishments for them.

  A crime is an offence where the state acts against the individual in order to defend a collective interest. Punishments for crimes are fines, probation, community service or a prison sentence.

Cybercrime – The use of any computer networks to commit crime.

Cybersquatting – The deliberate registration of a domain name knowing that it is a name used by an existing party.

Defamation – The act of damaging the reputation of another by means of false or malicious communications, whether written or spoken.

Delict – A wilful wrong, similar to the common law concept of tort.

Denial-of-service attack (DoS) – Massive quantities of otherwise normal messages or page requests are sent to an internet host, with the result that the server is overloaded, is unable to deal with legitimate requests and in effect becomes unavailable.

Dooced – Being sacked for something you wrote on your personal blog or website.

Droit de suite ('artist's resale right') – A right which entitles authors and their successors in title to a percentage of the sale price, net of tax, whenever original works of art, in which copyright subsists, are re-sold in transactions involving art market professionals.

Escrow agreement – See **technology escrow agreement**, below.

Interdict – A Scottish term for a temporary restraint.

Legal deposit – The legal requirement for publishers to deposit with the British Library and the five other legal deposit libraries.

Lending – Making available for use for a limited period of time and not for direct or indirect economic or commercial advantage.

Libel – A written defamation.

Orphan works – Works where the rights holder is either difficult or even impossible to identify or locate.

Pharming – The ability to connect to a PC with the intention of retrieving 'sensitive' information and keystrokes, in order to trap log-in names and passwords.

Phishing – The fraudulent acquisition, through deception, of sensitive personal information such as passwords and credit card details, by masquerading as someone trustworthy with a genuine need for that information.

Precedent – The principle of deciding cases by reference to previous judicial decisions.

Prescribed library – The definition of prescribed library (as set out in Part A of Schedule 1 to The Copyright [Librarians and Archivists] [Copying of Copyright Material] Regulations 1989: SI 1989/1212) makes it clear that the library must be not-for-profit. The list set out in the Regulations includes:

- public libraries
- national libraries
- libraries of educational establishments
- parliamentary or governmental libraries
- local government libraries
- 'Any other library conducted for the purpose of facilitating or encouraging the study of bibliography, education, fine arts, history, languages, law, literature, medicine, music, philosophy, religion, science (including natural and social science) or technology, or administered by any establishment or organization which is conducted wholly or mainly for such a purpose' (see SI 1989/1212 Schedule 1 Part A (6)).
- Any library outside the UK which exists wholly or mainly to encourage the study of the above subjects.

Rental – Making something available for use for a limited period of time and for direct or indirect economic or commercial advantage.

Slander – Oral defamation; the use of the spoken word to injure another person's reputation.

Spoofed websites – A spoofed website is one which is deliberately designed to look like a legitimate site, sometimes using components from that legitimate site.

Spyware – A category of malicious software that is designed to intercept or take over control of a PC's operation without the knowledge or consent of the computer user. The term is used to refer to software that subverts the computer's operation for the benefit of a third party.

Sui generis – A Latin term which literally means 'of its own kind [or type]', constituting a class of its own. In relation to database rights it refers to the rights that were newly created in order to protect databases.

Technology escrow agreement – An arrangement between two or more contracting parties to provide an independent, trusted third party with the source code which would only be released by the trusted third party if particular contractual provisions are triggered (such as in the event of a service provider going into administration). It is a means of protecting against software vendor failure.

Tort – A civil wrong that provides individuals with a cause of action for damages in respect of the breach of a legal duty.

Walled gardens – Internet portals where the operators guarantee the quality of sites that can be accessed through them.

Introduction

The readership of this book is envisaged to include practitioners and academics. The book uses cases to illustrate legal principles and contextualize specific regulations in a deliberate attempt to present the reader with an approachable, digestible text to give them the information they need.

As far as practitioners are concerned, the book is aimed primarily at library and information professionals, but will also be of interest to staff working in the publishing and IT sectors, as well as anyone with an information governance role.

The book contains a number of figures and tables, including checklists. These are all designed to present relevant information on a topic in a succinct format, enabling readers to assimilate key points at a glance. Throughout the book, extensive notes and references are provided and most chapters provide a list of sources of further information. And there is a list of further reading for the book as a whole, listing a number of titles on various aspects of information law.

For academics this book provides a comprehensive picture of the law as it affects information management as well as an exploration of the fundamental principles that underlie practice.

The book is designed to be as accessible as possible with an index, a table of cases, a table of legislation, and a glossary of terms. The aim is to make it as easy as possible for readers to dip into the contents of the book when they have a particular issue or problem to research. In order to aid navigation the book uses symbols to identify two types of content. These are: (Tip) and Useful resource.

- denotes short pieces of advice which, if followed, should help the reader to reduce the level of exposure to legal risks.
- denotes material which it is felt should be drawn to the attention of the reader as being especially useful and of real practical value. Examples from the chapter on copyright include a copyright risk management calculator; guidance on what would constitute 'commercial' copying; and a tool to quickly check if your CLA licence covers particular titles.

When the first edition was published in 2003 it consisted of 12 chapters and 222 pages; this grew to 14 chapters and 278 pages in the second edition of 2006 (with the addition of chapters on the reuse of public sector information, human rights, and legal deposit) and it has now grown to 17 chapters, with a new chapter covering patents and trade marks; and a chapter looking at other legal issues relevant to librarians, which covers topics as diverse as the legal implications of cloud computing, stocking extremist/controversial literature, and the duty of local authorities to provide a comprehensive library service. The section on privacy has been expanded into a chapter in its own right.

The law is all-pervasive and has an impact on a wide range of information work. One way or another the law governs a whole wealth of different aspects of library and information management. Here are just a few examples:

1 The June 2008 CILIP survey on police, surveillance and libraries found that, of the 55 completed questionnaires received from library services in England, Wales and Scotland, 75% of the respondents reported incidents of police or other security agency activity with regard to libraries and their users. This raises a number of matters of professional ethics covering the issues of privacy, censorship, and freedom of access to information (see Section 17.2).

2 The use of fingerprints to manage book loans in school libraries raises a number of privacy issues (see Figure 11.2).

3 A member of the library staff at Manchester's Central Library stole rare books valued at £175,000 in order to sell them on the internet (see BBC News Online, 2006 and Section 17.5).

4 A librarian who refused to serve a library user whom she caught sharing sexual fantasies on a library computer was reported to be facing disciplinary action as a result whilst the library user was given an apology by the head of library services (See *The Times*, 2005 and Section 15.7).

5 A librarian at the University of Kent was the target of online bullying by students using the social networking site Facebook to ridicule him, referring to him as the 'little fat library man' (see BBC News Online, 23 July 2007).

6 In 2007 a report by think tank The Centre for Social Cohesion claimed that public libraries were inundated with extremist Islamic literature. The story was covered on an edition of 'Newsnight' (See BBC News Online, 2007). The Museums Libraries and Archives Council (MLA) subsequently developed guidance on the stocking of extremist material (see Section 17.4).

7 Local authorities are required under the Public Libraries and Museums Act of 1964 to provide a comprehensive library service. Library campaigners in a number of locations around the country have mounted legal challenges to library closures in the wake of cutbacks. A report in the *The Bookseller* told of how campaigners in Doncaster, Oxford and Lewisham were considering the use of judicial reviews. In the case of Brent libraries a judicial review ruled that the process the council had followed in reaching a decision to close six of its libraries had been reasonable (Bailey & Others v London Borough of Brent [2011] EWHC 2572 (Admin)). (See Further Legal Challenges to Library Closures Planned, *The Bookseller*, 10 January 2011; Section 17.7; and *Judicial Review for Gloucestershire Libraries Closure*, BBC News Online, 7 July 2011, www.bbc.co.uk/news/uk-england-gloucestershire-14064413.

CHAPTER 1

General law and background

Contents

1.1   Legal system

The United Kingdom consists of three distinct jurisdictions, each with its own court system and legal profession: England and Wales, Scotland, and Northern Ireland. The UK joined the European Economic Community (EEC) (now the European Union [EU]) in 1973, which means that we are required to incorporate European legislation into UK law, and to recognize the jurisdiction of the European Court of Justice (ECJ) in matters of EU law. The ECJ, broadly speaking, hears two types of case. One type relates to disputes between member states or actions brought by the Commission against member states. The other is 'preliminary rulings', where a court in a member state refers a point of EU law – the case then returns to the court of origin for a decision in light of the ruling.

When the Labour Party came to power in 1997, they embarked on a number of constitutional reforms. These included the introduction of freedom of information legislation, the implementation of the European Convention on Human Rights (ECHR) into UK law, and a programme of devolved government. We now have a separate Scottish Parliament and Welsh Assembly. Northern Ireland already had its own Assembly.

The Scottish Parliament legislates in areas of domestic policy, but matters best dealt with at UK level remain reserved to the UK Parliament and government. These include defence, foreign affairs, economic and fiscal policy, social security, employment law, and aspects of transport and energy policy.

The Government of Wales Act 1998 gave the Welsh Assembly powers to legislate in domestic areas and the Assembly's powers were strengthened under the

Government of Wales Act 2006, which sets out in Schedule 5 those areas that have been devolved. This excludes foreign affairs and defence, taxation, overall economic policy, energy, immigration and nationality. Legislation put forward by the Welsh Assembly Government is subject to scrutiny and approval by the National Assembly for Wales. Initially, the National Assembly didn't have full law-making powers and the Welsh Assembly could only pass subordinate legislation. However, a referendum was held on 3 March 2011 in which 63.49% of the votes cast were in favour of the motion: 'Do you want the Assembly now to be able to make laws on all matters in the 20 subject areas it has powers for?' (see www.aboutmyvote.co.uk/PDF/Wales-Referendum-Booklet-English-Final.pdf). As a result, the Welsh Assembly will be able to make laws, known as Acts of the Assembly, on all matters in the subject areas, without needing the UK Parliament's agreement.

The UK is a signatory of the ECHR (Council of Europe, 1950) and this was incorporated into UK law through the Human Rights Act 1998.

There is no written constitution as such for the UK. The constitutional law of the UK consists of statute law and case law. In November 2010 a draft Cabinet manual was published setting out the main laws, rules and conventions affecting the conduct and operation of government (Cabinet Office, 2011). Some commentators see this as a step towards a written constitution, whilst others see it merely as a document explaining how government operates.

In addition there are international treaties and conventions to which the UK is a signatory, which have binding force.

There are two basic systems of law: the common law system, which is used in England and Wales; and the civil law system, which is used by most of Continental Europe and parts of Latin America. The legal systems of England, Wales and Northern Ireland are very similar. Scotland has a hybrid system of civil and common law.

1.1.1   Common law system

English law is called common law because it aims to be the same, whichever court makes the decision. It began soon after the Norman Conquest of 1066, when the king and court travelled around the country hearing grievances. The common law system is based on the principle of deciding cases by reference to previous judicial decisions (known as 'precedents'), rather than to written statutes drafted by legislative bodies. A body of English law evolved from the 12th century onwards.

Reported cases present specific problems out of which a point of law is extracted. Formulation of the law is bottom-up from a specific event to a general principle. Judicial decisions accumulate around a particular kind of dispute and general rules or precedents emerge. These precedents are binding on other courts at the same or a lower level in the hierarchy. The same decision must result from another situation in which the material or relevant facts are the same. The law evolves by means of opinion changing as to which facts are relevant; and by novel situations arising.

1.1.2   Civil law system

The civil law system is used by most of Continental Europe and parts of Latin America. The law is written down in statutes in a very logical and organized (codified) way across all the subject areas. In such systems, precedent is not normally recognized as a source of law, although it can be used as a supplementary source. This results in a top-down system of a codified law book, which is based upon broad principles and then broken down into legal topics similar to those of the common law countries.

In the civil law system, case law is illustrative, as the court relies more on commentaries from professors and judges published in books and journal articles. The civil law system – which is based on ancient Roman law – arose from many countries being given the Napoleonic code when occupied during the Napoleonic era. Since then national laws have diverged, but remain basically similar.

1.2   Court system

England and Wales, Scotland, and Northern Ireland have their own hierarchy of courts, although they are all divided into two sections – criminal and civil.

1.2.1   England and Wales

The lowest criminal courts are the Magistrates' Courts, which deal with minor offences. More serious cases are heard in the Crown Court in front of a judge and jury. The Crown Court also hears cases that are appealed from the Magistrates' Courts on factual points. Cases can be appealed on points of law to the High Court (Queen's Bench Division [QBD]). Appeals against conviction and sentence go to the Court of Appeal, Criminal Division(CACD).

Civil cases at first instance are heard in the County Courts for minor claims. More serious cases are dealt with by the High Court, which is divided into three divisions:

1 The QBD hears civil claims involving tort, such as personal injury, other negligence actions and contracts.
2 The Chancery Division hears cases involving areas such as land, wills, and trusts; as well as intellectual property, company and tax cases.
3 The Family Division hears cases relating to family law, such as divorce.

Cases may be appealed to the Court of Appeal (Civil Division), and in turn these may be appealed to the Supreme Court. It should be noted, however, that appeals can only be brought with permission – either from the judge hearing the original case or from a Court of Appeal judge.

The Supreme Court hears appeals on arguable points of law of the greatest public importance, for the whole of the United Kingdom in civil cases, and for England, Wales and Northern Ireland in criminal cases. In October 2009 it replaced the system of Law Lords operating as a committee of the House of Lords as the highest court in the United Kingdom. Moving the UK's top court from Parliament was an integral part of demonstrating its independence from government.

In December 2010 the Supreme Court published a set of interim practice guidance on the use of live text-based forms of communication (including Twitter) from court for the purposes of fair and accurate reporting which said that the Justices of the Supreme Court were content with legal teams, journalists and members of the public communicating to the outside world what is happening in the courtroom; the exceptions being cases where there are formal reporting restrictions in place, family cases involving the welfare of a child, and cases where publication of proceedings might prejudice a pending jury trial. In such instances notices placed at the doors of the courtroom will indicate that restrictions are in place. The guidance was limited to the Supreme Court and took into account its unique role as the highest appeal court in the land. A consultation document on the use of live text-based forms of communication from the Supreme Court was launched in February 2011.

1.2.1.1 Judicial reviews

The QBD of the High Court has a supervisory role in which it is responsible for supervising subordinate bodies and tribunals in the exercise of their powers. This is achieved primarily by means of the procedure known as judicial review in which the decisions of any inferior court, tribunal or other decision-making public body may be challenged or called into question on any one of three possible grounds:

1 Illegality: where the decision-maker acted beyond their powers.
2 Unfairness: where there has been a procedural irregularity or breach of natural justice, such as not permitting applicants to put their case properly, or bias.
3 Irrationality: where the decision that has been reached is one that no properly informed decision-maker could rationally reach.

A couple of examples relevant to library and information professionals of where judicial reviews have been used to challenge legislation include the case of R v. Ealing, London Borough Council, ex parte Times Newspapers Ltd [1987] 85 LGR 316 where the decision of several libraries to ban *The Times* on political grounds (specifically, in support of print workers in an industrial dispute) was challenged (see Section 17.7) because of their legal duty under the Public Libraries and Museums Act 1964 to provide a comprehensive library service. A more recent example was British Telecommunications PLC and TalkTalk Telecom Group PLC v. Secretary of State for Business Innovation and Skills [2011] EWHC 1021 (Admin) in which BT and TalkTalk applied for a judicial review of the provisions in the Digital Economy Act 2010 governing the online infringement of copyright.

1.2.1.2 Civil court procedure

Procedure in the civil courts is governed by the Civil Procedure Rules, which took effect in April 1999, after the Woolf Report 'Access to Justice', which instigated the most wide-ranging changes to civil litigation since the turn of the 20th century. These were developed from a number of overriding objectives: the Rules sought to change the adversarial nature of litigation and to introduce a fairer, faster and cheaper system of civil justice in which the courts exercised more control over the proceedings.

1.2.2   Scotland

There are three levels of court procedure in criminal matters in Scotland. The lowest criminal courts are the District Courts, which are presided over by justices of the peace and in some cases stipendiary magistrates. These courts deal with minor offences such as breach of the peace and shoplifting, and their powers to sentence are limited.

Next are the Sheriff Courts, which deal with minor offences (where a sheriff presides), while more serious offences, except murder and rape, are dealt with by a sheriff sitting with a jury. A sheriff sitting alone has limited sentencing powers in comparison to a sheriff sitting with a jury.

The most serious criminal offences in Scotland are heard by the High Court of Justiciary. The principal forms of civil procedure in Scotland are small claims, summary cause and ordinary procedure in the Sheriff Court, and Court of Session procedure.

Small claims are intended to be simple and cheap and designed for claims where the value of the claim is up to (and including) £3000. Summary cause is for sums over £3000 and up to (and including) £5000. An ordinary cause action is a court procedure dealing with claims which have a value of more than £5000 or civil cases in the Sheriff Court that involve complicated law. Ordinary cause procedure and Court of Session procedure are more formal with full written pleadings.

The Outer House of the Court of Session can hear most types of civil case. The Inner House of the Court of Session is generally the court of appeal from the Outer House, sheriffs and certain tribunals. Thereafter appeals in civil cases can be made to the Supreme Court.

1.2.3   Northern Ireland

The highest court in Northern Ireland is the Court of Judicature, which consists of the Court of Appeal, the High Court and the Crown Court. There are then the lower courts: the County Courts with criminal and civil jurisdiction, and the Magistrates' Courts. Cases which start in either the Crown Court or the High Court can be appealed to the Court of Appeal in Belfast; and, where leave is given, to the Supreme Court of the United Kingdom. Cases which start in either the County Courts or the Magistrates' Courts can only be appealed as far as the Court of Appeal in Belfast; and, unlike the equivalent in England and Wales, this is not split into a Civil Division and a Criminal Division.

1.2.4   Tribunals

In addition to the courts there are also a number of specialized tribunals, which hear appeals on decisions made by various public bodies and government departments. Tribunals cover areas such as employment, immigration, social security, tax and land. Three tribunals relate to areas of law covered in this book:

1 The First-Tier Tribunal (Information Rights), formerly the Information Tribunal, hears appeals arising from decisions and notices issued by the Information Commissioner under the Freedom of Information Act 2000, the Data Protection Act 1998, the Privacy and Electronic Communications (EC Directive) Regulations 2003, and the Environmental Information Regulations 2004.
2 The Investigatory Powers Tribunal considers all complaints against the Intelligence Services (security service, Secret Intelligence Service [SIS] and Government Communications Headquarters [GCHQ]), and those against law enforcement agencies and public authorities in respect of powers granted by The Regulation of Investigatory Powers Act 2000 (RIPA); and considers proceedings brought under Section 7 of the Human Rights Act 1998 against the intelligence services and law enforcement agencies in respect of these powers.
3 The other tribunal relevant to the topics covered in this book is the Copyright Tribunal (see Section 2.5). In October 2010 the government announced its intention to merge the Copyright Tribunal with the Ministry of Justice's Tribunals Service.

1.3   Sources of law

Statutory legislation and case law are the primary sources of law, with textbooks, journal articles, encyclopedias, indices and digests making up a body of secondary sources.

Legislation in the UK can apply to the country as a whole; or, bearing in mind the impact of devolved government, there can also be Scottish legislation, Welsh legislation, and Northern Irish legislation.

United Kingdom primary legislation consists of public and general Acts; and local and personal Acts – such as ones that are of specific and limited nature – for example, the Manchester City Council Act 2010. Acts of Parliament typically have a section just before any schedules which is headed 'short title, commencement, extent' and which outlines the short title the Act is known by, the arrangements for the coming into force of the Act, and whether the Act applies to particular countries. Either there will be an extent section at the end of the Act setting out the geographical extent of the Act; or else it will be silent on the matter, in which case the Act applies to the whole of the UK.

When considering Acts of Parliament, one needs to ask whether an Act is yet in force – few Acts come into force immediately on being passed. The reader should look for a commencement section at the end of the Act (which would appear before any schedules). It will either give a specific day for commencement or else it will refer to 'a day to be appointed' which will then be prescribed in one or more commencement orders in the form of Statutory Instruments. If the Act doesn't contain a commencement section, this means that the Act came into force on the date it received the Royal Assent. Where an Act has been brought into force, the question to ask is whether the Act is still – wholly or partly – in force. This isn't always easy to establish. For example, an Act could be repealed by another Act, but one would then need to check whether the repealing Act has yet come into force.

There are a number of commercially available annotated versions of statutes such as Halsbury's Statutes, or the Blackstone's Statutes Series, or those available on the online services LexisNexis (www.lexisnexis.com) or Westlaw (www.westlaw.co.uk).

1.3.1   Progress of UK government legislation

UK government Bills can start in either the House of Commons or the House of Lords, although Bills whose main purpose is taxation or expenditure start in the House of Commons. Some Bills may have been preceded by a consultation document (Green Paper) and/or by a statement of policy (White Paper), although this is optional. Bills are broken up into clauses whereas Acts of Parliament are broken up into sections. In the introductory part of the Act it will set out its purpose in a series of provisions. For example, the Digital Economy Act 2010 (www.legislation.gov.uk/ukpga/2010/24/introduction) says:

An Act to make provision about the functions of the Office of Communications; to make provision about the online infringement of copyright and about penalties for infringement of copyright and performers' rights; to make provision about internet domain registries.

Her Majesty's Government's (HMG) code of practice on consultations (Better Regulation Executive, 2008) says that an impact assessment should be carried out where appropriate; and an earlier edition of the code of practice on written consultations (Cabinet Office, 2000) said that it would be appropriate where the regulatory proposals may create burdens for business, charities or voluntary organizations.

Bills are drafted by lawyers in the Office of the Parliamentary Counsel, which is part of the Cabinet Office. The Daily Order Paper contains a Notice of Presentation of the Bill and this is the first reading of the Bill. The Minister or a government whip then names a day for the Bill's second reading. The Bill is then allocated a Bill number and is printed by The Stationery Office (TSO) – for example, Localism Bill [HC] Bill 126 of Session 2010/11. The text of Bills can also be found on the internet (parliament.uk, 2011a). Explanatory notes are published to accompany Bills. These normally include a summary of the main purpose of the Bill and a commentary on individual clauses and schedules; for example, Localism Bill Explanatory Notes [HC] Bill 126-EN of Session 2010/11.

The second reading debate is announced by the Leader of the House in a Business Statement. The second reading is the time for the House to consider the principles of the Bill. The debate on second reading is printed in Hansard (parliament.uk, 2011b). After the second reading, the Bill has its Committee stage. This would normally take place in a Standing Committee, but it may be taken in a committee of the whole House or a Special Standing Committee depending on the nature of the Bill.

The next stage is the consideration or report stage. The House can make further amendments to the Bill at that stage, but does not consider the clauses and schedules to which no amendments have been tabled. The final Commons stage of the Bill is the third reading. This enables the House to take an overview of the Bill as amended in Committee. No amendments can be made at this stage. Once it has passed its third reading in the Commons, the Bill is then sent to the House of Lords.

The legislative process in the House of Lords is broadly similar to that in the House of Commons. However, there are a few important differences:

1 After the second reading, Bills are usually submitted to a committee of the whole House.
2 There is no guillotine, and debate on amendments is unrestricted.
3 Amendments can be made at the third reading as well as at committee and consideration stage.

The House of Lords and House of Commons must finally agree the text of each Bill. In practice, in order for this to happen a Bill can travel backwards and forwards between the two Houses several times. If the Lords have not amended a Commons Bill, they must inform the Commons of that fact.

Once the text of a Bill has been approved by both Houses, the Bill is then submitted for Royal Assent. The UK Parliament website (2011a) can be used in order to monitor the progress of Bills through Parliament.

Statutory Instruments are regulations, orders or rules made under the authority of an Act of Parliament. They often provide the detail required for the application of the Statute such as what forms to fill in, the level of fees to be paid or provisions for the commencement of an Act (i.e. when it comes into force). Statutory Instruments are 'revoked' rather than 'repealed'.

1.3.1.1 Sunset clauses

The Coalition Government (which came to power in May 2010) intends to ensure that each new regulation is subject to a sunset clause under which the regulations will be regularly reviewed. This will ensure that where regulations are no longer needed or impose disproportionate burdens on business or civil society they can be removed; whilst in other cases it will help to ensure that regulations are kept up to date. The first statutory review should normally be carried out and published no later than five years after the regulation comes into force; and where the regulation is subject to automatic expiry this should be no later than seven years after the regulations come into force.

In addition to primary legislation in the form of Acts of Parliament and secondary legislation in the form of Statutory Instruments, there is also a body of what one might refer to as 'quasi-legislation' and other regulatory materials. This would include statutory codes of practice, departmental circulars, and material emanating from governmental or non-governmental bodies that would have relevance in legal proceedings – particularly where questions of standards or reasonableness are in issue (see, for example, the codes of practice in Section 8.3).

1.3.2 Law reports

Cases in the courts are reported in numerous series of law reports. Until 1865, case reporting in England was undertaken by private court reporters, and the resultant publications were known as the nominate reports, because they were usually known by the name of the reporter. These have been gathered together in a collection called the English Reports. In 1865 the reporting of cases was systematized by the Incorporated Council of Law Reporting, which started publishing series of reports organized according to the court, collectively known as The Law Reports. These are recognized as being the most authoritative in the hierarchy of reports.

The main series of law reports in England and Wales are:

- The Law Reports 1865– (in four separate series: Chancery Division [Ch.], Appeal Cases [AC], Family Division [Fam.], Queen's Bench [QB])
- Weekly Law Reports 1954–
- All England Law Reports 1936– .

In Scotland, the Scottish Council of Law Reporting (a non-profit-making body) produces the most authoritative reports, but commercial publishing companies undertake most reporting.

The main reports are the Session Cases and these commenced in their present form in 1907. Previously, like the English Law Reports, the reports were known by the names of the court reporter and were collectively referred to as the nominate reports.

The other common reports are:

- Scots Law Times
- Scottish Civil Law Reports 1987–
- Scottish Criminal Case Reports 1981–
- Green's Weekly Digest 1986– .

In Northern Ireland the official law reports are the Northern Ireland Law Reports. There are also the Northern Ireland Judgments Bulletin, the Irish Reports and the Irish Law Times Reports.

In addition, there are many specialized reports covering different areas of law. The most comprehensive list of citations in the UK is Donald Raistrick's *Index to Legal Citations and Abbreviations* (2008).

The starting point for research on English law is Halsbury's Laws of England, and in Scotland it is Stair's Institutions of the Law of Scotland. When using sources of legal information it is vital to make sure that the books, journal articles or web pages you use are up to date, or that at the very least you are aware of the changes that have taken place since they were written.

 Bear in mind that the law is changing rapidly in the areas covered by this book. The free web-based sources may not have been annotated or amended, so it is often necessary to use commercial subscription services in order to get the most up-to-date information.

Textbooks and other secondary sources aren't formal sources of law, but they do nevertheless have relevance in the courts. Writings by highly regarded authors are frequently cited in court as persuasive sources.

There are a number of guides to law libraries and legal research. These include:

Clinch, P. (2010) *Legal Research: a practitioner's handbook*, Wildy, Simmonds & Hill.

Holborn, G. (2001) *Butterworths Legal Research Guide*, 2nd edn, Butterworths.

Knowles, J. (2009) *Effective Legal Research*, 2nd edn, Sweet & Maxwell.

Pester, D. (2003) *Finding Legal Information: a guide to print and electronic resources*, Chandos Publishing.

Thomas, P. A. and Knowles, J. (2001) *Dane & Thomas: how to use a law library*, 4th edn, Sweet & Maxwell.

1.3.3   Public international law

The law governing the legal relations between states is known as 'public international law' and it is distinct from internal domestic law. Public international law covers topics such as the recognition of states, the law of war, treaty making and diplomatic immunity. It can also apply to individuals where it operates at an international level but only through international courts and tribunals. This covers areas such as the law on asylum, human rights or war crimes. Sources of public international law include treaties and the case law of international courts and tribunals.

1.3.4   Websites

1.3.4.1 Parliamentary websites

- United Kingdom Parliament: www.parliament.uk.
- Northern Ireland Assembly: www.niassembly.gov.uk.
- Welsh Assembly Government : www.wales.gov.uk.
- Scottish Parliament: www.scottish.parliament.uk.
- Tynwald (Parliament of the Isle of Man): www.tynwald.org.im.

1.3.4.2 Government, legislation and law report sites

- Directgov is a portal to the websites of central government: www.direct.gov.uk.
- The texts of statutes and Statutory Instruments can be found here: www.legislation.gov.uk.
- TSO is an online index to TSO publications: www.tso.co.uk.
- Government News Network contains press releases of central government departments: http://nds.coi.gov.uk.
- Parliament website for Bills: http://services.parliament.uk/bills.
- BAILII (British and Irish Legal Information Institute) provides access to British and Irish legal cases and legislation: www.bailii.org.
- Supreme Court judgments: www.supremecourt.gov.uk/news/latest-judgments.html.

- Her Majesty's Courts Service: www.hmcourts-service.gov.uk.
- Scottish Court Service: www.scotcourts.gov.uk.
- Northern Ireland Courts and Tribunals Service: www.courtsni.gov.uk.

1.4   European Union

The first source of EU law are the treaties establishing the Communities and the Union, the subsequent amending treaties, and the treaties of accession of additional member states. Under the normal principles of public international law, the treaties require incorporation into UK domestic law. However, the novel feature of the European Communities Act 1972 was that it gave effect to all future obligations under Community law without further enactment. The second source of EU law is the secondary legislation made at Brussels, which forms part of UK law, as does the third source, the decisions of the ECJ at Luxembourg. The body of European Union law is known as the 'acquis communitaire'. European law consists of four main strands – treaties, regulations, directives and decisions – described in further detail in Sections 1.4.1 and 1.4.2.

1.4.1   Primary legislation

'Treaties' are referred to as the 'primary' legislation of the Community as they form the constitution and give the structure of institutions and extent of powers. The principles of European law derive from the 1957 Treaty of Rome, but this has been amended by a number of other treaties such as the Maastricht Treaty 1992 and the Treaty of Amsterdam 1997.

1.4.2   Secondary legislation

'Regulations' are binding in their entirety. They are directly applicable and do not need to be transposed into national law by the respective member states in order for them to take effect. An example of a regulation would be Regulation (EC) No 864/2007 on the law applicable to non-contractual obligations (Rome II).

'Directives' are the main form of substantive law. They are formulated by the European Commission, where they are subject to extensive consultation and are thereafter passed by a combination of the parliament and the Council of Ministers. Directives only state the effects to be achieved and many directives leave the practical application to national discretion, so one needs to be aware of the non-harmonized details. Directives only take effect when enacted into national laws, which usually takes several years. The period of implementation is normally prescribed by each directive.

Taking the copyright directive 2001/29/EC as an example: the directive was published in the Official Journal on 22 June 2001 and Article 13 of the directive states that 'member states shall bring into force the laws, regulations and administrative provisions necessary to comply with this directive before 22 December 2002'. In fact, the European Commission was keen for the copyright directive to come into force at roughly the same time as the electronic commerce directive, and for that reason the time allowed for implementation was 18 months rather than the period of 2 years that had been expected.

With the copyright directive, Article 5 on exceptions and limitations is an example of harmonized and non-harmonized details within a directive. Article 5 has one compulsory exception where the law is harmonized throughout the European Union, but the directive then provides for a series of optional exceptions from which member states can choose the ones that they wish to implement. Because those exceptions are optional, the law isn't harmonized across the Union as each member state can select a different mix of exceptions to implement within their own countries.

'Decisions' are from the Commission or the Council of Ministers, not from the ECJ. These are generally of restricted application and importance. Normally these are addressed to member states.

1.4.3   Gold plating

The United Kingdom is often said to be guilty of 'gold plating' with regard to European legislation, a term which refers to the practice of national bodies exceeding the terms of European Community directives when implementing them into national law. In the United Kingdom business lobbyists argue that the government often tags additional measures onto the back of European directives and in so doing puts UK business at a competitive disadvantage in relation to other EU states where directives are implemented more literally.

In a Department for Business Innovation and Skills press release of 15 December 2010 the government announced that it would put an end to gold plating and would instead copy out the text of European directives directly into UK law, saying that this direct copy out principle will mean that the way European law is interpreted will not unfairly restrict British companies.

HMG have set out a number of guiding principles that are aimed at ensuring the UK systematically transposes directives so that burdens are minimized and UK businesses are not put at a disadvantage to their European competitors (Department for Business, Innovation and Skills, 2011). One of the principles says that the government will include a statutory duty for ministerial review every five years.

1.5   Legal concepts/terminology

1.5.1   Criminal law

A crime is defined as an offence where the state acts against the individual to defend a collective interest. Criminal law is the branch of law that defines crimes and fixes punishments for them. The punishments are fines, probation, community service (which are seen as alternatives to custody) or a prison sentence. Also included in criminal law are rules and procedures for preventing and investigating crimes and prosecuting criminals, as well as the regulations governing the constitution of courts, the conduct of trials, the organization of police forces and the administration of penal institutions. In general, the criminal law of most modern societies classifies crimes as: offences against the safety of the society; offences against the administration of justice; offences against the public welfare; offences against property; and offences threatening the lives or safety of people.

1.5.2   Civil law

Civil law deals with disputes between individuals or organizations. The state's role is simply to provide the means by which they can be resolved. 'Civil law', in the context of distinguishing between civil law on the one hand and criminal law on the other, has a different meaning to that of the legal system known as the 'civil law system', which is used in most of Continental Europe (see Section 1.1.2). A civil claim results in a remedy, such as the payment of damages by way of compensation being granted to one party against the other, or restitution – injunction/interdict.

1.5.3   Tort (England, Wales, Northern Ireland)/Delict (Scotland)

When a contract (see Section 1.5.4) cannot apply, third-party agreements called torts might apply. These encompass mainly obligations and duties of care. These duties of care are owed to those foreseeably affected by one's actions, balanced by a concern not to extend this to remote and generalized effects. A standard test of reasonableness has to be applied, whereby you must take reasonable care to avoid all acts and omissions that you can reasonably foresee would be likely to injure your neighbour.

Torts are essentially civil wrongs that provide individuals with a cause of action for damages in respect of the breach of a legal duty. They include negligence, and, as far as information professionals are concerned, professional negligence covers things like the accuracy of information; and they would also include defamation. In deciding whether an information professional's actions were negligent, they would be judged against the actions of their fellow professionals (see Chapter 14).

Basically, rights in tort are civil rights of action that are available for the recovery of unliquidated damages by persons who have sustained injury or loss from acts or statements or omissions of others in breach of a duty or in contravention of a right imposed or conferred by law, rather than by contract. Damage includes economic as well as physical damage.

1.5.4   Contract law

A contract, in law, is an agreement that creates an obligation binding upon the parties involved. It is a promise or set of promises that the law will enforce. To constitute a valid contract, there must be two or more separate and definite parties to the contract. There must be an offer, acceptance, intention to create legal relations (and capacity to do so) and consideration (although consideration is not required in Scotland) supporting those promises. There has to be a mutual exchange of promises for a contract to arise.

In general, contracts may be either oral or written. Certain classes of contracts, however, in order to be enforceable, must be written and signed. These include contracts involving the sale and transfer of real estate, and contracts to guarantee or answer for the miscarriage, debt or default of another person.

In England, Wales and Northern Ireland, the Supply of Goods and Services Act 1982 implies terms into a contract, such as implying that the service must be carried out with reasonable care and skill. Customers in Scotland continue to rely on their common law rights. However, please note that the parties can agree that the implied rights should not apply to the provision of the service but any exclusion or restriction shall be subject to the terms of the Unfair Contract Terms Act 1977 (UCTA), www.legislation.gov.uk/ukpga/1977/50.

Under the UCTA a person cannot exclude or restrict his liability for death or personal injury resulting from negligence. Only if the exclusion clauses satisfy a test of reasonableness can someone exclude or restrict liability for other loss or damage resulting from negligence. It would be for the party seeking to impose a contract term to demonstrate to the court that it was reasonable, should they be challenged.

It should be noted, however, that the UCTA specifically excludes intellectual property rights from its main provisions. In Schedule 1 it says that so far as section 2 (negligence liability), section 3 (liability arising in contract), section 4 (unreasonable indemnity clauses), and section 7 (miscellaneous contracts under which goods pass) are concerned, they do not apply to any contract so far as it relates to the creation or transfer of a right or interest in any patent, trade mark, copyright [or design right], registered design, technical or commercial information or other intellectual property, or relates to the termination of any such right or interest.

The Unfair Terms in Consumer Contracts Regulations 1999: SI 1999/2083 provides that a term which has not been individually negotiated in a consumer contract is unfair if, contrary to the requirement of good faith, it causes a significant imbalance in the rights and obligations of the parties to the detriment of the consumer.

Chapter 6 considers contracts and licensing in more detail, especially as they relate to the work of information professionals, such as contracts for searching online databases or having access to proprietary information.

1.5.5 Property

The concept of property is formulated as an exclusionary right to prevent others from making use of either tangible or intangible 'things'. Intellectual property laws, for example, cover the areas of copyright, patents, trade and service marks, and designs. They specify rights to control who may copy, perform, show or play a work, reproduce an invention, or benefit from the creative promotion of a brand.

These property rights are qualified rather than absolute rights. The interests of other stakeholders, or a broad public interest will override, limit or in some way modify what can be done. Hence there will be exceptions to the exclusive intellectual property rights (IPRs).

1.6   Conclusions

It is important to recognize that where legal matters are concerned there are very few clearly right or wrong answers, hence the reason for many issues having to be resolved in court. Dealing with legal issues is often a matter of risk management and how organizations and individuals can minimize the risk of legal action being taken against them.

Throughout the UK, the law is uniform in many respects. The laws of England, Wales and Northern Ireland are particularly close, although there are a number of differences with the law of Scotland. This book is based upon the laws of the UK, and, whilst it will be of interest to information professionals working in other parts of the world, the reader should bear in mind that it is written from a UK perspective.

References

Better Regulation Executive (2008) *Code of Practice on Consultation*, www.berr.gov.uk/files/file47158.pdf.

Cabinet Office (2000) Referred to in www.bis.gov.uk/files/file47158.pdf.

Cabinet Office (2011*) Draft Cabinet Manual*, www.cabinetoffice.gov.uk/resource-library/cabinet-manual.

Council of Europe (1950) *The European Convention on Human Rights*, HRI, www.hri.org/docs/ECHR50.html.

Department for Business, Innovation and Skills (2011) *Transposition Guidance: how to implement European directives effectively*, www.bis.gov.uk/assets/biscore/better-regulation/docs/t/11-775-transposition-guidance.

Parliament.uk (2011a) *Bills Before Parliament 2010–11*, http://services.parliament.uk/bills.

Parliament.uk (2011b) *Hansard*, www.parliament.uk/business/publications/hansard.

Raistrick, D. (2008) *Index to Legal Citations and Abbreviations*, 3rd edn, Sweet & Maxwell.

CHAPTER 2

Copyright

Contents

2.1   General principles

Copyright is the right to prevent the copying of work that has been created by intellectual effort. It protects information and ideas where these have been reduced into the form of a 'work' (see Figure 2.1). Copyright is augmented by 'database right' – a *sui generis* right to prevent extraction and reutilization of all or a substantial part of a database.

Copyright subsists in:

- original literary, dramatic, musical or artistic works
- sound recordings, films or broadcasts
- the typographical arrangement of published editions.

Article 27 of the Universal Declaration of Human Rights (UN, 2011), adopted by the United Nations General Assembly on 10 December 1948, says:

(1) Everyone has the right freely to participate in the cultural life of the community, to enjoy the arts and to share in scientific advancement and its benefits.

(2) Everyone has the right to the protection of the moral and material interests resulting from any scientific, literary or artistic production of which he is the author.

Literary works	Books, poems, tables, compilations, computer programs, words of a song, letters, memoranda, e-mails
Artistic works	Paintings, drawings, diagrams, maps, charts, plans, engravings, etchings, lithographs, woodcuts, photographs, sculptures, collages, works of artistic craftsmanship
Dramatic works	Plays, libretto of an opera, works of dance/ choreography, mime
Musical works	Musical notation
Films	Videos
Broadcasts	Television and radio broadcasts, whether terrestrial, satellite
Typographical arrangement	Layout of published editions

Figure 2.1 *What is protected by copyright?*

There are clearly tensions between the need to give authors protection for their work and the need to allow people access to material for the betterment of society, to promote education, science and scholarship. That is why the monopoly rights that the law confers on the owners of copyright have a number of built-in safeguards. These include a number of permitted acts or copyright exceptions such as fair dealing (see Section 2.4.1). Another safeguard is putting a limit on the period of copyright protection, after which works enter the public domain. (The public domain comprises the body of all creative works in which no person or organization has any proprietary interest.)

Copyright protection is automatic. It is not necessary to go through a registration process before copyright can be claimed. The corollary of this is that there isn't a comprehensive database of works protected by copyright with details of their rights owners.

Legal deposit (see Chapter 3) is not a prerequisite for claiming copyright protection. One myth is that if there is no copyright symbol on a work then it is not protected by copyright. Most countries (164 states as at October 2011) around the world are signatories to the Berne Convention for the Protection of Literary and Artistic Works 1886 (www.wipo.int/treaties/en/ip/berne/), and this provides for the automatic protection of works, without any formality. The Universal Copyright Convention (UCC) of 1952 does require the use of the © symbol in order for works to have protection, but apart from the Lao People's Democratic Republic and Cambodia all the other signatories to the UCC are also signatories of the Berne Convention; and as Cambodia is a member of the World Trade Organization it is obliged to observe the terms of the Berne Convention which stipulates that copyright protection is automatic.

> Even though copyright protection is automatic, it is nevertheless advisable to put a copyright notice on a work that you create because this will serve as a reminder to those who make use of that work of the need to respect your rights. You could use the copyright notice to tell potential users both the nature and the amount of copying that you are willing to permit. For example: 'You are allowed to redistribute this newsletter in its entirety, on a non-commercial basis. This includes making it available (in full and as published) on your corporate intranet. However, individual sections may not be copied and/or distributed without the prior written agreement of the publishers.'

2.1.1 Copyright ownership

In general, the author of a work is the first owner of any copyright in it. However, where the work is made by an employee in the course of their employment, the employer is the first owner of any copyright in the work subject to any express written agreement to the contrary. This only applies to employees, not to contractors, so the mere fact that a work has been commissioned and paid for does not give the ownership of the copyright to the commissioning party. It is important, therefore, to ensure that appropriate mechanisms are in place to deal with the ownership of the rights in content. For example, an organization may wish to publish information on a website. That information may come from a number of sources such as external developers, consultants and internal employees. The organization in question will therefore need to be sure that it secures assignments of rights from any third parties, and it should also be certain that any employees created the content during the course of their employment. It is all too often the case in practice that assignments are not obtained, which can cause problems if the organization wishes to sell, copy or license any of the copyright. It is therefore of the utmost importance that organizations regularly audit their rights to ascertain any ownership difficulties.

2.2   Economic and moral rights

Section 16(1) of the Copyright, Designs and Patents Act 1988 (CDPA) sets out the 'economic' rights that a copyright owner has. These are the exclusive rights to:

* copy the work (which includes storing the work electronically)
* issue copies of the work to the public
* rent or lend the work to the public

- perform, show or play the work in public
- communicate the work to the public (by electronic means)
- make an adaptation or translation of the work.

If anyone other than the copyright owner does any of these activities without permission or licence, unless it is under one of the statutory exceptions, it would be a primary infringement of the copyright.

There are also some acts that could be said to be secondary infringements (CDPA ss22–6):

- importing an infringing copy
- possessing or dealing with an infringing copy
- providing the means for making infringing copies
- permitting the use of premises for infringing performance
- providing apparatus for infringing performance.

In addition to a series of economic rights, the author has a number of moral rights (see sections 77–85 of the CDPA):

- the right of paternity
- the right of integrity
- the right to object to false attribution
- the right of disclosure.

The right of paternity is the right of the author to be identified as such. This right of attribution or paternity is not infringed unless the author has asserted their right to be identified as the author of the work. That is why you will often find a statement at the beginning of a book along the lines of: 'Joe Bloggs asserts his right to be identified as the author of this work in accordance with the terms of the Copyright, Designs and Patents Act 1988 (CDPA).'

The right of integrity is the right of the author to prevent or object to derogatory treatment of their work. The right to object to false attribution is the right of persons not to have literary, dramatic or musical works falsely attributed to them; and this right applies both to copyright owners and non-copyright owners alike. The right of disclosure is the right to privacy of a person who commissions the taking of a photograph or the making of a film for private and domestic purposes.

There are a number of remedies available for copyright infringement, both civil and criminal. The Copyright, etc. and Trade Marks (Offences and Enforcement) Act 2002 was passed in order to harmonize and rationalize enforcement provisions dealing with copyright and trade mark theft. The maximum penalties for wilful copyright infringement were brought into line with those already provided for wilful trade mark infringement. Consequently, people could potentially face up to ten years in prison, where previously the maximum prison sentence was two years.

Section 42 of the Digital Economy Act 2010 increased the maximum statutory fine for offences under sections 107 (criminal liability for making or dealing with infringing articles) and 198 (criminal liability for making, dealing with or using illicit recordings) of the CDPA to £50,000.

The range of available remedies for infringement are set out in Chapter VI of the CDPA. These include damages, an injunction, delivery up of infringing copies, an account of profits, or an undertaking to take out an appropriate licence.

2.2.1 Risk management

Where copyright infringement occurs, people need to consider the risks involved. They should take into account not only the financial consequences of infringement, but also the potential risk of having a public relations disaster on their hands, and the damage that could be done to their organization's reputation.

⁌ Useful resource

A Joint Information Systems Committee (JISC)-funded project made available a risk-management calculator for open educational resources (web2rights, 2011) designed to help people understand the levels of risk associated with publishing open educational materials, www.web2rights.com/OERIPRSupport/risk-management-calculator/.

2.3 Legislative framework

The legislative and regulatory framework for UK copyright consists of four key components. These are:

1 International treaties and conventions to which the UK is a signatory.
2 European directives which the UK as a member state of the EU is obliged to implement.
3 UK legislation in the form of Acts of Parliament and Statutory Instruments.
4 Case law, which clarifies how the law applies in a particular set of circumstances.

2.3.1 Berne Convention

The 1886 Berne Copyright Convention for the Protection of Literary and Artistic Works is the main international agreement governing copyright. Most countries including the UK are signatories (164 states as at October 2011). A full contents list of the treaty can be found at www.wipo.int/treaties/en/ip/berne/trtdocs_ wo001.html. Under the convention authors are entitled to some basic rights of protection for their intellectual output.

Berne recognizes the need for people to have access to protected works and it allows exceptions and limitations to the exclusive rights (see Table 2.1), although these must pass a three-step test (see Figure 2.2). The test is significant, because a substantially similar form of words is used in Article 5(5) of Copyright Directive 2001/29/EC, which was implemented in the UK through the Copyright and Related Rights Regulations 2003 (SI 2003/2498). In short it means that any copyright exceptions or permitted acts are only allowed within UK copyright law so long as they meet this three step-test.

Table 2.1   Exclusive rights set out in the Berne Convention (as amended in Paris, 1971)

• translation	(article 8)
• reproduction	(article 9)
• public performance	(article 11)
• communication to the public	(article 11)
• recording of musical works	(article 13)
• broadcasting	(article 11)
• cinematic adaptations	(article 14)
• adaptations, arrangements, and other alterations	(article 12)
• moral rights	(article 6)

1.	that the exception only applies in special (defined) cases
2.	provided that such reproduction does not conflict with the normal exploitation of the work
3.	and does not unreasonably prejudice the legitimate interests of the author

Figure 2.2 *Berne three-step test*

The Berne Convention is based upon three principles:

1 Reciprocal protection. Among Berne members, each state must protect the works of others to the same level as in their own countries, provided the term accorded is not longer than that for its own works.
2 Minimum standards for duration and scope of rights are the author's life plus 50 years or, for anonymous works, 50 years after making available to the public.
3 Automatic protection, with no registration.

2.3.2 Universal Copyright Convention

The UCC was agreed at a 1952 UNESCO conference in Geneva. The main features of the Convention are that:

1 Works of a given country must carry a copyright notice to secure protection in other UCC countries – it was this convention that established the copyright symbol © (as mentioned previously, the use of the © symbol is only required for works of the Lao People's Democratic Republic to be protected, because all the other signatories are also signed up to the Berne Convention which says that copyright protection is automatic [Cambodia is not a signatory to the Berne Convention but is required to follow the Berne Convention by virtue of its membership of the World Trade Organization]).
2 Foreign works must be treated as though they are national works – the 'national treatment' principle.
3 There must be a minimum term of protection of life plus 25 years.
4 The author's translation rights may be subjected to compulsory licensing.

The two conventions are not mutually exclusive, and the UK is also a member of the UCC.

2.3.3 Trade-Related Aspects of Intellectual Property Rights

The World Trade Organization (WTO) signed an agreement in 1994 which had an annex known as Trade-Related Aspects of Intellectual Property Rights (TRIPS) (WTO, 1994). This is designed to ensure that intellectual property rights do not themselves become barriers to legitimate trade.

The three main features of the agreement are:

1 The minimum standards of protection to be provided by each member on:
   a. the subject matter to be protected
   b. the rights to be conferred
   c. permissible exceptions to those rights
   d. the minimum duration of protection.
2 The production of general principles applicable to all IPR enforcement procedures in order that rights holders can effectively enforce their rights.
3 The agreement that disputes between WTO members about TRIPS obligations will be subject to the WTO's dispute settlement procedures.

The TRIPS agreement is often described as one of the three 'pillars' of the WTO, alongside the Agreements on Trade in Goods (GATT) and Trade in Services (GATS).

There is a TRIPS council comprising all WTO members, which is responsible for monitoring the operation of the agreement, and how members comply with their obligations to it. The UK is a signatory of TRIPS.

2.3.4 World Intellectual Property Organization Copyright Treaty

The World Intellectual Property Organization (WIPO) is a United Nations body that is responsible for administering many of the international conventions on intellectual property. In December 1996 around 100 countries adopted the WIPO Copyright Treaty and the WIPO Performances and Phonograms Treaty. The WIPO Copyright Treaty of 1996 introduced a new right of communication to the public, and it also gave legal protection and legal remedies against circumvention of technological measures, in order to prevent unauthorized access to works. The European directive on the harmonization of certain aspects of copyright and related rights [2001/29/EC] implemented the 1996 WIPO treaties in the European Union.

2.3.5 Anti-Counterfeiting Trade Agreement

The Anti-Counterfeiting Trade Agreement (ACTA) seeks to improve the global enforcement of intellectual property rights through the creation of common enforcement standards and practices and more effective international co-operation. ACTA aims to achieve this by establishing shared international standards on how countries should act against large-scale infringements of intellectual property rights.

ACTA has three main objectives:

1 Better co-ordination of international co-operation.
2 Establishing best practice in enforcement methods.
3 Providing a more coherent legal framework.

ACTA has been negotiated by Australia, Canada, the EU, Japan, Mexico, Morocco, New Zealand, Republic of Korea, Singapore, Switzerland and the United States. Eight countries signed the treaty on 1 October 2011, and it remains open for signature until 1 May 2013. But at the time of writing (November 2011) ACTA is not yet in force.

The treaty has been controversial for a number of reasons, not least because of the way it sidestepped existing institutions such as WIPO, and its negotiations were shrouded in secrecy.

2.3.6 European directives on copyright matters

Changes to UK copyright law are often the result of developments at a European level. The aim of the European Commission is to harmonize copyright laws in the member states in order to achieve a level playing field for copyright protection across national borders so that the Single Market can become a reality for new products and services containing intellectual property. There have been a number of European directives on copyright over the past two decades:

2.3.6.1 On the legal protection of computer programs [2009/24/EC replaces 91/250/EEC]

Computer programs are protected as literary works, which gives them the full protection of the Berne Convention. The term 'computer program' includes preparatory design work leading to the development of a program, provided that the nature of the preparatory work is such that a computer program can result from it at a later stage.

2.3.6.2 On rental and lending right [2006/115/EC replaces 92/100/EEC]

Authors and performers have an exclusive right to authorize or prohibit rental and lending of their works. 'Rental' means making available for use for a limited period of time and for direct or indirect economic or commercial advantage. 'Lending' means making available for use for a limited period of time and *not* for direct or indirect economic or commercial advantage. Libraries are generally allowed to lend books. (Section 40A of the CDPA states that copyright is not infringed by the lending of a book by a public library if the book is within the public lending right scheme, and section 36A of the CDPA says that copyright in a work is not infringed by the lending of copies of the work by an educational establishment.) See www.legislation.gov.uk/ukpga/1988/48/content.

2.3.6.3 Harmonizing the term of copyright protection [2006/116/EC replaces 93/98/EEC]

This extends the term of protection for copyright literary, dramatic, musical and artistic works and films from 50 to 70 years after the year of the death of the author; and gave a new right – publication right – to works in which copyright had expired and which had not previously been published.

2.3.6.4 On the legal protection of databases [96/9/EEC]

This introduces a new form of *sui generis* property protection for databases to prevent unfair extraction and reutilization of their contents (see Section 2.6.4).

2.3.6.5 On the harmonization of certain aspects of copyright and related rights [2001/29/EC]

This enables the EU and its member states to ratify the provisions of the two 1996 WIPO treaties – the Copyright Treaty and the Performers and Producers of Phono - grams Treaty – and updated the law to incorporate new technology, including internet practices.

2.3.6.6 On the resale right for the benefit of the author of an original work of art (droit de suite) [2001/84/EC]

This provides an artist with a right to receive a royalty based on the price obtained for any resale of an original work of art, subsequent to the first transfer by the artist. The right does not apply, however, to resales between individuals acting in their private capacity, without the participation of an art market professional; and to resales by persons acting in their private capacity to museums that are not-for-profit and are open to the public.

Resale of a work of art incurs a royalty of between 0.25% and 4% depending upon the sale price. However, the total amount of resale royalty payable on the sale must not in any event exceed 12,500 EUR. The directive has been implemented in the UK through The Artist's Resale Right Regulations 2006 SI 2006/346 and came into force for living artists on 1 January 2006. The Artist's Resale Right (Amendment) Regulations 2009 SI 2009/2792 delayed until January 2012 the application of the 2006 Regulations to the estates of deceased artists in the UK.

The royalty payment is payable where the resale involves art dealers or other art market professionals as sellers, buyers or intermediaries. This royalty is not payable where the resale takes place directly between private individuals or where the resale price is below a certain limit.

2.3.6.7 On the enforcement of intellectual property rights [2004/48/EC]

This requires all member states to apply effective, dissuasive and proportionate remedies and penalties against those engaged in counterfeiting and piracy and to create a level playing field for rights holders in the EU.

Having published a range of measures to tighten up copyright law over the past two decades, it is clear that there is now a focus on enforcing intellectual property rights in order to ensure that those earlier measures have maximum impact. In addition to directive 2004/48/EC on the enforcement of intellectual property rights, in July 2005 the European Commission published COM(2005) 276 final on criminal measures aimed at ensuring the enforcement of intellectual property rights; and this was followed in April 2006 by an Amended proposal for a directive on criminal measures aimed at ensuring the enforcement of IPR COM(2006) 0168 final.

2.3.6.8 Directive amending 2006/116/EC on the term of protection of copyright and certain related rights [2011/77/EC]

This extends the term of protection of the rights of performers and phonogram producers on music recordings within the EU from 50 to 70 years. It also harmonizes the method of calculating the term of protection of songs and other musical compositions with words created by several authors. The term of protection will expire 70 years after the death of the last person to survive: the author of the lyrics or the composer of the music.

In view of the introduction of so many directives on copyright, the Commission issued a staff working paper in July 2004 (SEC[2004] 995) (EC, 2004) on the review of the European Community (EC) legal framework in the field of copyright and related rights. It assessed whether there were any inconsistencies in the definitions or in rules on exceptions and limitations between the different directives and whether these hampered the operation of the acquis (that is to say the body of Community law) or whether they had a harmful impact on the fair balance of rights and other interests, including those of users and consumers.

2.3.7 UK legislation

The principal UK copyright legislation is the CDPA, which came into force on 1 August 1989. The CDPA has been amended on a number of occasions by the Broadcasting Acts of 1990 and 1996, the Copyright, etc. and Trade Marks (Offences and Enforcement) Act 2002, the Copyright (Visually Impaired Persons) Act 2002, the Legal Deposit Libraries Act 2003, the Digital Economy Act 2010 and by secondary legislation (Statutory Instruments) which interpret and modify the CDPA, including:

- SI 1992/3233 – The Copyright (Computer Programs) Regulations 1992
- SI 1995/3297 – The Duration of Copyright and Rights in Performances Regulations 1995
- SI 1996/2967 – The Copyright and Related Rights Regulations 1996
- SI 1997/3032 – The Copyright and Rights in Databases Regulations 1997
- SI 2003/2498 – The Copyright and Related Rights Regulations 2003
- SI 2006/1028 – The Intellectual Property (Enforcement, etc.) Regulations 2006
- SI 2008/677 – The Copyright and Performances (Application to Other Countries) Order 2008
- SI 2009/2745 – The Copyright and Performances (Application to Other Countries) (Amendment) Order 2009
- SI 2010/2694 – The Copyright, Designs and Patents Act 1988 (Amendment) Regulations 2010.

The Intellectual Property Office is responsible for developing and carrying out UK policy on all aspects of intellectual property. They develop UK law on intellectual property, and promote UK interests in international efforts to harmonize and simplify intellectual property law. The Copyright and IP Enforcement Directorate of the Intellectual Property Office deals with policy on copyright.

2.3.8   Supplementary case law

No matter how well a piece of legislation is drafted, there will always be grey areas of interpretation or situations requiring further clarification about how the law applies to a particular set of circumstances, so the fourth component in the regulatory and legislative regime for copyright is that of case law. Under the English common law tradition, case law plays a key role.

Many copyright cases are not settled in court, but are instead agreed informally as out of court settlements. In these instances, no legal precedent is set, and we are usually none the wiser as to the terms of the settlement. According to a PWC report (PWC, 2011), there have been 67 fair dealing decisions in the courts since 1978 – an average of two a year.

2.4   Acts permitted in relation to copyright works

Chapter III of the CDPA covers acts permitted in relation to copyright works, otherwise known as exceptions. All of the UK's copyright exceptions have to conform to directive 2001/29/EC on the harmonization of certain aspects of copyright and related rights in the information society. Article 5(5) of the directive states that 'the exceptions and limitations [...] shall only be applied in certain special cases which do not conflict with a normal exploitation of the work or other subject matter and do not unreasonably prejudice the legitimate interests of the author'. This is based on the Berne three-step test (see Figure 2.2).

The main copyright exceptions of interest to librarians have been fair dealing for research and private study, and library privilege, which relate only to copying undertaken for non-commercial purposes.

2.4.1   Fair dealing

Fair dealing is effectively a 'defence' against accusations of infringement rather than a licence to copy (see Figure 2.3). Section 29(1) of the CDPA says that 'Fair dealing with a literary, dramatic, musical or artistic work for the purposes of *research*

- Fair dealing has not been defined by statute.
- It must fit into one of the following four categories:
  1. research for a non-commercial purpose
  2. private study
  3. criticism and review
  4. reporting current events.
- In the case of research for a non-commercial purpose or private study, multiple copying would not be fair dealing.
- Courts are left to decide what constitutes 'fair dealing' on a case-by-case basis.

Figure 2.3 *What is fair dealing?*

for a non-commercial purpose does not infringe any copyright in the work provided that it is accompanied by a sufficient acknowledgement', while section 29(1C) says that 'Fair dealing with a literary, dramatic, musical or artistic work for the purposes of *private study* does not infringe any copyright in the work'. Tucked away in a section of minor definitions (s178) there is a definition which makes it clear that private study is also non-commercial: ' "Private study" does not include any study that is directly or indirectly for a commercial purpose.' The problem is that the CDPA does not define what is meant by the phrase 'fair dealing'. It is therefore left for the courts to decide on a case-by-case basis whether or not a particular instance of copying was fair – a point made by Lord Denning in Hubbard v. Vosper [1972] 2 QB 84 CA, which pre-dates the CDPA.

The term 'fair dealing' is commonly thought to mean that the copying must not unfairly deprive the copyright owner of income for their intellectual property. Copyright owners earn income not just from sales of the original work, but also from copying undertaken under licensing schemes operated by collective licensing societies such as the Copyright Licensing Agency (CLA). This income is a just return for the creative work of the author and the financial investment made by the publisher.

Section 16 of the CDPA makes clear that copyright is not infringed unless the whole or a substantial part of a work has been copied. The problem is that the legislation doesn't define 'substantial', but what we are clear about is that 'substantial' is not viewed in purely quantitative terms. It is also related to the qualitative nature of the extract being copied.

2.4.1.1 What is substantial?

Every situation will be different, but here are five examples from legal cases:

1 Eleven-word extracts from newspaper articles can infringe copyright (ECJ judgment in Infopaq v. Dankse Dagblades Forening, Case C-5/08, 16 July 2009).
2 An extract of 250 words from James Joyce's *Ulysses*, which represented less than a thousandth of the work (Sweeney v. MacMillan Publishers Ltd [2001] EWHC Ch 460). They were substantial because their inclusion made the text original and distinct.
3 Four lines of Kipling's 32-line poem *If* (Kipling v. Genatosan 1917). The lines were important lines because they formed an essential part of the crescendo in the poem.
4 Fifty-four lines from a computer program which constituted 0.03% of the program (Veritas Operating Corp v. Microsoft Corp, 2008).
5 Thirty seconds from an hour-long interview (Pro Sieben Media AG v. Carlton TV 1998 [1998] FSR 43). The case involved a documentary produced by

Carlton TV entitled *Selling Babies* which attacked cheque-book journalism. Pro-Sieben had arranged an exclusive contract for an interview with Mandy Allwood who was pregnant with octuplets. The documentary used a 30-second sample of the Pro-Sieben interview with a clip showing Ms Allwood and her boyfriend purchasing eight teddy bears. The Pro-Sieben logo was displayed on the clip although there was no acknowledgement of their ownership of the copyright.

When making decisions it is helpful to bear in mind the much cited dictum of Judge Petersen in University of London Press Limited v. University Tutorial Press Ltd (1916) 2 Ch. 601: 'What is worth copying is prima facie worth protecting.'

Key points about fair dealing

If you rely on the fair dealing exceptions to justify copying activity, then you should minimize the risks of copyright infringement by considering the following points:

1 To be considered 'fair dealing', the copying must fit within one of the following four categories:
   a. research for a non-commercial purpose s29(1)
   b. private study s29(1C)
   c. criticism and review s30(1)
   d. reporting current events s30(2) (this does not cover photographs).

2 Multiple copying for the purpose of non-commercial research or private study would not normally be considered to be fair, nor would systematic single copying. Therefore the copying should normally be restricted to making a single copy.

3 The CILIP copyright poster states that the agreed safe copying limit is one chapter or 5% of extracts from a published work; or one article from any one issue of a journal or periodical.

4 If the copying is likely to have a significant economic impact upon the copyright owner, then it would not be considered to be fair dealing.

5 Ask yourself whether you intend to copy a 'substantial' part. The legislation does not define what is meant by 'substantial', although it is clear from case law that it relates not just to quantity but also to quality. For example, if you were to copy a two-page executive summary from a market-research report and that contained the most valuable findings from the report, the rights owner might argue that the copying was unfair.

6 What is the purpose of the copying? If the copying is undertaken to support research for a commercial purpose, then fair dealing for research cannot be used as a defence (see Figure 2.4).

> - Copying for a commercial purpose has not been defined by statute.
> - The ECJ has the final say.
> - The test is whether the research is for a commercial purpose, not whether it is done by a commercial body.
> - When deciding whether or not research has a non-commercial purpose, businesses will only need to consider what is known at the time of copying.
> - Some research in a commercial environment could be classed as non-commercial.

Figure 2.4 *What constitutes copying for a commercial purpose?*

◆ Useful resource

There are no formal guidelines as to what would count as commercial copying, although The British Library and the CLA produced joint guidance (CLA, 2003) on the changes to UK copyright law that came about through SI 2003/2498 (www.cla.co.uk/data/corporate_material/submissions/2003_cla_and_bl_joint_note_on_changes_to_copyright_law_nov03.pdf).

The legislation does not provide us with a definition of copying 'for a commercial purpose', but the meaning was explored in the case HM Stationery Office v. Green Amps Ltd [2007] EWHC 2755 (Ch).

It would ultimately be for the ECJ to decide precisely what research for a commercial purpose means. We do, however, have a number of helpful pointers. The test is whether the research is for a commercial purpose, not whether it is done by a commercial body. Research carried out may have no immediate commercial goal but may possibly have an unforeseen commercial application at a later date. However, the law cannot expect you to do more than decide what the case is on the day you ask for the copy. If there is no commercial purpose on the day the copy is requested, then it would seem reasonable for the user to sign the copyright declaration form as non-commercial (see Figure 2.7), which is required for all copying under the library regulations (SI 1989/1212). If it is known that research is directly funded by a commercial organization and related to a product or service that will be going into the market, then it is likely to be for a commercial purpose.

Where the copying is undertaken within the scope of the fair dealing provisions, this would normally require acknowledgement. However, section 30(3) does say that 'no acknowledgement is required in connection with the reporting of current events by means of a sound recording, film or broadcast where this would be impossible for reasons of practicality or otherwise'.

Copyright legislation does not set out percentages or numbers of words that can legitimately be copied under the exceptions. The only place where a percentage is given is largely irrelevant because it relates only to educational establishments, and is only applicable where there is no licensing scheme in place; and as there is a CLA licensing scheme in place, the exception is of limited value. Section 36 of the CDPA on reprographic copying by educational establishments of passages from published works says that:

> Not more than one per cent of any work may be copied by or on behalf of an establishment by virtue of this section in any quarter, that is, in any period 1st January to 31st March, 1st April to 30th June, 1st July to 30th September or 1st October to 31st December. [...] Copying is not authorised by this section if, or to the extent that, licences are available authorising the copying in question and the person making the copies knew or ought to have been aware of that fact.
> (www.legislation.gov.uk/ukpga/1988/48/section/36)

The recommended limits set out in Figure 2.5 should be given with a health warning to the effect that they are merely guidance, and a court would make a judgment about what was fair dealing based on the circumstances of each individual case. They are based on the premise that fair dealing copying for non-commercial research or private study purposes should observe the same limits that are set out in the Library Regulations (The Copyright [Librarians and Archivists] [Copying of Copyright Material] Regulations SI 1989/1212 as amended by SI 2003/2498); the 5% limit for books is based on guidance in the CILIP copyright poster (CILIP, 2010).

Fair dealing for research for non-commercial purposes and private study only
Books: Up to a maximum of 5% of extracts or one complete chapter
Journals: One article from a single issue of a journal

Figure 2.5 *Guidance on what you are allowed to copy (Source: CILIP, 2010)*

2.4.2   The library provisions in the CDPA

Sections 38–43 of the CDPA deal with copying by librarians and archivists, and they should be read in conjunction with SI 1989/1212 – The Copyright (Librarians and Archivists) (Copying of Copyright Material) Regulations 1989 as amended.

Library privilege applies to staff who work in 'prescribed libraries' and who carry out photocopying on behalf of their users (see Figure 2.6). Schedule 1 of SI 1989/1212 sets out which libraries are 'prescribed'. These include:

- public libraries
- national libraries
- libraries in educational establishments
- parliamentary and governmental libraries

Only applies to 'prescribed' (not-for-profit) libraries.
- Provides an indemnity for librarians copying on behalf of their users so long as the conditions are met.
- Only applies to copying for non-commercial research purposes or private study.
- Library users must sign a statutory declaration form.
- It is important to retain the statutory declaration because it is the librarian's indemnity. The minimum period that these should be kept for would be six years plus the current year, taking account of the Limitation Act 1980.
- Librarians should be cautious about giving out advice to their users on what constitutes copying for a non-commercial purpose. They must not knowingly be party to advising or telling people how to fill in the declaration or they could be jointly liable

Figure 2.6 *Library privilege*

- local authority libraries
- libraries whose main purpose is to encourage the study of a wide range of subjects (including libraries outside the UK).

The regulations specifically exclude libraries that are conducted for profit.
Libraries have special privileges to copy:

- For their readers (ss38–9).
- For other libraries (s41):
  — any library in the UK can supply a copy of an item, but only 'prescribed libraries' can receive copies.
- For preservation (s42) under the following conditions:
  — the work is in the permanent collection for reference or lending only to other libraries and archives
  — the copy made will only be used for these purposes
  — where it is not reasonably practicable to purchase a copy of the item.
- For replacement (s42) of all or part of a work for a prescribed library provided that each of the following conditions as set out in the Library Regulations (SI 1989/1212) are met:
  — the copy is required to replace an item that has been lost, damaged or destroyed
  — the work being replaced was in the permanent collection for reference or lending only to other libraries
  — the copy made will only be used for these same purposes
  — a copy cannot reasonably be purchased
  — the requesting library provides a declaration that it is a prescribed library and stating the purposes for which it requires the copy (i.e. if the item has been lost, destroyed or damaged)

— the requesting library pays a sum equivalent to but not exceeding the cost (including a contribution to the general expenses of the library or archive) attributable to its production.

Libraries have special privileges to copy certain unpublished works (s43):

* If the document was deposited before it was published.
* If the copyright owner has not prohibited copying.
* If the reader pays a sum equivalent to but not exceeding the cost (including a contribution to the general expenses of the library or archive) attributable to their production.
* If a statutory declaration is signed, which must state that:
  — the work was not published before it was deposited
  — the copy is for research for a non-commercial purpose or private study and will not be further copied
  — a copy has not previously been supplied.

Library privilege covers copying undertaken by library staff on behalf of their users, whether they are local users or interlibrary users. The individual users themselves cannot claim it. Library privilege covers literary, dramatic or musical works, including typographical arrangements and illustrations, but it does not cover artistic works.

Under library privilege, library staff can make one copy of an article from an issue of a periodical; or a reasonable proportion of a non-periodical work provided that a number of conditions are met:

* The user must sign the necessary statutory declaration form.
* The user must pay an appropriate sum so that the library is able to recover the costs of production of the copy.
* No more than one article from a periodical issue can be copied or a reasonable proportion of a non-periodical work.
* The librarian must be satisfied that the criteria set out in the legislation are met.

The statutory declaration form (see the sample copyright declaration form in Figure 2.7) which library users are required to sign must state that:

* a copy has not previously been supplied (by any librarian)
* the copies are for research for a non-commercial purpose or private study and will not be further copied
* they are not aware that anyone with whom they work or study has made, or intends to make, at or about the same time as this request, a request for substantially the same material for substantially the same purpose.

DECLARATION: COPY OF ARTICLE OR PART OF PUBLISHED WORK

To:
    The Librarian of...Library
    [Address of Library]

Please supply me with a copy of:
    * the article in the periodical, the particulars of which are
    [   ]

    * the part of the published work, the particulars of which are
    [   ]

required by me for the purposes of research for a non-commercial purpose or private study.

2. I declare that:
(a) I have not previously been supplied with a copy of the same material by you or any other librarian;
(b) I will not use the copy except for research for a non-commercial purpose or private study and will not supply a copy of it to any other person; and
(c) to the best of my knowledge no other person with whom I work or study has made or intends to make, at or about the same time as this request, a request for substantially the same material for substantially the same purpose.

3. I understand that if the declaration is false in a material particular the copy supplied to me by you will be an infringing copy and that I shall be liable for infringement of copyright as if I had made the copy myself.

                            † Signature ....
                            Date ....

Name ....
Address ....
     ....
     ....
* Delete whichever is inappropriate
† This must be the personal signature of the person making the request. A stamped or

Figure 2.7 *Sample copyright declaration form*

The Library Regulations (SI 1989/1212) do not require the declaration form to be precisely the same as the one that appears in Schedule 2 to the SI, but that it is 'substantially in accordance' with that form (see Figure 2.7). If the declaration is false the copy is an infringing copy and the reader is responsible.

Whilst it is certainly the case that librarians have previously relied upon the fair dealing and library privilege exceptions as their main justification for the copying of copyright works, the CDPA does contain over 50 exceptions. For example, there are exceptions relating to public administration which permit copying for Parliamentary and judicial proceedings (s45), Royal Commissions and statutory enquiries (s46), material open to public inspection or on an official register (s47), material communicated to the Crown in the course of public business (s48), public records (s49) and acts done under statutory authority (s50). The Copyright (Visually Impaired Persons) Act 2002, which was implemented in October 2003, introduced two new copyright exceptions. These are outlined in the chapter on disability discrimination (see Section 16.2).

More often than not, the business community will experience difficulty trying to fit their copying into any of the copyright exceptions or permitted acts, and they are advised to look to the copyright licences offered by the collective licensing societies as a possible solution.

2.5   Licensing

What copyright law does not allow can often be done with the copyright owner's consent through an appropriate licence – usually in exchange for payment. The CDPA allows for the setting-up of collective licensing bodies such as the CLA or the Newspaper Licensing Agency (NLA). Where there is a dispute between a collecting society and users or groups representing users, these can be referred to the Copyright Tribunal that is administered by a Secretary who is a civil servant working in the Intellectual Property Office. The decisions of the Copyright Tribunal are appealable to the High Court (or in Scotland to the Court of Session) only on a point of law. Details of Copyright Tribunal cases can be found on the Intellectual Property Office website at www.ipo.gov.uk/ctribunal.htm.

2.5.1   Copyright Licensing Agency

The CLA is one of the UK's largest reproduction rights organizations. It is a not-for-profit company that was set up in 1983 by the Publishers Licensing Society (PLS) and the Authors' Licensing and Collecting Society (ALCS). The CLA also works closely with the Design and Artists Copyright Society (DACS). The CLA licences permit photocopying, scanning and digital reuse of extracts from print and digital publications and some free-to-view websites.

The CLA offers a range of licences, according to the type of organization. The licences available include ones for business, law firms, pharmaceutical companies, public administration, higher education and schools. There is also a licence available for press cuttings agencies. To see details of the full range of licences available from the Copyright Licensing Agency see www.cla.co.uk/licences/licences_available.

As required by s136 of the CDPA (implied indemnity in schemes or licences for reprographic copying), licence holders are given an indemnity against liability for infringement for reprographic copying provided that the licence terms are complied with.

⚬ Useful resource

The CLA maintains a 'list of excluded categories and excluded works' (www.cla.co.uk/licences/excluded_works/excluded_categories_works), which lists the publishers and/or the individual titles that cannot be copied under the terms of the licence agreement. It also covers a number of 'excluded categories' such as printed music, workbooks, work cards or assignment sheets, maps, charts, and newspapers.

⚬ Useful resource

Does my CLA licence cover this title? (www.cla.co.uk/licences/titlesearch)

 Even if a work isn't specifically mentioned in the CLA's list of excluded works, care should be taken to see if the work itself has a note on it about copyright, because one of the excluded categories covers any work on which the copyright owner has expressly and prominently stipulated that it may not be copied under a CLA licence.

In January 2011 a Multinational Licence was launched, which means that the CLA is able to license global organizations with headquarters based in the UK. This digital licence is especially useful for large organizations that require consistent copyright terms across all global sites, and also for companies that have subsidiary offices based in territories where there is no collective licence available for commercial organizations.

The CLA's licence fee is usually based on a rate per professional employee, and the interpretation of what is meant by a 'professional employee' will differ from sector to sector. There is one licence available from the CLA which is not based upon a rate per professional employee, and that is the small business licence that is available for businesses employing up to 50 employees. Businesses are charged a flat fee which is based upon the total number of staff. There are two bands – one for businesses employing up to 10 people, and the other for those employing between 11 and 50 employees. The small business licence incorporates the same terms as the business licence.

The CLA exists in order to collect licence fees from organizations wishing to make copies of items and then passes those fees on to authors, publishers, and visual artists. In order for the fee distributions to be fair to authors and publishers, it is necessary to gather information on what material is being copied. It is for this reason that licence holders are required to complete an information audit in which they tell the CLA what journals they subscribe to and what books they have purchased. Surveys are also undertaken to record what is being copied. The fees are then distributed to authors, publishers, and visual creators and artists, through the ALCS, the PLS and DACS, respectively.

2.5.2   Newspaper Licensing Agency

Set up in January 1996, the NLA operates a licensing scheme to collect royalties on behalf of newspaper publishers. The NLA licence covers UK national and regional papers, worldwide newspapers, select business titles, and online/digital versions of these. There are a number of different types of licence available such as the business licence, educational licence, public relations licence, professional partnerships licence, and the licence for media monitoring agencies.

The NLA licences cover paper copying (photocopying, faxing and printing), digital copying (scanning, e-mailing and hosting on an intranet) as well as the receipt and distribution of content received from a licensed media monitoring agency.

The NLA manages eClips, an online database of newspaper articles that is designed for media monitoring agencies and their clients. It is used by these agencies in order to deliver press articles electronically in PDF format to their clients. Another service offered by the NLA is Clipsearch (www.clipsearch.co.uk), an online newspaper archive of over 9 million articles from more than 140 newspapers dating back to 2006.

The Newspaper Licensing Agency offers two services for schools which are designed to make the use of newspaper material in schools as easy as possible. Firstly, there is a free licence for schools in the UK, which permits copying in paper format; and secondly there is an online service allowing schools access to newspaper clippings in PDF format (www.newspapersforschools.co.uk).

NLA v. Meltwater and PRCA [2010] EWHC 3099 (Ch)

Meltwater provide a media monitoring service to clients. Websites are scanned for the occurrence of particular words or phrases that the client wishes to monitor, and where the word/phrase appears Meltwater sends the client a hyperlink to each relevant article, along with the opening words of the article, and an extract from the article showing the context within which the word or phrase appears.

During 2009 the NLA proposed two new licensing schemes, one for media monitoring organizations and the other for end-users of those monitoring services. The NLA contended that end-users would need to take out an NLA licence if they wanted to make use of media monitoring services; otherwise they would be infringing copyright in the material by receiving and reading Meltwater News because by clicking on a link to the article they would be making a copy of the article within the meaning of section 17 of the CDPA 1988, and by forwarding Meltwater News or its contents to clients they would be issuing copies to the public within the meaning of section 18 of the CDPA 1988.

In December 2009 Meltwater Group announced that it had referred the NLA to the Copyright Tribunal over the reasonableness of those licences. At the time of referring the dispute to the Copyright Tribunal, Jorn Lyseggen, CEO of Meltwater Group, said: 'The NLA's attempt to license our clients is essentially a tax on receiving these internet links. This fee is not only unjust and unreasonable, it is contrary to the very spirit of the internet.' (www.meltwater.com/about/press-room/news-releases/meltwater-takes-the-nla-to-uk-copyright-tribunal-over-proposed-hyperlink-ta).

Meanwhile, the NLA launched a High Court action in order to get legal clarity on aggregator and end-user licences. David Pugh of the NLA said: 'The Copyright Tribunal will rule on the commercial aspects of NLA web licensing. [...] But the High Court is the proper place to decide on the legality of our web licences.' (www.nla.co.uk/uploads/public/Press%20Releases/100524%20NLA%20press%20statement%20and%20background%20information.pdf)

But it is worth bearing in mind firstly the sheer scale of the use which is being made of the content because it would seem that a single end-user could well receive text from some 50,000 articles per annum; and secondly that the newspaper publishers have devoted very substantial resources in developing their websites and to the selection, arrangement and presentation of the material on them. Meltwater is making millions of pounds from its own activities, which include 'scraping' the publishers' websites for information.

The judge was asked to rule on the following issues:

1. Is a newspaper headline capable of being a freestanding original literary work?
   Mrs Justice Proudman said: 'In my opinion headlines are capable of being literary works, whether independently or as part of the articles to which they relate.'
2. If the text extract constitutes a 'substantial part' of the article as a literary work.
   'On the basis of Infopaq, the text extract and indeed the text extract excluding the headline ... are capable of being substantial enough for the purposes of s. 16 (3).'
3. Do the PRCA (Public Relations Consultants Association) and its members need a web end-user licence from the NLA or its members in order to lawfully use and receive Meltwater's service?
   The conclusion reached was that, without a licence, end-users are infringing the publishers' copyright.
   Mrs Justice Proudman said: 'When an End-user clicks on a Link (to) a copy of the article on the Publisher's website which appears on the website accessible via that Link (a copy) is made on the End-user's computer.... it seems to me that in principle copying by an End-user without a licence through a direct Link is more likely than not to infringe copyright'.

> The judgment of the High Court was published in November 2010; and the Court
> of Appeal upheld the decision of the High Court (Newspaper Licensing Agency Ltd
> & Ors v Meltwater Holding BV & Ors [2011] EWCA Civ 890 (27 July 2011).
>   The Copyright Tribunal decision examined whether or not the terms of the licence
> are reasonable. At the time of writing (November 2011) the case hearings had been

2.5.3   Design and Artists Copyright Society

Formed in 1983, DACS represents visual creators, artists and photographers. It licenses the use of artistic works such as photographs, sculptures, charts, maps, cartoons and diagrams. DACS also pursues cases of copyright infringement on behalf of its members.

Many artists create their works as a result of a commission, and they might directly administer and control their primary rights, but they may not be able to control their secondary rights. DACS manages this for them through 'Payback', an annual service that distributes royalties to visual artists whose work has been reproduced in UK books or magazines or on certain television channels.

DACS lobbied on behalf of its members for the introduction of Artist's Resale Right (*droit de suite*) under which an artist gets a percentage each time a work is sold after the first sale (see Section 2.3.6.6).

2.5.4   Ordnance Survey

The Ordnance Survey (OS) provides a licensing system for people to be able to make use of their mapping products (such as maps and aerial photographs). Customers ranging from solicitors, shopkeepers and estate agents through to engineers use these licences. Users pay an annual fee in order to be able to make unlimited copies of maps for internal business use or to publish OS mapping externally for display and promotion purposes, so long as this does not result in any direct financial gain from the use of the mapping.

➻ Useful resource

On 1 April 2010, OS launched OS OpenData, an online portal providing free and unrestricted access to a large range of mapping and geographic information (www.ordnancesurvey.co.uk/oswebsite/products/os-opendata.html). OS OpenData allows users to: download a wide range of mapping and geographic information for free reuse direct to their computers; view maps and boundary information for the whole country; develop web-map applications using OS's OS OpenSpace API (Application Programming Interface). In January 2011 Ordnance Survey announced that OS OpenData would now be governed by the Open Government Licence.

2.5.5 The National Archives

The National Archives is an executive agency of the Ministry of Justice. It incorporates HMSO, the Office of Public Sector Information, the Public Record Office, the Historical Manuscripts Commission, and the Statutory Publications Office. It is at the heart of information policy, setting standards, delivering access and encouraging reuse of public sector information (see Chapter 12). The agency provides online access to UK legislation, oversees the open government licence, manages the Information Fair Trader Scheme (see Section 12.1.3), maintains the government's Information Asset Register (see Section 12.1.2) and provides advice and guidance on official publishing and Crown Copyright.

Ordnance Survey Northern Ireland v. Automobile Association (2001)

OS launched a High Court action against the Automobile Association (AA) in 1996 after they were caught copying dozens of OS maps. Cartographers at OS trapped the copiers by putting faults, such as tiny kinks in rivers, in dozens of maps. These faults helped to prove that 26 million published guides, which the AA claimed as its own work, were straightforward copies.

In 2000 the AA had already admitted breaching Crown Copyright of 64 maps and agreed to pay £875,000 compensation. In this separate case, more than 500 publications were involved with more than 300 million copies printed.

Outcome: The AA agreed to pay £20 million in compensation. The money was paid over a period of two years and covered backdated royalties, interest, legal costs and an advance on the AA's coming royalties for the next year.

In September 2010, The National Archives launched the Open Government Licence. As a consequence, Crown Copyright material, which was previously available for reuse under waiver conditions, can now be reused under the terms of the Open Government Licence. The licence replaced the Click-Use Licence for Crown Copyright material.

Under the terms of the Open Government Licence (www.nationalarchives. gov.uk/doc/open-government-licence/), where content has been expressly made available under the Open Government Licence, users are free to:

- copy, publish, distribute and transmit the information
- adapt the information
- exploit the information commercially, for example by combining it with other information, or by including it in their own product or application.

There are a number of conditions that need to be met by users of Crown Copyright material under the terms of the Open Government Licence:

- Acknowledge the source of the information by including any attribution statement specified by the Information Provider(s) and, where possible, provide a link to the licence.
- Ensure that they do not use the information in a way that suggests any official status or that the Information Provider endorses them or their use of the information.
- Ensure that they do not mislead others or misrepresent the information or its source.
- Ensure that their use of the information does not breach the Data Protection Act 1998 or the Privacy and Electronic Communications (EC Directive) Regulations 2003.

The National Archives issues guidance to government departments, agencies and all users of Crown-Copyright-protected material (see www.nationalarchives. gov.uk/information-management/our-services/copyright-guidance.htm).

As far as Parliamentary copyright is concerned, a significant amount of content covered by parliamentary copyright is covered by the Open Parliament Licence (www.parliament.uk/site-information/copyright/open-parliament-licence/). What the licence does not cover, though, are:

- the Crowned Portcullis
- images featured on Art in Parliament
- Parliamentary archives
- Parliamentary photographic images
- live and archive video or audio broadcasts.

2.5.6   Creative Commons

Creative Commons licences try to achieve a point in-between all rights reserved and no rights reserved. They can be summed up as 'some rights reserved' because the content owner reserves some rights of control. The licences try to make it as easy as possible to understand what they cover by adopting four symbols; and each licence consists of a combination of these symbols, e.g. BY ND (attribution, no derivative works). These symbols and their definitions are:

1 Attribution (BY). You let others copy, distribute, display and perform your copyrighted work — and derivative works based upon it — but only if they give credit the way you request.
2 No derivative works (ND). You let others copy, distribute, display and perform only verbatim copies of your work, not derivative works based upon it.
3 Non-commercial (NC). You let others copy, distribute, display and perform

your work — and derivative works based upon it — but for non-commercial purposes only.

4 Share alike (SA). You allow others to distribute derivative works only under a licence identical to the licence that governs your work. Licences cannot feature both the SA and ND options because, by its very nature, the SA requirement applies only to derivative works.

Creative Commons aims to make copyrighted material more accessible in the digital environment and does this by getting content owners who participate in the Commons to label their material with a CC symbol representing the terms upon which the material may be reutilized. This enables users to see straightaway precisely what rights they have to reproduce, communicate, cut, paste and remix the content.

◆ Useful resource

There is a Creative Commons add-in for Microsoft Office available for download from the Microsoft website, which makes it easy for licence information to be embedded in Microsoft Word, Excel and PowerPoint documents. Where documents which have licensing information embedded in their metadata are published to the internet, this machine-readable data makes it possible for search engines to provide search forms where a user can specify that they want to limit their search to Creative Commons licensed content. See www.microsoft.com/download/en/details.aspx?displaylang=en&id=18413

The Open Government Licence (see Sections 12.1.1 and 2.5.5) is interoperable with widely used models such as Creative Commons and Open Data Commons and as such supports the inclusion of machine-readable description and semantic web properties.

A Creative Commons licence cannot make infringing material lawful. If a section of material is included in a Creative Commons licensed work and there wasn't a licence in place or any other permission to use it, then this may be a breach of copyright. In such circumstances the Creative Commons licence would be invalid with regard to the infringing elements of the licensed work and any additional use of the infringing elements would be a further breach of copyright.

In a 2009 discussion paper, Andrew Charlesworth said that it was unclear to what extent the Creative Commons copyright licensing system had been taken up by the general public, or the extent to which non-expert users of the licensing system truly understand the practical implications of the licences that they are creating or the extent of the permissions they are granting (Charlesworth, 2009). They might also not be aware that Creative Commons licences only deal with copyright, and not with issues such as privacy (see britishlibrary.typepad.co.uk/files/digital-lives-legal-ethical.pdf).

Chang v. Virgin Mobile USA LLC 2009 WL 111570 (N.D. Tex. January 16, 2009)

A photograph of Alison Chang was posted on Flickr under a Creative Commons Attribution 2.0 licence. The photograph of the teenager was then used by Virgin Australia in an advertising campaign. Alison Chang's parents brought a lawsuit, claiming that Virgin violated their daughter's right to privacy by using a photograph of her for commercial purposes without her or her parents' permission. The photographer also sued on the grounds that the Creative Commons failed 'to adequately educate and warn him [...] of the meaning of commercial use and the ramifications and effects of entering into a license allowing such use'. See Lawsuit Against Virgin Mobile and Creative Commons – FAQ http://creativecommons.org/weblog/entry/7680. The claims against the Creative Commons Corporation were subsequently withdrawn and the case against Virgin Australia in the US courts was dismissed for lack of jurisdiction.

This case illustrates the lack of understanding of the purpose of a Creative

There have been a number of court cases in a variety of different countries which have established the enforceability of Creative Commons licences:

- In Lichodmapwa v. L'asbl Festival de Theatre de Spa (2010), a Belgian court awarded Lichodmapwa 4,500 EUR for infringement of a song ('Abatchouck') released under a CC BY-NC-ND licence. Lichodmapwa claimed that the theatre company had violated all three of the licence conditions when it used an extract from the song in a commercial advert without any attribution.
- In 2007 Bulgarian blogger Elenko Elenkov filed a lawsuit against the newspaper *24 Hours* for using one of his photos licensed under a CC BY-SA licence without mentioning him or the licence used.
- Adam Curry v. Weekend. In 2006 a Dutch court ruled that photographs that had been posted on Flickr under a CC licence should not have been repro - duced by the Dutch magazine without permission. The publisher faces a fine of 1,000 EUR if they publish any of Curry's pictures without permission again.
- Avi Reuveni v. Mapa Publishing Ltd (2011). An Israeli court enforced CC BY-NC-ND licences relating to fifteen copyrighted photographs which had been uploaded to Flickr and awarded the plaintiffs the equivalent of US $12,500 in damages. The defendant was also ordered to pay half of the plaintiff's court fees and $2,500 for the plaintiff's legal costs.

➡ Useful resource

OpenAttribute (http://openattribute.com) provides a set of tools for a range of platforms to make it as easy as possible for people to comply with the terms of the licences so that reusing and properly attributing open content is as easy as cut and paste.

⊷ Useful resource

It is possible to monitor the use that is made of Creative Commons licensed content using Tynt's tracer tool available at www.tynt.com. The tool can be used by authors of CC content to monitor who is copying and pasting their content.

2.6 Digital copyright

Works which are published in electronic form, such as electronic journals, PDF documents on the internet, online databases or websites, are protected by copyright law.

2.6.1 Internet

In a single web page there can be many different copyrights. For example, the textual articles, HTML coding and metadata are literary works; the graphics are artistic works; and the sound files containing musical works are protected as sound recordings. The web page would benefit from the exclusive right of the copyright owner to communicate their work to the public by electronic means.

People wishing to undertake copying of material on the internet which falls outside any of the permitted acts should check to see if there is a copyright notice on the web page. If the copying they wish to undertake is not covered in the copyright notice, or if there is no copyright notice on the website, then they should ask for permission by contacting the webmaster.

Librarians need to be mindful of both copyright and database right when copying material on the internet. Many websites will fall under the definition of a database which appears in The Copyright Rights in Databases Regulations 1997 (SI 1997/3032) and will therefore have the protection of database right (see Section 2.6.4). An important legal case that dealt with database right is that of British Horseracing Board (BHB) v. William Hill EWCA (Civ) 863. The ECJ judgment (C-203/02) shows that in order for database right to apply there must have been a substantial investment in the *obtaining, verification and presentation* of the contents of the database; and that this must be distinct from any investment involved in the *creation* of the contents of the database.

Copying in relation to any description of work includes the making of copies which are transient or are incidental to some other use of the work (CDPA s17[6]). When you look at a web page, for example, you will have automatically made more than one copy simply by virtue of the way in which the technology works – the copy that you see on the screen as well as the copy that is automatically saved to your web browser's cache, even before you think about downloading or printing a copy. It is for this reason that directive 2001/29/EC has one mandatory exception. Article 5.1 requires member states to provide an exception to the reproduction right for certain temporary acts which are transient or incidental, and so SI 2003/2498 inserts s28A into the CDPA:

> Copyright in a literary work, other than a computer program or a database, or in a dramatic, musical or artistic work, the typographical arrangement of a published edition, a sound recording or a film, is not infringed by the making of a temporary copy which is transient or incidental, which is an integral and essential part of a technological process and the sole purpose of which is to enable—
> (a) a transmission of the work in a network between third parties by an intermediary; or
> (b) a lawful use of the work;
> and which has no independent economic significance.
> (www.legislation.gov.uk/ukpga/1988/48/section/28A, and a footnote shown in the link also gives the full reference to the relevant piece from SI 2003/2498)

2.6.2   Right of communication to the public

The copyright owner has an exclusive right to communicate their work to the public. It covers broadcasting the work and also making the work available by electronic transmission so that members of the public may access it from a place and at a time individually chosen by them. If you want to include another person's content on your website it is essential that you obtain their permission.

Remedies available to a copyright owner who finds that someone has made use of his or her content without permission include damages and an injunction to stop the inclusion of the material on the website.

2.6.3   Hyperlinking and deep linking

Hyperlinking is an integral part of the way in which the web works, allowing people either to jump from one website to another or to navigate from one page within a site to another page on the same site. There have been quite a number of legal cases that have considered the use of hyperlinks, and in particular deep links, and whether or not these are legitimate.

The NLA introduced a new licence for media monitoring organizations which took effect from 1 September 2009, and another for licensing those who receive and use media monitoring company services which took effect from 1 January

2010. In the case NLA v. Meltwater and PRCA [2010] EWHC 3099 (Ch) the High Court considered the question of whether a commercial end-user infringes copyright by linking to an online article. The court concluded that if an end-user didn't have a licence, more likely than not they would be making an unauthorized copy on their computer. The judgment was upheld by the Court of Appeal in July 2011 (NLA v Meltwater [2011] EWCA Civ 890 (27 July 2011)).

In June 2005 the Department for Trade and Industry published a consultation document on the *Electronic Commerce Directive: the liability of hyperlinkers, location tool services and content aggregators* (DfTI, 2005). This set out three types of hyperlink:

1 'Linking' which takes you to the home page of a particular website. This is also known as 'shallow linking'.
2 'Deep linking' is a link that takes you directly to a specific page (or part of a page) of a website at a lower level in the website's page hierarchy than the home page.
3 'Framing' occurs where a webpage is linked to what appears in a 'frame' of the original website visited, when the Uniform Resource Locator (URL) remains that of the original site.

The use of deep links can be problematic for a number of reasons:

1 If the website that you are linking to has banner advertisements on the home page for which the site owner gets an income based upon the number of 'click-throughs', then you should avoid linking to a page further down within the site because it could be argued that, by deep linking within the site, you are depriving the site owner of income.
2 By deep linking to a page within a site, you might be said to be encouraging people to go directly to a page when the site owner might want you to see a set of terms and conditions before viewing any pages on their site. Indeed, by getting people to circumvent the page containing terms and conditions of use, you might actually be stopping people from seeing if the site owner has clearly stated in those terms and conditions that deep linking is not permitted.
3 Linking may be judged to be an infringement of database right. In Stepstone v. OFiR [2000 EBLR 87], a German court took the view that Stepstone's website, which provided a database of job vacancies, was protected by database right, and that OFiR's activities amounted to the repeated and systematic extraction of insubstantial parts of Stepstone's database, which prejudiced Stepstone's legitimate interests.
4 The use of frames technology can also be problematic. With frames it is possible to link from one website to another without users realizing that they have linked through to an external site. This could suggest a false association

with the other site, or lead to an accusation of passing off someone else's content as though it were your own.

The law is still uncertain in this area, but avoiding the use of deep linking altogether would be an overreaction to the perceived risks. See Figure 2.8 for issues to bear in mind.

- Make it clear what is being done and who you are linking to.
- Avoid using frames technology that could result in you appearing to pass off someone else's content as your own.
- Ideally the hyperlink should open up in a new page.
- Use a disclaimer about the content of external sites.
- Check the website's terms and conditions for the sites you wish to link to.
- Do not circumvent anti-linking measures.
- Link to the home page if sufficient.
- Avoid commercially unfair deep linking (i.e. that will lead you to benefit commercially at the expense of the owner of the site you are linking to).
- Inform the content owner that you wish to link to their site. This is a matter of good 'netiquette' and may lead to them creating a reciprocal link from their website.
- Don't link to content which infringes copyright, is defamatory or libellous, is blasphemous, is obscene, incites racial hatred, or encourages terrorist activity.

Figure 2.8 *Points to consider when deep linking*

2.6.4   Database regulations

The Copyright and Rights in Databases Regulations (SI 1997/3032) came into force on 1 January 1998. They implement council directive 96/9/EC on the legal protection of databases. The regulations introduced a new right – database right – which subsists if there has been a substantial investment in obtaining, verifying and presenting the contents of the database. In order for a database to qualify additionally for full copyright protection, it must be the author's own intellectual creation by virtue of the selection and arrangement of the contents. Some databases might qualify for both copyright and database right. The regulations do not consider a 'database' to be limited to electronic information, but rather as any collection of independent works, data or other materials which are arranged in a systematic or methodical way and are individually accessible by electronic or other means. Collections of data such as directories, encyclopedias, statistical databases, online collections of journals, multimedia collections and many websites would fit this definition of a database.

As with copyright, there are a number of exceptions to database right. However, the number of exceptions is far fewer than is the case for copyright. Fair dealing with a database is permitted so long as the person extracting the material is a lawful user of the database, that their purpose is illustration for teaching, research or private study and not for any commercial purpose, and that the source is indicated. The regulations state that 'the doing of anything in relation to a database for the purposes of research for a commercial purpose is not fair dealing with the database' (www.legislation.gov.uk/uksi/1997/3032/part/II/made). This was the first time that such a distinction had been made in UK copyright law, and this principle was extended in SI 2003/2498 to cover other copyright-protected material.

Schedule 1 of the Regulations sets out a number of exceptions to database right for public administration and these relate to:

- Parliamentary and judicial proceedings
- Royal Commissions and statutory inquiries
- material open to public inspection or on an official register
- public records
- acts done under statutory authority.

In the case of copyright, the protection for a database would normally be for 70 years from the end of the year of death of the author if there is one, or the end of the year of first publication if there isn't a personal author. In the case of database right, the period of protection would be for 15 years from its creation or from its being made available to the public if this occurs during the 15-year period. Importantly, a substantial new investment would qualify the database for a new 15-year term of protection. Many 'databases' are maintained continually and this can involve a significant investment. As such, they can potentially end up being protected for an indefinite period.

2.6.5 Archiving and preservation of digital content

Section 42 of the CDPA allows prescribed libraries to make a copy of a literary, dramatic or musical work held in their permanent collection for the purpose of preservation and replacement. These provisions assist libraries and archives who may wish to minimize the wear and tear of fragile items or to replace lost, destroyed or damaged items in their permanent collections.

The *Gowers Review of Intellectual Property* (HM Treasury, 2006) noted that archiving and preservation arrangements are far more stringent in the UK than those in place in many other countries in so far as they relate to:

- the classes of works that can be copied
- the number of copies that can be made
- the ability to format shift.

Currently, in the UK, the classes of work within the scope of section 42 do not include sound recordings, films or broadcasts. These limitations create practical problems for prescribed organizations who have an interest in preserving content that is stored on unstable media that deteriorates with age (such as film). This is precisely the kind of content for which the preservation costs are considerable if they are left to deteriorate over a period of many years. The situation is further exacerbated by an inability to format shift to a more stable medium.

Prescribed bodies are only entitled to take a single copy, but in order to ensure the preservation of materials, it is essential that the law is changed so as to accommodate as many copies being made over the life of the item in question as are necessary for the ongoing preservation of those materials – bearing in mind that with technological developments there will inevitably be a need to transfer from one format to another in order to get around the problem of technological obsolescence.

The *Gowers Review* (HM Treasury, 2006) proposed that the section 42 (of the CDPA) exception be expanded to allow copies of sound recordings, films and broadcasts to be made. It further proposed that these prescribed bodies be able to format shift to address the problem that occurs where works are held on unstable media, and that the making of more than a single copy be permitted where successive copying may be required to preserve permanent collections in an accessible format.

The aim was to allow libraries and archives to use technology to preserve valuable material before it deteriorates or the format in which it is stored becomes obsolete. The *Gowers Review* recommendations to expand section 42 have not been implemented; but the May 2011 report *Digital Opportunity: a review of intellectual property and growth* (Hargreaves, 2011) said that the exception for archiving falls well short of current needs:

> Libraries are inhibited in preserving content through digitization, that they cannot preserve all categories of works and that as a result, works continue to deteriorate. This makes no sense and it should be uncontroversial to deliver the necessary change by extending the archiving exception, including to cover fully audio-visual works and sound recordings.   (Hargreaves, 2011)

2.6.6   Licensing of electronic resources

One of the problems with electronic information is that its use is normally governed by a licence or contract rather than by copyright law, and these licences often differ on key points from one supplier to another. It is for this reason that a number of initiatives have been undertaken to try and come up with a standard licence for electronic resources.

❧ Useful resources

These initiatives include John Cox Associates (www.licensingmodels.org), ICOLC (International Coalition of Library Consortia) (www.library.yale.edu/consortia/statement.html), the NESLi2 licence for journals (www.jisc-collections.ac.uk/nesli2), and the Zwolle principles (http://copyright.surf.nl/copyright). Also see Section 6.3.

With digital information, as with hard-copy information, it is important to make a distinction between single copying and multiple copying. If, for example, you send an e-mail containing a scanned item in which you do not own the rights to several people, you will have undertaken multiple copying, and the exceptions for fair dealing for a non-commercial purpose or for private study would not cover this.

2.6.7 Digital rights management systems

Digital rights management (DRM) systems can provide a technological solution for rights owners wishing to ensure that their intellectual property is not copied or redisseminated in an unauthorized manner. They provide robust and reliable tamper-proof mechanisms for controlling the use of copyright material. There are two key elements to a DRM system, which can be summed up by the formula DRM = RMI + TPM. That is, a DRM system consists of both rights management information as well as a technical protection measure.

In principle, the copyright exceptions or permitted acts apply to digital information. However, if the rights owners have made use of technical measures to prevent access to their work(s), the copyright exceptions are rendered worthless, because it would be illegal to try and break any copy protection that is in place. SI 2003/2498 implements the provisions of directive 2001/29/EC into UK law, making it an offence to break through a technical protection measure or to remove or alter electronic rights management information.

CDPA 1988 s296ZE sets out the remedy that is available where effective technological measures prevent a person from carrying out a permitted act. Basically, the person affected can issue a notice of complaint to the Secretary of State for Business Innovation and Skills if they believe that they are entitled to make use of a copyright exception but are being prevented from doing so because of a technical measure attached to a work. The Secretary of State can then give directions to the publisher to rectify the situation.

2.6.8 Digital signatures and copyright declaration forms

Section 7 of the Electronic Communications Act 2000 implemented the provisions of directive 1999/93/EC relating to the admissibility of electronic signatures as evidence in legal proceedings, while The Electronic Signatures Regulations 2002 (SI

2002/318) implemented the provisions relating to the supervision of a certification-service provider,[1] their liability in certain circumstances and data protection requirements concerning them. These regulations define 'electronic signatures' as 'data in electronic form which are attached to or logically associated with other electronic data and which serve as a method of authentication'. (www.legislation.gov.uk/uksi/2002/318/regulation/2/made)

 The Library Regulations (SI 1989/1212) (www.legislation.gov.uk/uksi/1989/1212/contents/made) require the requester to sign the statutory declaration form. Therefore, a librarian must not sign the declaration form on behalf of the user.

Schedule 2 to the Library Regulations says that 'this must be the personal signature of the person making the request. A stamped or typewritten signature, or the signature of an agent, is NOT acceptable' (www.legislation.gov.uk/uksi/1989/1212/schedule/2/made). The Library Regulations are compatible with the use of e-signatures because they require that the signature must be in 'writing', and 'writing' is defined in the CDPA s178 as including any form of notation or code, whether by hand or otherwise.

Librarians can receive copyright declaration forms that have been signed electronically. The problem is that they must fulfil the requirements for a personal signature. The signature has to have a unique link to the requester that cannot easily be used by others. In short, this means that the signature must be linked to an authentication system, and it is unclear which systems would be deemed to fulfil the necessary legal requirements. (For further information see the statement by the Libraries and Archives Copyright Alliance (LACA) concerning electronic signatures on copyright declaration forms (LACA, 2002).)

2.6.9   The implications for libraries of the Digital Economy Act 2010

Sections 3–18 of the Digital Economy Act (DEA) 2010 cover the infringement of copyright. They were primarily introduced in order to tackle illicit peer-to-peer file-sharing and it is these sections that were the subject of a judicial review heard in the High Court in March 2011 (British Telecommunications PLC and TalkTalk Telecom Group PLC v. Secretary of State for Business Innovation and Skills [2011] EWHC 1021 (Admin)). In April 2011 the High Court ruled in favour of the Government in all but one regard – the judge ruled that internet service providers (ISPs) could be made to pay a share of the cost of operating the Act's mass notification system between rights holders and ISPs and the appeals process, but not Ofcom's costs from setting up, monitoring and enforcing it. But in October 2011 BT and TalkTalk were given leave to appeal against the Court's ruling.

There are three key players especially relevant to how the system established under the DEA and the Ofcom code (2010) will work:

1 Communications provider: 'A person who provides an electronic communications network or an electronic communications service.' (Communications Act, 2003, s405) (www.legislation.gov.uk/ukpga/2003/21/section/405)
2 ISP: 'A person who provides an internet access service.' An internet access service is defined as 'an electronic communications service that – (a) is provided to a subscriber; (b) consists entirely or mainly of the provision of access to the internet; and (c) includes the allocation of an IP address or IP addresses to the subscriber to enable that access.' (DEA, 2010, s16) (www.legislation.gov.uk/ukpga/2010/24/section/16)
3 Subscriber: 'In relation to an internet access service [...] a person who – (a) receives the service under an agreement between the person and the provider of the service; and (b) does not receive it as a communications provider' (DEA s16) (www.legislation.gov.uk/ukpga/2010/24/section/16)

Initially, only fixed-line ISPs with over 400,000 subscribers fall within the definition of ISP.

Most of the operational details of the copyright infringement provisions are not defined in the Act itself, but are instead set out in a series of regulatory codes produced by Ofcom. The copyright infringement provisions of the DEA will come into force once Ofcom's initial obligations regulatory code is approved by Parliament.

Under the regime established by the DEA and the accompanying code, rights holders gather together lists of Internet Protocol (IP) addresses that they believe have infringed their copyrights. They then send each IP number to the appropriate ISP along with a 'copyright infringement report' (CIR). The ISP is then required to send a notification to the subscriber that the IP address associated with them has been reported by copyright holders as being used to infringe copyright.

The next stage involves the rights holder requesting a 'copyright infringement list' from the ISP. This contains an anonymous list of all subscribers who have reached the threshold set out in the Ofcom code with regard to the number of copyright infringement reports for their works. The rights holder can then approach a judge to gain a court order to identify some or all of the subscribers on the list, and with that information launch copyright infringement litigation against them.

ISPs are required to provide Ofcom with a quality assurance report detailing the processes by which they match IP addresses to subscribers in order to ensure that these are both robust and accurate.

The notification procedure proposed in the draft code ensures that a subscriber's identity is not disclosed directly or indirectly to a copyright owner without the express written consent of the subscriber. A copyright owner would need to apply to a court to obtain such a disclosure.

In order for rights owners to establish who is responsible for illicit file-sharing activity, they have on a number of occasions gone to court and made use of a device known as a 'Norwich Pharmacal order' in order to force ISPs to divulge the names of internet subscribers whose IP addresses are said to have been responsible for the infringing activity. If the court grants the order, legal action can be pursued against the alleged wrongdoer. Norwich Pharmacal orders are used when someone wishes to sue in respect of some wrong, but doesn't know the identity of the person who did it. If an innocent third party is in possession of information that can identify the alleged wrongdoer, then the claimant can ask the court to order the third party to produce the identifying information. If the court grants the order the plaintiff is then able to pursue legal action against the alleged wrongdoer on the basis of the disclosed information.

After a minimum of one year the Secretary of State can lay down an order for ISPs to impose 'technical measures' on subscribers who meet the copyright infringement report threshold. These measures may limit internet access in a number of ways. As well as suspending it entirely, these measures include:

- Blocking:
  — sites or URLs
  — protocol blocking
  — port blocking.
- Bandwidth capping (capping the speed of a subscriber's internet connection and/or capping the volume of data traffic which a subscriber can access).
- Bandwidth shaping (limiting the speed of a subscriber's access to selected protocols/services and/or capping the volume of data to selected protocols/ services).
- Content identification and filtering.

Ofcom is required to establish an independent appeals body to hear cases; although if a technical measure has been applied, there will be a further right of appeal to the First-Tier Tribunal. The appeals body will be able to award costs or compensation in favour of a subscriber whose appeal against a copyright infringement report is successful.

The grounds of appeal may include that:

- the apparent infringement to which the CIR relates was not an infringement of copyright
- the CIR does not relate to the subscriber's IP address at the time of the apparent infringement

- the act constituting the apparent infringement to which a CIR relates was not done by the subscriber and the subscriber took reasonable steps to prevent other persons infringing copyright by means of his/her internet access service.

On 30 August 2011, James Frith reported on the Slightly Right of Centre blog (www.slightlyrightofcentre.com) that the government had requested that Ofcom make DEA appeals harder and that the grounds for appeal be narrowed.

The appeals body may require any information it considers necessary from copyright owners and ISPs to assist it in reaching its determination. Any failure to provide information will be a breach of the Code and actionable accordingly.

The Act gives Ofcom the responsibility of enforcing ISPs' obligations. A fine of up to £250,000 can be levied on an ISP if it is found to be in contravention of those obligations; the limit can be raised by the Secretary of State with Parliament's consent.

 Practical steps that libraries can take in order to comply with the DEA
Libraries should take steps to prevent their internet connection from being used to share copyright content illegally. It is in their interests to do so because the Ofcom code makes clear that the appeals body must find in favour of the subscriber if:

- the act constituting the apparent infringement to which the CIR relates was not done by the subscriber, and
- the subscriber took reasonable steps to prevent other persons infringing copyright by means of the internet access service.

Measures libraries can use in order to reduce the risk of copyright infringements occurring include the following:

Secure Wi-Fi networks
Where libraries offer wireless internet access it is harder to tackle infringement than is the case with wired internet access, especially at the higher levels of bandwidth but there are a number of steps that can be taken to limit infringement:

- changing the administrator password
- turning off the network's name or Service Set Identifier (SSID)
- enabling Wi-Fi Protected Access (WPA) encryption
- if the router has this feature, reducing the range of the signal in order to limit the distance from your location that the signal can reach.

Wireless internet access can be vulnerable to use by criminals with hackers 'piggybacking' onto the internet connection, stealing usernames and passwords, and undertaking illegal activities including copyright infringement.

Procedure for receiving reports of copyright infringement

Libraries could implement and advertise a rapid and effective process for receiving reports of copyright infringement, identifying and dealing with the users responsible for any copyright infringement (see the JANET guidance at www.ja.net/documents/publications/factsheets/ 077-investigating-copyright-complaints.pdf).

Acceptable use policy

Libraries should have an acceptable use policy in place, and make sure that it covers all types of uses of the institutional IT facilities and systems, whether they be on- or off-site; whether they be permanent staff, freelancers, students, visitors or contractors. In order to be effective, the policy needs to be drawn to the attention of users and it needs to be enforced. Take disciplinary procedures and where appropriate legal action against those who breach the organization's acceptable use policy or code of conduct. It is also important to ensure that the policy is enforced in a consistent manner.

Authentication

Libraries can make sure that users are required to authenticate themselves before gaining unrestricted internet access and that logs are kept as appropriate, whilst conforming to the requirements of the Data Protection Act. If libraries were to be classed as internet service providers at some stage in the future, it would be essential to know who had committed a particular act of copyright infringement in order to notify them that a copyright infringement report had been received relating to their internet usage.

A few sources of information on user authentication and managing the identity of users are:

www.jisclegal.ac.uk/Themes/IdentityManagement.aspx;
www.ja.net/documents/publications/technical-guides/logfiles.pdf; and
www.ja.net/documents/publications/factsheets/041-user-authentication.pdf.

Monitor and manage new software installations

An easy way to prevent users file-sharing from a particular machine is to prevent them from being able to install the 'BitTorrent client' software required for file-sharing. This isn't possible for wireless networks, where users use their own hardware.

Education

Libraries can reduce the risk of copyright infringements by educating users on the correct and incorrect uses of copyright materials of all kinds. Ensure that all users of the organization's applications, software, systems or networks (including remote users and visitors) are aware of these policies and the need to comply with them, for example by providing a landing page that requires active consent to terms and conditions, prior to access being permitted. Software such as the 'u-Approve' module in Shibboleth may be beneficial for institutions wishing to implement such a process.

Monitoring

To minimize copyright infringements, monitor, manage and where necessary block unacceptable or inappropriate websites and track web traffic and user activities.

Blocking access to websites

Section 17 of the DEA provides powers for the Secretary of State to introduce provisions relating to court injunctions in respect of an internet site which the court is satisfied is being used for copyright infringement; while section 18 of the Act sets out a requirement that before such a process can take effect there would be specific Parliamentary debate and scrutiny. A Department for Culture Media and Sport (DCMS) press notice dated 1 February 2011 (entitled 'Ofcom to review aspects of Digital Economy Act') stated that Jeremy Hunt, Secretary of State for Culture Media and Sport, had referred to Ofcom the question as to whether or not these measures are possible and that they would work, saying: 'Before we consider introducing site blocking we need to know whether these measures are possible' (DCMS, 2011).

The Secretary of State must be satisfied before making the request that the location is 'having a serious adverse effect on businesses or consumers' (17(3)(a)), that the injunction 'is a proportionate way to address that effect' (17(3)(b)), and that 'making the regulations would not prejudice national security or the prevention or detection of crime' (17(3)(c)).

In deciding whether to grant an injunction, the court is required (under section 17(5) of the DEA) to consider:

- Any evidence presented of steps taken by the service provider or the operator of the location to prevent infringement.
- Any evidence of steps taken by the copyright owner to facilitate lawful access to the material.
- Any representations made by a Minister of the Crown.

- Whether the injunction would be likely to have a disproportionate effect on any person's legitimate interests.
- The importance of freedom of expression.

In Ofcom's findings, published in August 2011 as '"Site blocking" to reduce online copyright infringement', it concluded that 'sections 17 and 18 of the Digital Economy Act 2010 are unlikely to be able to provide for a framework for site blocking which would be effective' (Ofcom, 2011).

2.6.10 Hargreaves review of intellectual property and growth

In November 2010 David Cameron asked Ian Hargreaves to chair a review of the UK's intellectual property laws with a view to developing proposals on how the UK's intellectual property framework can further promote entrepreneurialism, economic growth and social and commercial innovation. The resulting report (Hargreaves, 2011) set out ten main recommendations, covering the suite of IPRs, not just copyright (see Box 2.1).

The report considered whether the more comprehensive American approach to copyright exceptions, based upon the so-called 'fair use defence', would be beneficial in the UK. It concluded that importing fair use wholesale was unlikely to be legally feasible in Europe and that the UK could achieve many of its benefits by taking up copyright exceptions already permitted under EU law and arguing for an additional exception, designed to enable EU copyright law to accommodate future technological change where it does not threaten copyright owners.

Box 2.1   Recommendations in the report of the Hargreaves independent review of IP and growth relevant to copyright

Digital Copyright Exchange

The setting up of a cross-sectoral Digital Copyright Exchange and the appointment of a senior figure to oversee its design and implementation by the end of 2012.

The Hargreaves report said that the government had a severely time-limited opportunity to bring about in the UK the best copyright licensing system in the world, and proposed a range of incentives and disincentives to encourage rights holders and others to take part in the exchange. For example, making DEA sanctions apply only to infringements involving works available through the exchange; and stipulating that orphan works searches be required to check the licensing exchange as part of a diligent search.

Orphan works

The report said that the government should legislate to enable licensing of orphan works: establish extended collective licensing for mass licensing of orphan works, and introduce a clearance procedure for use of individual works. In both cases, a work should only be treated as an orphan if it cannot be found by search of the databases involved in the proposed Digital Copyright Exchange.

Enforcement of IPR in the digital age

The government should pursue an integrated approach based upon enforcement, education and, crucially, measures to strengthen and grow legitimate markets in copyright and other IP-protected fields. In order to support rights holders in enforcing their rights the government should introduce a small claims track for low monetary value IP claims in the Patents County Court (which will be renamed the Intellectual Property County Court).

Text mining and data analytics

The government should introduce a UK exception under the non-commercial research heading to allow use of analytics for non-commercial use, as well as promoting at EU level an exception to support text mining and data analytics for commercial use.

The Hargreaves report took the view that text mining is one current example of a new technology which copyright should not inhibit, but does. The current non-commercial research 'Fair Dealing' exception in UK law will not cover use of these tools, and in any event text mining of databases is often excluded by the contract for accessing the database.

Regulation of the collecting societies

Collecting societies should be required by law to adopt codes of practice, approved by the Intellectual Property Office (IPO) and the UK competition authorities, to ensure that they operate in a way that is consistent with the further development of efficient, open markets.

Make use of the exceptions available in the copyright directive

The UK does not currently exploit all the exceptions available. Most notably, we do not have exceptions for:

* private copying
* parody and pastiche
* the exception for archiving falls well short of current needs
* the exception for non-commercial research doesn't currently cover all forms of

copyright work.

Format shifting/private copying

EU law permits Member States to introduce an exception for private copying, provided that fair compensation is paid. In other EU countries private copying exceptions are supported by levies on copying equipment, but the schemes vary greatly in terms of the size of levies, what they are charged on, and how the revenues are used.

The UK has a thriving market for personal media devices which rely on private copying. The Hargreaves report sees no economic argument for adding an extra charge to these devices in order to authorize reasonable private acts that are part of the normal use of devices:

> We are not aware of strong evidence of harm to rights holders done by this kind of private copying in the normal course of using digital equipment to play works. There is considerable evidence of overall public benefits from consumer use.   (Hargreaves, 2011, 48)

Expand the archiving exception

The archiving exception should be extended to cover fully audio-visual works and sound recordings. At present, libraries are inhibited in preserving content through digitization as they cannot preserve all categories of works and as a result works continue to deteriorate.

> We may well find that this public digital archive turns out to have considerable economic as well as social and cultural value, but this will not happen if our cultural institutions are prevented from securing it through digitization.
> (Hargreaves, 2011, 50)

No exception to copyright should be overridden by contract

The government should change the law to make it clear no exception to copyright can be overridden by contract.

2.7   Copyright clearance

Copyright is an automatic right. There is no formal process that a creator has to go through before copyright is granted. As a result there isn't a comprehensive register available for locating the creator or rights holder in a work in order to seek their explicit permission to copy material. And even if there were, it would have to be kept up to date if people were to rely on it bearing in mind that ownership can change over time.

 Consider whether or not clearance is required, because there are a number of reasons why copyright clearance might not be necessary, such as:

- where the material is in the public domain (although it is important to remember that both the typographical rights and the copyright relating to the content itself must have expired)
- it is a government publication covered by the Open Government Licence
- the copying may be covered by a licence that your organization already holds
- it is governed by a Creative Commons licence.

You will need to consider who owns or controls the rights in the material. This could be:

- the creator of the material or his/her heirs
- the creator's employer
- anyone else to whom the rights in the material have been sold, or otherwise transferred or licensed
- a collective licensing society which has been asked to collect fees on behalf of the rights holder.

For a work that has been commercially published, the starting point for permission seeking would be the publisher. If they don't hold the rights, they can generally refer you to whoever they think holds the rights. If, for whatever reason, they were not the rights holder, then the next step would be to try and locate the author. Another thought is to contact the appropriate collecting society.

Organizations such as the PLS (www.pls.org.uk), the ALCS (www.alcs.co.uk) and DACS (www.dacs.co.uk) are responsible for distributing monies to their members and as such they need to have up-to-date and accurate records, and they might be able to help with tracing a particular rights owner.

The Society of Authors (www.societyofauthors.net) manages the estates of a number of well known authors.

If after a lot of searching you have still not been able to trace the rights owner, you might consider placing an advertisement in a relevant journal.

2.7.1 Databases of rights owners

•◆ Useful resources

There are a number of databases that can be used in order to trace rights owners. These include:

- **WATCH (Writers Artists and their Copyright Holders)**
  http://tyler.hrc.utexas.edu
  WATCH primarily contains the names and addresses of copyright holders or contact persons for authors and artists whose archives are housed, in whole or in part, in libraries and archives in North America and the United Kingdom. The objective in making the database available is to provide information to scholars about whom to contact for permission to publish text and images that still enjoy copyright protection.

- **FOB (Firms Out of Business)**
  http://tyler.hrc.utexas.edu/fob.cfm
  FOB is a companion to WATCH. It aims to record information about printing and publishing companies, magazines, literary agencies and similar organizations that are no longer in existence, and the successor organizations that might own any surviving rights.

- **ARROW (Accessible Registries of Rights Information and Orphan Works towards Europeana)**
  www.arrow-net.eu
  ARROW aims to support the EC's i2010 Digital Libraries initiative by finding ways to clarify the rights status of orphan and out-of-print works, so that they can be cleared for digitization and inclusion in the Digital Library.

- **MILE (Metadata Image Library Exploration)**
  www.mileproject.eu
  MILE is co-ordinated by The Bridgeman Art Library. It aims to promote European cultural heritage and make digital art more accessible by improving metadata. There are three components to the project: metadata classification, metadata search and retrieval, and IPRs as metadata.

When contacting the rights holder in order to obtain permission, provide them with the following information:

- author and title of the extract you want to reproduce

- page range
- date of publication (plus volume and issue numbers for journals)
- ISBN/ISSN
- publisher's name
- number of copies to be made.

You might also include:

- format of the copies
- levels of protection available (e.g. individual passwords are needed to be able to access the file)
- whether you subscribe to the journal or hold copies of the book
- your reference to the request (to identify it quickly).

 If you are going to request copyright clearance from rights holders on a regular basis you should consider developing a standard form for this purpose.

If you have tried all avenues to trace the publisher and the author, and failed, then the decision to digitize the materials comes down to a risk assessment.

↔ Useful resource

There is a risk management calculator available on the Web2rights website (www.web2rights.com/OERIPRSupport/risk-management-calculator), which shows the low, medium or high indicative risk value.

 If you do decide to go ahead without permission, you should first have made every 'reasonable' effort in order to trace the rights holder and have kept good records of your efforts. That way, if you are challenged about the copying you have done, it will help to show that you were acting in good faith. But there isn't currently an exception available that would let you go ahead and copy without the permission of the rights owner on the basis that you had undertaken a reasonable search.

2.7.2   Orphan works

'Orphan work' is the term that has come to be used in order to describe a work where the rights holder is either difficult or even impossible to identify or locate. The orphan works problem tends to be more prevalent amongst older works where the copyright term far exceeds the 'commercial' life. It also tends to be the case that the less commercially successful a work has proved to be, the more administrative effort is required to search for possible authors.

Examples of orphan works can include the following:

- obscure works of literature or art
- copyright works coming to the end of their protection period
- anonymous or pseudonymous works
- works not traditionally published
- works no longer commercially published.

The orphan work issue is linked to the lack of appropriate attribution of authorship in many creative sectors. It is especially problematic in the area of visual art and photography.

Where people wish to make use of a work that is protected by copyright, and that use would not be covered by one of the copyright exceptions or permitted acts, it requires the permission of the copyright holder. The problem with orphan works is that if a library undertakes a reasonable search for the copyright owner but the rights owner still cannot be located, they would be taking an incalculable risk if they did decide to go ahead with the copying. Indeed, the risk of liability for copyright infringement is enough to prevent many stakeholders from making use of the work; and as such it is a major obstacle to large-scale digitization projects.

There are a number of factors which can lead to a work being an orphan work:

1 When there is no information about the author on the work itself. Books and journals will normally have ISBNs and ISSNs, respectively, but for some types of material there won't be any markings along similar lines. It is highly likely that there won't be any information about the author on photographs, for example. In addition to ISBNs and ISSNs, there are a number of other identifier systems. They include:
   a   ISAN for audio-visual material
   b   ISMN for sheet music
   c   ISWC for musical scores
   d   ISRC for sound recordings.
2 The term of copyright is dependent upon the date of the death of the author. It isn't always easy to know when an author died, and therefore, to know when the work comes out of copyright protection.
3 The author is known, but has died, and there is no information about his or her heirs.
4 The company that held the copyright no longer exists. Indeed the *Gowers Review* (HM Treasury, 2006) uses the word 'abandonware' to describe when businesses go bankrupt or merge, and where any information about copyright

ownership gets lost.

5 The author is no longer the rights owner.

The question arises as to what to do if the copyright owner cannot be identified; or where the copyright owner has been identified, but can't be located; or where they don't respond to your request; or where they are uncertain about the ownership of the rights.

There are a number of options available, but depending on which option is selected, there may be risks attached. Options include:

- Don't digitize the material under any circumstances.
- Digitize the content but continue to make efforts to find the owners.
- Include a disclaimer in the material that you digitize.
- Take out indemnity insurance.

Reading the British Library's annual accounts for 2010–11 (www.bl.uk/aboutus/annrep/2010to2011/accounts/accounts.pdf, page 79), for example, one finds a couple of paragraphs about the British Library Newspaper Digitisation Project:

> The British Library has undertaken the digitisation of millions of pages from the archive using a commercial partner to take on the costs of digitisation in return for being able to exploit the digitisations commercially.
>
> The supplier has warranted in the contract with the British Library that use of the digitisations will not infringe copyright, or give rise to any possible action for defamation and has undertaken to cover any liability falling on the Library as a result of any such claims (in addition to the cost of defending the action) up to £5m.

Possible solutions to orphan works, which have been considered over the last few years, include:

1 Dealing with orphan works as with abandoned or ownerless property (*bona vacantia*). This would require primary legislation and it would be desirable to have the EC's endorsement for such a scheme.
2 Amending the Information Society directive (2001/29/EC) to allow for an explicit exception to cover orphan works. At present, the list of exceptions and limitations in Article 5 of the directive doesn't cater for orphan works, and without amending the directive it is not possible for any Member States of the EU to introduce a defence covering orphan works into their list of permitted acts or exceptions.
3 The EC introducing a new orphan works directive, which would allow for licensing solutions for each country, and for these to be mutually recognizable

(as set out in *Proposal for a directive of the European Parliament and of the Council on certain permitted uses of orphan works*, European Commission, 2011, COM(2011)289 final, http://ec.europa.eu/internal_market/copyright/docs/orphan-works/ proposal_en.pdf.)

4 Establishing extended licensing schemes operated by the collective licensing societies which would permit uses of orphan works that would otherwise infringe; however, this needs legislation to exonerate any organization (such as a collecting society) offering a scheme from civil and, potentially, criminal liability. Such an option would need to resolve the issue of what happens to any monies collected where no rights owner comes forward.

In May 2011, the EC published a proposal for a draft directive on orphan works (COM(2011)289 final), the main purpose of which is to create a legal framework to ensure the lawful, cross-border online access to orphan works contained in online digital libraries or archives operated by a variety of institutions in pursuance of the public interest mission of those institutions.

The organizations covered by the proposed directive will only be able to use the orphan works in order to achieve the aims of their public interest missions – notably preservation, restoration and the provision of cultural and educational access to works contained in their collections.

The aim of the draft directive is for there to be a system of mutual recognition of the orphan status of a work throughout the EU, thus obviating the need for multiple diligent searches. This approach allows libraries and other beneficiaries to enjoy legal certainty as to the 'orphan status' of a particular work.

In order to establish that a work has 'orphan' status, libraries, educational establishments, museums or archives, film heritage institutions and public service broadcasting organizations are required to carry out a prior diligent search in the Member State where the work was first published.

The proposal covers books, journals, newspapers, magazines or other writings which are in the collections of publicly accessible libraries, educational establishments, museums or archives; as well as cinematic or audio-visual works contained in the collections of film heritage institutions; and cinematographic, audio or audio-visual works produced by public service broadcasting organizations before 31 December 2002 and contained in their archives.

The sources appropriate for each category of works will be determined by each Member State and includes the sources listed in the annex to the proposal. For example, in the case of books this would include legal deposit, ARROW, WATCH and the ISBN; and in the case of newspapers and magazines it would include associations of publishers, authors and journalists, legal deposit, and the relevant collecting society.

2.8   Open access

Open access is an alternative to the traditional method of publishing scholarly papers. It refers to the availability of peer-reviewed literature to the public on the internet free of charge, permitting any user to read, download, copy, distribute, print, search or link to the full texts of the articles.

This is the ideal that was set out in the landmark 2002 Budapest Open Access Initiative statement (www.soros.org/openaccess/read.shtml).

In October 2003, the Berlin Declaration on Open Access to Knowledge in the Sciences and Humanities was signed by the Max Planck Society and a number of other large German and international research organizations.

Signatories to the Berlin Declaration agreed to make progress by:

• Encouraging their researchers or grant recipients to publish their work according to the principles of open access.
• Encouraging cultural institutions to support open access by providing their resources on the internet.
• Developing means and ways to evaluate open access contributions in order to maintain the standards of quality assurance and good scientific practice and by advocating that such publications be recognized in promotion and tenure evaluation.

Open access can be achieved in one of two ways:

1 Articles are published in open access journals which don't levy a subscription charge to the user.
2 The articles are deposited in a subject-based or an institutional electronic repository that is accessible from remote locations without any access restrictions.

Just as with the traditional publishing market, some open access journals are peer-reviewed. This is when the papers are submitted, reviewed, authenticated and finally published. Open access journals are subject to thorough quality controls, and many are supported by editors who organize the refereeing process.

Academic institutions aren't able to stock all of the journal titles that are relevant to their research staff for a number of reasons which, when considered together, amount to the so-called 'serials crisis'. The serials crisis was a key driver for the adoption of open access as it emphasized:

• the large number of journals published
• that journal prices increase at a much faster pace than the rate of inflation
• constraints on library budgets.

Financial considerations are, however, not the only driver for the adoption of open access. In fact, one of the main motives is to grant academic peers and scientific collaborators rapid access to discoveries in their same field of study by publishing online.

There are a number of different models for open access, including one that is known as 'author pays'. Under the 'author-pays' model, the author has to pay a fee in order to have their article published. Whilst the author has to pay for the article to be published, under this model the user doesn't have to pay anything to access the item.

The general principles of open access require authors to grant an irrevocable right for anybody to download, copy, redistribute and view the content that is submitted. Copyright still subsists within the published material, and there are a number of important considerations that need to be kept in mind:

- Any copying and redistribution of the content should always include the proper attribution of the author.
- The author's moral right of integrity does not permit modification of a work.
- The copyright policy would not normally permit printing of the material in large numbers, especially if this was for commercial use; although a suitable number of private printouts is generally permitted.

➼ Useful resources

The SHERPA website has drawn together links to the publishers' copyright policies and self archiving: www.sherpa.ac.uk/romeo/.

There is also a directory of open access journals, which can be found at: www.doaj.org.

2.9   Ethical and professional issues and conflicts

Library and information service professionals find themselves in a difficult situation playing the role of 'piggy in the middle', acting as guardians of intellectual property whilst at the same time being committed to supporting their users' needs to gain access to copyright works and the ideas that they contain.

CILIP's Ethical Principles and Code of Professional Practice for Library and Information Professionals (2009) states that information professionals should strive to achieve an appropriate balance within the law, between demands from information users, the need to respect confidentiality, the terms of their employment, the public good and the responsibilities outlined in the Code. It also says that information professionals should defend the legitimate needs and interests of information users, while upholding the moral and legal rights of the creators and distributors of intellectual property. The key point here is that the commitment to providing their users with information has to be tempered by the need to do so within the limits of the law, which includes respecting copyright law.

Similarly, the European Information Researchers Network (EIRENE) Code of Practice for Information Brokers (EIRENE, 1993) also deals with a number of copyright-related issues stating that 'a broker shall abide by copyright law' (A.3) and that they shall 'clarify their copyright position vis-à-vis the information suppliers and inform the client of their copyright obligations as regards the information provided' (B.1).

It is not the role of the librarian or information professional to police the copying undertaken by their users on behalf of rights owners. For example, the CLA make clear in their guidance about the Sticker Scheme for walk-in users of public libraries that librarians are not required to monitor private copying or police the use of the scheme. It is for each patron at a self-service copier to decide whether or not their copying is for commercial purposes and, if so, whether to ask for a sticker.

However, librarians should do everything they can to ensure copyright compliance within their organization. This could, for example, include:

- Putting up the CILIP posters next to photocopying machines or publicly accessible computers.
- Including guidance about copyright on your intranet.
- Developing a set of frequently asked questions (FAQs) about copyright which cover the activities that users are most likely to wish to undertake.
- Making the users of electronic products aware of the key points of the terms and conditions of the licence agreement(s).

2.10　Further information

British Library intellectual property page
　Website: www.bl.uk/ip.

CILIP
　7 Ridgmount Street, London WC1E 7AE
　Tel.: 020 7255 0620 (CILIP Information Services)
　E-mail: info@cilip.org.uk (members only).
　Website: www.cilip.org.uk

Copyright Licensing Agency
　Saffron House, 6–10 Kirby Street, London EC1N 8TS
　Tel.: 020 7400 3100

Fax: 020 7400 3101
E-mail: cla@cla.co.uk
Website: www.cla.co.uk.

Design and Artists Copyright Society

33 Great Sutton Street, London EC1V 0DX
Tel.: 020 7336 8811
Fax: 020 7336 8822
Website: www.dacs.org.uk.

European Commission – Copyright and Neighbouring Rights

http://ec.europa.eu/internal_market/copyright/index_en.htm.

Intellectual Property Office

Enquiry Unit Tel.: 0845 9500505
E-mail: enquiries@ipo.gov.uk
Website: www.ipo.gov.uk.

IPR helpdesk

www.ipr-helpdesk.org (a project of the European Commission DG Enterprise and Industry).

National Archives

The Licensing Division, St Clements House, 2–16 Colegate, Norwich
NR3 1BQ
Tel.: 01603 723 000
Contact form: www.nationalarchives.gov.uk/contact/contactform.asp
Website: www.nationalarchives.gov.uk.

Newspaper Licensing Agency

Wellington Gate, Church Road, Tunbridge Wells TN1 1NL
Tel.: 01892 525273
Fax: 01892 525275
E-mail: copy@nla.co.uk
Website: www.nla.co.uk.

Ordnance Survey

Customer Service Centre (Copyright), Romsey Road, Southampton
SO16 4GU
Tel.: 08456 050505
E-mail: customerservices@ordnancesurvey.co.uk
Website: www.ordnancesurvey.co.uk.

World Intellectual Property Organization
Copyright and Related Rights Sector, 34 chemin des Colombettes, CH-1211 Geneva 20, Switzerland
Tel.: 0041 22 338 9111
Fax: 0041 22 338 9070
E-mail: copyright.mail@wipo.int
Website: www.wipo.int.

References

Charlesworth , A. (2009) *Digital Lives: legal and ethical issues*, British Library.

CILIP (2009) *Ethical Principles and Code of Professional Practice for Library and Information Professionals*,
www.cilip.org.uk/get-involved/policy/ethics/pages/principles.aspx.

CILIP (2010) *Copyright Posters*,
www.cilip.org.uk/get-involved/advocacy/copyright/posters-forms/
pages/default.aspx.

CLA (2003) *Note on Changes to UK Copyright Law*,
www.cla.co.uk/data/corporate_material/submissions/2003_cla_and_bl_joint_
note_on_changes_to_copyright_law_nov03.pdf.

DCMS (2011) Ofcom to review aspects of Digital Economy Act, press notice,
www.culture.gov.uk/news/media_releases/7756.aspx.

DfTI (2005) *Electronic Commerce Directive: the liability of hyperlinkers, location tool services and content aggregators*,
www.berr.gov.uk/files/file13986.pdf, and
http://webarchive.nationalarchives.gov.uk/+/www.berr.gov.uk/consultations/
page13985.html.

EC (2004) *Commission Staff Working Paper on the Review of the EC Legal Framework in the Field of Copyright and Related Rights*,
http://ec.europa.eu/internal_market/copyright/docs/review/
sec-2004-995_en.pdf.

EIRENE (European Information Researchers Network) (1993) *Code of Practice for Information Brokers*,
www.jiscmail.ac.uk/cgi-bin/webadmin?A2=LIS-UKEIG;df511604.99.

Hargreaves, I. (2011) *Digital Opportunity: review of intellectual property and growth*,
www.ipo.gov.uk/ipreview-finalreport.pdf.

HM Treasury (2006) *The Gowers Review of Intellectual Property*, TSO.

LACA (2002). *Electronic Signatures on Copyright Declaration Forms*,
www.cilip.org.uk/get-involved/advocacy/copyright/advice/Pages/
esignatures.aspx.

Ofcom (2011) *'Site Blocking' to Reduce Online Copyright Infringement: a review of sections 17 and 18 of the Digital Economy Act*, http://stakeholders.ofcom.org.uk/binaries/internet/site-blocking.pdf.

PWC (2011) *Economic Analysis of Copyright, Secondary Copyright and Collective Licensing*,
www.alcs.co.uk/Documents/Downloads/PWC-Final-report.

UN (1948) *Universal Declaration of Human Rights*,
www.un.org/en/documents/udhr.

web2rights (2011) *OER IPR Support Risk Management Calculator*,
www.web2rights.com/OERIPRSupport/risk-management-calculator.

WTO (1994) *Agreement on Trade-Related Aspects of Intellectual Property Rights*,
www.wto.org/english/tratop_e/trips_e/t_agm0_e.htm.

Notes

1 A person who issues certificates or provides other services related to electronic signatures.

CHAPTER 3

Legal deposit

Contents

3.1   Introduction

There has been a rapid growth in the publication of material in non-print forms in recent years, and, unless these forms of publishing are covered by the legal deposit legislation, the danger is that we might lose an important part of the UK's national heritage. The legal deposit legislation set out in the Copyright Act 1911 was designed to ensure that the legal deposit libraries received a copy of everything published in the UK. However, only covering material that was printed in hard copy, the Act has long since ceased to be adequate to ensure the continuation of a comprehensive archive of the nation's published material. For that reason a number of people lobbied for the scope of the legislation to be extended which ultimately led to the passing of the Legal Deposit Libraries Act 2003 (LDLA). The problem, though, is that there has been no legislation to implement the provisions of the Act with regard to digital content at the time of writing (November 2011).

Around the time of the 2010 general election, CILIP published a manifesto in which one of the six priorities they identified was to 'Ensure the legal deposit system works effectively so that the nation's digital heritage can be enjoyed and exploited effectively by future generations' (CILIP, 2010).

3.2   General principles

'Legal deposit' is the legal requirement for publishers to deposit with the British Library and the five other legal deposit libraries (see Figure 3.1 overleaf) a single copy of each publication. The system is governed by the LDLA.

British Library
National Library of Scotland
National Library of Wales
Bodleian Library, Oxford
Cambridge University Library

Figure 3.1 *Legal deposit libraries*

The Legal Deposit Libraries Bill received Royal Assent on 31 October 2003, and the provisions for print publications commenced on 1 February 2004, with the coming into force of the Legal Deposit Libraries Act (Commencement) Order 2004: SI 2004/130. The DCMS is the relevant government department or principal owner of the Act and they are responsible for legislation in this field.

The LDLA sets out a 'duty to deposit' under which anyone who publishes in the UK a work to which the Act applies, 'must, at his own expense, deliver a copy of it to an address specified (generally or in a particular case) by any deposit library entitled to delivery under this section' (s1(1) of the Legal Deposit Libraries Act 2003) (see Figure 3.2).

- Duty on publishers to deposit (ss1-3).
- New and alternative editions – deposit restricted to one edition and one medium (s2).
- Printed publications – carried over with only minor amendments from 1911 Act affecting BL (s4) and five other libraries (s5).
- New consequential exceptions to the Copyright Designs and Patents Act 1988 and Copyright and Rights in Databases Regulations 1997 (s8).
- Exemptions from liability for publishers in respect of breach of contract (s9).

Figure 3.2 *Layout of the LDLA*

3.2.1   Print material

The LDLA re-enacted (with minor amendments) the obligation in the Copyright Act 1911 to deposit printed publications in the six legal deposit libraries. A copy of each book or serial or other printed publication which is published in the UK is required to be deposited, free of charge, in the British Library. The copy must be delivered to the British Library within a month of publication, and the copy must be of the same quality as the best copies published in the United Kingdom at that time. The British Library Board must provide a receipt for the deposited printed works received. In addition, the other five legal deposit libraries (Figure 3.1) are each entitled to receive, on request, one free copy of any book or other printed publication published in the UK providing that they make a claim in writing within a year of the date of publication.

In respect of works that are published in print, the Act applies to:

- books (including pamphlets, magazines and newspapers)
- sheet music or letterpress
- maps, plans, charts or tables
- any part of any such work.

3.2.2 Non-print material

On 4 July 2003 the then Arts Minister, Estelle Morris, said that the LDLA legislation would be 'implemented slowly, incrementally, and above all, selectively' (Hansard, 2003). People may well have underestimated just how true those words were, given the length of time that has already elapsed and the fact that even now the provisions relating to electronic content haven't been enacted through Statutory Instruments.

The LDLA gives the Secretary of State specific powers to make regulations which will cover the deposit (or harvesting) of publications in different formats. The Secretary of State has powers to extend the system of legal deposit to cover various non-print media as they develop, including offline publications such as CD-ROMs and microforms, online publications such as electronic journals or blogs, and other non-print materials.

If the work is published in a medium other than print, then the Act only applies if the work is of a 'prescribed description' and these descriptions will be specified by regulation.

The 2003 Act was drafted so that it would be flexible enough to cover the diverse and complex nature of the publishing industry in the 21st century. It ensures that forms of publication developed in the future can be incorporated into legal deposit, without the need to return to primary legislation.

A consultation paper was published in September 2010 incorporating a set of Draft Legal Deposit Libraries (Non-print Publications) Regulations 2011 (DCMS, 2010). Whilst specific types of non-print publications are listed in the draft Regulations, the list is non-exhaustive because the government didn't want to preclude new types of publications which may develop in the future. In April 2011, the DCMS published the *Government Response to the Public Consultation on the Draft Regulations and Guidance for Non-Print Legal Deposit* (DCMS, 2011) in which they said that it wasn't viable to go forward with the Regulations as currently drafted without evidence demonstrating that they were proportionate.

There was general support amongst respondents to the consultation for the need to ensure that the nation's non-print published output (and thereby its intellectual record and future published heritage) is preserved as an archive for research purposes and the use of future generations. However, opinion was divided on the support for the Regulations as drafted.

The Legal Deposit Libraries were broadly supportive of the draft Regulations. However, they did have concerns with:

* the inclusion of embargoes in the draft Regulations
* publishers having the overriding say on the format of the content deposited
* copyright restrictions
* the definition of published in the UK
* restrictions on access to content following the expiry of copyright
* the inclusion of the Sunset Clause.

Other libraries, archivists and researchers generally mirrored the issues raised by the Legal Deposit Libraries while also calling for wider access to content; and the inclusion of audio and video content.

Respondents from the library community were in favour of the Regulations being extended to Trinity College Dublin, providing the Secretary of State is satisfied that restrictions on the use of the deposited material under Irish law are not substantially less than in the UK.

The publishing sector recognized that the government had listened to them and had gone a long way to try and meet their concerns regarding non-print legal deposit. However, they still had significant concerns about:

* access to content
* cost
* data security
* definitions
* duplication of archives
* governance
* long-term access and use
* technical implications
* the inclusion of Trinity College Dublin.

One of the key objectives of the consultation was to try and clarify the costs to business of the Regulations as drafted in order to ensure that the cost of deposit to publishers should not be disproportionate to the public benefit of deposit, as required under the LDLA. However, it is because of a lack of evidence from both libraries and publishers to support the case that the Regulations do not impose a disproportionate burden that the DCMS does not believe that it is viable to go forward with the Regulations as currently drafted without the necessary evidence of proportionality.

Nevertheless, the government does intend to develop draft regulations to include only offline content, and online content that can be obtained through a harvesting process. A number of news articles interpreted this to mean that only free websites would be covered by the legislation. However, the DCMS has made clear that they intend to cover both content that is freely available and that which has access restrictions (this could include paid-for content). They will also look to include online content that is substantially the same as a printed work, removing the need to deposit print and reducing the costs to the publishing sector.

3.3   Voluntary deposit of non-print publications

At the end of 1997 the Secretary of State for Culture, Media and Sport set up a working party under the chairmanship of Sir Anthony Kenny to advise on how an effective national archive of non-print material might be achieved. The working party reported in July 1998, concluding that in the longer term only statutory deposit could secure a comprehensive national published archive. It was clear that further work was needed, consulting the publishing industry, working on the definitions of material to be covered, and also looking at the impact such legislation would have on business. As a result, the Secretary of State requested that a code of practice for the voluntary deposit of non-print publications should be drawn up and agreed between publishers and the deposit libraries (BL, 2010).

The code of practice covers microform and other offline electronic media (such as CD-ROM or DVD); but it does not cover online publications or 'dynamic' databases and other continuously updated publications. The voluntary scheme for offline media is still ongoing.

3.4   Enforcement

Section 3 of the LDLA sets out the provisions regarding enforcement. If a publisher fails to deposit, the library will be able to apply to the county court (or to the sheriff court in Scotland) for an order requiring deposit. In those instances where such an order would not be effective or appropriate, the court may make an order requiring the publisher to make a payment of not more than the cost of making good the failure to comply.

3.5   Copyright and use of legal deposit material

Section 7 of the LDLA provides that the libraries, persons acting on their behalf and readers may not do any of the following activities unless authorized by regulations: using the material, copying it, adapting any accompanying computer program or database, lending it to a third party, transferring it to a third party, or disposing of it.

The regulations may in particular make provision for the *purposes* for which the deposited material may be used; the *time at which readers may first use the material* (thereby allowing embargoes to be established); and the *description of readers that may use the material* at any one time (which will enable cross-library limits to be imposed if there is a secure network, in addition to limiting the number of people that may access the material simultaneously in any particular library).

The LDLA inserts section 44A into the CDPA. It additionally inserts a new exception to database right into the Copyright and Rights in Databases Regulations 1997 (SI 1997/3032) in respect of activities permitted by regulations made under section 7 (see Figure 3.3).

---

(1) Copyright is not infringed by the copying of a work from the internet by a deposit library or person acting on its behalf if–
    (a) the work is of a description prescribed by regulations under section 10(5) of the 2003 Act,
    (b) its publication on the internet, or a person publishing it there, is connected with the United Kingdom in a manner so prescribed, and
    (c) the copying is done in accordance with any conditions so prescribed.
(2) Copyright is not infringed by the doing of anything in relation to relevant material permitted to be done under regulations under section 7 of the 2003 Act.
(3) The Secretary of State may by regulations make provision excluding, in relation to prescribed activities done in relation to relevant material, the application of such of the provisions of this Chapter as are prescribed.
(4) Regulations under subsection (3) may in particular make provision prescribing activities–
    (a) done for a prescribed purpose,
    (b) done by prescribed descriptions of reader,
    (c) done in relation to prescribed descriptions of relevant material,
    (d) done other than in accordance with prescribed conditions.
(5) Regulations under this section may make different provision for different purposes.
(6) Regulations under this section shall be made by statutory instrument which shall be subject to annulment in pursuance of a resolution of either House of Parliament.
(7) In this section-
    (a) 'the 2003 Act' means the Legal Deposit Libraries Act 2003;
    (b) 'deposit library', 'reader' and 'relevant material' have the same meaning as in section 7 of the 2003 Act;
    (c) 'prescribed' means prescribed by regulations made by the Secretary of State.

Figure 3.3 *CDPA Section 44A: Legal deposit libraries*

(www.legislation.gov.uk/ukpga/1988/48/section/44A)

3.6   Online defamation

Section 10 of the LDLA provides that any liability of the deposit libraries for defamation resulting from prescribed activities relating to deposited works will arise only where they know or ought to know that the material is defamatory and have had a reasonable opportunity to prevent activities giving rise to the claims for defamation.

Section 10(1) of the Act says:

> A deposit library, or a person acting on its behalf, is not liable in damages, or subject to any criminal liability, for defamation arising out of the doing by a relevant person of an activity listed in section 7(2) in relation to a copy of a work delivered under section 1.   (www.legislation.gov.uk/ukpga/2003/28/section/10)

References

British Library (BL) (2010) *Self-regulated Code for the Voluntary Deposit of Microform and Offline (Hand Held) Electronic Publications*,
www.bl.uk/aboutus/stratpolprog/legaldep/offlinevoluntary/offline.html.

CILIP (2010) *Manifesto*,
www.cilip.org.uk/get-involved/policy/statements/Documents/
ManifestoA4%28web%29.pdf.

DCMS (2010) *Consultation on the Legal Deposit of Non-Print Works*,
www.dcms.gov.uk/images/publications/Cons-non-print-legal-deposit-
2011.pdf.

DCMS (2011) *Government Response to the Public Consultation on the Draft Regulations and Guidance for Non-Print Legal Deposit*,
www.culture.gov.uk/publications/8029.aspx.

Hansard (2003) *Hansard*, 4 July 2003,
www.publications.parliament.uk/pa/cm200203/cmhansrd/vo030704/
debtext/30704-22.htm.

CHAPTER 4

Breach of confidence

Contents

4.1   General principles

The common law tort of breach of confidence deals with unauthorized use or disclosure of certain types of information and provides protection for that information to be kept secret. This branch of the law is based upon the principle that a person who has obtained information in confidence should not take unfair advantage of it. The main means used to achieve this is the interim injunction (interdict in Scotland), which is an order of the court directing a party to refrain from disclosing the confidential information. A document may be considered confidential where there is:

- an obligation of non-disclosure within a particular document
- a duty in certain papers involving professional relationships
- a duty of confidence, which arises where a reasonable individual may determine that a document contains confidential material.

Breach of confidence is most commonly used to prevent publication of private material. The law protects confidential information from unauthorized disclosure, and an injunction may be granted unless you can show that the publication is in the public interest, usually by exposing some wrongdoing. The injunction can in extreme circumstances be against the whole world, such as the injunction granted to protect the new identities of the killers of James Bulger.

In the James Bulger case, Dame Elizabeth Butler-Sloss gave the killers of James Bulger the right to privacy throughout their life. The media were already prevented from publishing their identities as a result of information obtained from those who owed the pair a duty of confidence, such as police officers and probation service officials; but Dame Elizabeth went further and said the pair had an absolute right to privacy. In another legal case from May 2003 the child killer Mary Bell and her daughter won a High Court injunction guaranteeing them lifelong anonymity.

There are three elements of a breach of confidence. In Coco v. Clark [1969] RPC 41, Mr Justice Megarry said:

1 The information must have 'the necessary *quality of confidence*' – namely, it must not be something which is public property and public knowledge.
2 The information must have been imparted in circumstances imposing an *obligation of confidence.*
3 There must be an unauthorized use of that information to the *detriment* of the party communicating it.

If someone wishes to seek redress for disclosure of confidential information, then each of these elements must be present. Furthermore:

1 Companies use breach of confidence to protect sensitive commercial information and trade secrets.
2 Governments use breach of confidence to protect information they regard as secret.
3 Individuals use it for the same purpose and also to protect their privacy.

The duty of confidence is, as a general rule, also imposed on a third party who is in possession of information that he knows is subject to an obligation of confidence.[1] If this were not the law, the right would be of little practical value. There would, for example, be no point in imposing a duty of confidence in respect of the secrets of the marital bed if newspapers were free to publish those secrets when they were betrayed to them by the unfaithful partner in the marriage. Similarly, when trade secrets are betrayed by a confidant to a third party, it is usually the third party who is to exploit the information, and it is the activity of the third party that must be stopped in order to protect the owner of the trade secret.

The use of breach of confidence by individuals wishing to protect their privacy was boosted by the implementation of the ECHR in UK law through the Human Rights Act 1998 (HRA), because this Act gives individuals a right to privacy.

Between February and April 2003, the Culture, Media and Sport Select Committee held an inquiry into privacy and media intrusion and whether there was a need for legislation on privacy. The inquiry did not aim to come to the aid of public figures who have problems with the press; rather, they were concerned with ordinary people whose lives can be affected, perhaps adversely, by their relations with the media. About 11 years had elapsed since the previous inquiry on this topic by the then National Heritage Committee.

The government's response to the Select Committee Report made clear that they didn't accept a need for a new law in this area:

> The Government believes that people have a right to a private life, but that right is not absolute. Equally, the right to freedom of expression is not absolute. Where there is conflict between the two, they must be weighed against each other. The Government remains committed to supporting self-regulation as the best possible form of regulation for the press, and as the best possible way of balancing those sometimes-conflicting demands. There is, however, room for improvement in any regulatory system, and the Committee's report has effectively opened up debate on what the improvements in this system might be. We believe that such debate is healthy and constructive, and that it should lead to a positive outcome.
>
> (The Government's Response to the Fifth Report of the Culture,
> Media and Sport Select Committee on 'Privacy and Media Intrusion'
> (HC 458-1) Session 2002–2003 Cm 5985.)

In 2009 the Culture, Media and Sport Select Committee held an inquiry into press standards, privacy and libel. This was published in February 2010 (House of Commons, 2010). The Select Committee's report concluded that for now matters relating to privacy should continue to be determined according to the common law, with all the flexibility that it permits, rather than for it to be set down in statute.

In July 2011 the Prime Minister announced a two-part inquiry investigating the role of the press and police in the phone-hacking scandal (see www. levesoninquiry.org.uk/). In April 2011 Prime Minister David Cameron said that he was uneasy about the way in which the courts were issuing super-injunctions to

---

Kaye v. Robertson [1991] F.S.R 62

A reporter and a photographer tricked their way into the private hospital room of the actor Gorden Kaye who was lying there semi-conscious (he had been injured after a tree fell onto his car during the Burns Day storms of 1990). They did so in order to 'interview' and photograph him. The court held that there was no actionable right to privacy in English law and that no breach of confidence had taken place because there wasn't a recognized relationship between Mr Kaye and the journalists (such as that between a doctor and his patient) which could be used in order to impose an obligation to keep confidential what Mr Kaye had said.

This case might be seen as the low-point in the laws of privacy and breach of confidence; but since that time a lot has happened with the implementation of the HRA, and case law which has further refined and developed the laws relating to privacy and breach of confidence. Indeed, for a 'breach of confidence' action to succeed, there is no longer a need for there to be a confidential relationship.

prevent the media reporting allegations about the rich and famous; and in May 2011 speaking on ITV's *Daybreak* he said that the government and Parliament would now look at bringing in new legislation on privacy.

4.2   Obligation of confidence and the Freedom of Information Act

Section 41 of the Freedom of Information Act 2000 (FOIA) provides for an exemption for information provided in confidence. With the exemption, the duty to confirm or deny does not arise if, or to the extent that, the confirmation or denial that would have to be given in order to comply would constitute an actionable breach of confidence.

There are two components to the exemption:

1   The information must have been obtained by the public authority from another person. A person may be an individual, a company, a local authority or any other 'legal entity'. The exemption does not cover information which the public authority has generated itself, although another exemption may apply.
2   Disclosure of the information would give rise to an actionable breach of confidence. In other words, if the public authority disclosed the information the provider or a third party could take the authority to court.

For the precise wording of this exemption see Figure 4.1.

---

41. (1) Information is exempt information if–
　　　(a) it was obtained by the public authority from any other person (including another public authority), and
　　　(b) the disclosure of the information to the public (otherwise than under this Act) by the public authority holding it would constitute a breach of confidence actionable by that or any other person.
　(2)　The duty to confirm or deny does not arise if, or to the extent that, the confirmation or denial that would have to be given to comply with section 1(1)(a)

Figure 4.1 *Freedom of Information Act 2000, section 41, exemption*

There is guidance available on the exemption for information provided in confid - ence from the Information Commissioner and also from the Ministry of Justice:

- *Information provided in confidence*. Office of the Information Commissioner. Free - dom of Information Act awareness guidance no. 2 (version 4, September 2008).
- *Section 41 – Information provided in confidence*. Ministry of Justice. Exemptions guidance (May 2008).

This exemption qualifies the right of access under the Act by reference to the common law action for 'breach of confidence'. According to that action, if a person who holds information is under a duty to keep that information confidential, there will be a 'breach of confidence' if that person makes an unauthorized disclosure of the information. The concept of 'breach of confidence' has its roots in the notion that a person who agrees to keep information confidential should be obliged to respect that confidence. However, the law has now extended beyond this: the courts recognize that a duty of confidence may also arise due to the confidential nature of the information itself or the circumstances in which it was obtained.

The concept of 'breach of confidence' recognizes that unauthorized disclosure of confidential information may cause substantial harm. The law protects these interests by requiring the information to be kept confidential: if information is disclosed in breach of a duty of confidence, the courts may award damages (or another remedy) to the person whose interests were protected by the duty.

The s45 code of practice issued by the Secretary of State for Justice contains guidance on freedom of information and confidentiality obligations.[2] The guidance states that public authorities should bear clearly in mind their obligations under the FOIA when preparing to enter into contracts that may contain terms relating to the disclosure of information by them.

When entering into contracts with non-public authority contractors, public authorities may be under pressure to accept confidentiality clauses in order that information relating to the terms of the contract, its value and performance will be exempt from disclosure. Public authorities should reject such clauses wherever possible. Where, exceptionally, it is necessary to include non-disclosure provisions in a contract, an option could be to agree with the contractor a schedule of the contract that clearly identifies information not to be disclosed. But authorities will need to take care when drawing up any such schedule, and be aware that any restrictions on disclosure provided for could potentially be overridden by their obligations under the FOIA.

In some cases the disclosure of information pursuant to a request may affect the legal rights of a third party – for example, where information is subject to the common law duty of confidence or where it constitutes 'personal data' within the meaning of the Data Protection Act 1998 (DPA). Public authorities must always remember that, unless an exemption provided for in the DPA applies in relation to any particular information, they will be obliged to disclose that information in response to a request.

A public authority should only accept information from third parties in confidence if it is necessary to obtain that information in connection with the exercise of any of the authority's functions and it would not otherwise be provided. Acceptance of any confidentiality provisions must be for good reasons, capable of being justified to the Information Commissioner.

4.3   Remedies

The main means of ensuring that information obtained in confidence is not unfairly taken advantage of is the use of an injunction (interdict in Scotland). A prohibitory injunction can be used in order to direct the party to refrain from disclosing the information. There are a number of remedies available to the courts:

- fines
- court order to reveal source
- court order that a confidential matter be 'delivered up' or destroyed
- account for the profits where a person misusing confidential information may be asked to account to the person who confided the information
- damages claim by the person whose confidences have been breached in the publication of confidential material
- contempt of court action where injunction/interdict is breached.

4.4   Case law on breach of confidence

The past few years have witnessed a number of high-profile cases in which well known personalities have used the law relating to breach of confidence in order to try and protect their privacy.

Even a public figure is entitled to a private life, although they may expect and accept that their circumstances will be more carefully scrutinized by the media. If the claimant has courted attention, this may lead the claimant to have fewer grounds upon which to object to the intrusion.

In the late 1980s, the UK government used the law of confidence to try to silence former members of the security services (in particular Peter Wright, author of *Spycatcher*) and journalists trying to report their disclosures.

It has been established that the public have a legitimate interest to be weighed against other interests in knowing how they have been governed. Until quite recently it had always been accepted that Cabinet deliberations were confidential. Then, in October 2010, the government complied with a ruling by the First-Tier Tribunal (Information Rights) and disclosed the minutes of the 1986 Cabinet meeting where Michael Heseltine resigned over the Westland affair. The minutes had been requested by Martin Rosenbaum of the British Broadcasting Corporation (BBC) in February 2005. It was the first time that Cabinet minutes have been disclosed under the FOIA. The previous government vetoed the release of Cabinet minutes on the Iraq war and Cabinet sub-committee minutes on devolution from 1997. The government had fought disclosure of the material on the basis that revealing Cabinet minutes and internal disagreements would damage the convention of collective Cabinet responsibility. But, in December 2009, the Information Commissioner ruled in the case of the Cabinet minutes relating to the

Westland affair that the balance of the public interest lies in favour of disclosure of some of the information (ICO, 2009).

In Attorney General v. Jonathan Cape Ltd [1976] QB 752, which dealt with the publication of Richard Crossman's diaries, a case was taken by the Attorney General against the publisher for breach of confidence. It was held that the public interest in disclosure outweighed the protection of information given in confidence once the material was sufficiently old. In this particular case that period was taken to be ten years.

References

House of Commons (2010) *Culture, Media and Sport Committee - Second Report: press standards, privacy and libel*, www.publications.parliament.uk/pa/cm200910/cmselect/cmcumeds/362/36202.htm.

ICO (2009) Freedom of Information Act 2000 (Section 50) Decisions Notice, www.ico.gov.uk/upload/documents/decisionnotices/2009/fs_50088735.pdf.

Notes

1   See Prince Albert v. Strange (1840) 1 Mac & G 25 and Duchess of Argyll v. Duke of Argyll [1967] Ch 302.
2   Secretary of State for Justice, 'Code of practice on the discharge of public authorities' functions under part I of the Freedom of Information Act 2000, issued under section 45 of the Act. Lord Chancellor's Department, November 2004, www.justice.gov.uk/guidance/foi-guidance-codes-practice.htm.

CHAPTER 5

Patents, trade marks and design right

Contents

5.1   Introduction

Intellectual property can and does reside in everyday objects. The *Gowers Review of Intellectual Property* (HM Treasury, 2006) used the example of a coffee jar to show how even within what may at first seem to be a relatively straightforward object a bundle of rights will protect different aspects of that one object. In the case of the coffee jar, it could consist of the following:

- Patents may protect the contents of the jar, the lid and seal.
- Registered and unregistered design rights can also protect the lid and shape of the jar.
- Copyright can protect the label artwork.
- Trade marks can protect the shape of the jar, labels, colours used, and brand names.

The Intellectual Property Office's website used to use the example of a mobile phone to illustrate how the different types of intellectual property protection can protect a phone:

- Patents may protect the internal mechanism of the phone.
- Registered design right may protect the outward appearance and/or shape of the phone.
- Trade marks may protect the company name or logo.
- Database right may capture customer contact details.

- Know-how and knowledge management systems may have been involved in developing the silicon chip processors for the phone.
- Domain name registration protects the phone manufacturer's website address.
- Goodwill is likely to be important in attracting and retaining customers for this phone rather than for similar ones or services.
- Copyright may protect the operating instructions.

5.2   Patents

Patents are for inventions – new and improved products and processes that are capable of industrial application and which involve an inventive step that is not obvious to someone with knowledge and experience in the subject. They cover how things work, what they do, how they do it, what they are made of and how they are made. A granted patent gives the owner the right to prevent others from copying, manufacturing, selling or importing the invention without permission. See Figure 5.1 for databases accessing patents.

Patents have to be applied for and it can take several years following an application for a patent to be granted. Patents are also costly to obtain and then maintain. A firm challenging a patent can expect to pay £750,000 for a simple case, largely due to the costs of the adversarial system. Liability for the other side's costs could double this to £1.5 million. Their maximum lifetime is 20 years from the date when the patent was first applied for. They must be renewed every year after the 5th year for up to 20 years' protection.

Following enaction of the TRIPS agreement, if three conditions are fulfilled then an idea can be patented in any of the member countries of the World Trade Organization.

In order to be patentable an idea must be:

- New – not already in the public domain or the subject of a previous patent.
- Non-obvious – it should not be common sense to any accomplished practitioner in the field who having been asked to solve a particular practical problem would see this solution immediately.
- Useful, or applicable in industry – it must have a stated function, and could immediately be produced to fulfil this function.

In order for a patent application to be successful an invention must *not* be:
- a scientific or mathematical discovery, theory or method
- a literary, dramatic, musical or artistic work
- a way of performing a mental act, playing a game or doing business
- the presentation of information, or some computer programs
- an animal or plant variety

Esp@cenet: http://gb.espacenet.com.

IPO online patent services: www.ipo.gov.uk/types/patent/p-os/p-find.htm.

The United States Patent and Trademark Office (USPTO) Patent Full-Text Databases: http://patft.uspto.gov.

Google patents: www.google.com/patents.

Derwent World Patents Index gives details of over 14.8 million inventions, and provides access to information from more than 41 million patent documents: http://thomsonreuters.com/products_services/legal/legal_products/a-z/derwent_world_patents_index.

The International Patent Documentation Center (INPADOC) (produced by the European Patent Office) describes patents issued by 96 countries and patenting organizations: www.epo.org/searching/subscription/raw/product-14-11.html.

Free Patents Online: www.freepatentsonline.com.

Chemical Abstracts (CAS): www.cas.org.

Figure 5.1 *Databases for accessing patents*

- a method of medical treatment or diagnosis
- against public policy or morality.

Inventions must be kept confidential in order to be patentable. Inventors therefore need to keep their ideas secret before they apply for a patent otherwise they put at risk their chances of being granted a patent.

The mere existence of a patent may be sufficient in its own right to prevent others from trying to exploit an invention. But if someone does infringe a patent, then the patent registration gives the inventor the right to take legal action to stop them from exploiting the invention and it also gives the inventor the right to claim damages.

The patent gives the inventor the right to:

- sell the invention and all the associated intellectual property rights
- license the invention to someone else whilst retaining all the intellectual property rights
- discuss the invention with others in order to set up a business based around the invention.

A granted patent is a form of intellectual property, and just as with other property the inventor can buy or sell it; or the inventor can license it to others.

The patent bargain is formulated as a contract. The inventor contributes their invention and a detailed description and in return the government provides a limited time monopoly. The public benefit from the patent because the Intellectual Property Office publishes it after 18 months, which means that other people gain advance knowledge of technological developments which they will eventually be able to use freely once the patent ceases.

If an inventor doesn't patent their invention, potentially anyone could use, make or sell the invention without the permission of the inventor. The inventor could try to keep their invention secret, but this might not be possible or practicable for a product where the technology is on display.

Patents are territorial rights so if an inventor is granted a patent in the UK then they will have exclusive rights in the UK only, so long as they continue to pay the renewal fees. If they want protection in other countries they can apply for a patent in that country or through the European Patent Convention or the Patent Co-operation Treaty.

The patent is lodged at the national patent office (or with the European Patent Office), which for an agreed fee will allow others access to the patented knowledge as expressed in the patent document; and the office will police and facilitate the punishment of unauthorized usage.

In 2011 the European Commission published proposals to streamline patent protection across Europe (COM(2011)215/3) (EC, 2011). The proposals aim to cut the costs of obtaining protection across the whole of the European Union and every EU country with the exception of Spain and Italy have signed up to the proposals. However, it should be noted that the ECJ has ruled that a single litigation process on patent disputes would be incompatible with existing EU treaties.

In 2010, the British government published a consultation paper proposing to introduce a limit on the value of claims heard in the Patents County Court (PCC) (which will renamed the Intellectual Property County Court). The proposals were implemented in the Patents County Court (Financial Limits) Order 2011: SI 2011/1407 which said that the amount or value of the claim must not exceed £500,000, thereby reducing uncertainty and obviating the need for potentially protracted and costly transfer considerations. Having a limit in place has the effect of reducing costs for SMEs and entrepreneurs, who are most likely to litigate lower value IP-disputes. The principal purpose of a civil award of damages in the UK is not to punish the defendant but rather to compensate the claimant for the damage, loss or injury that they have suffered as a result of another's acts or omissions.

5.2.1   The legislative regime for patents

The Paris Convention for the Protection of Industrial Property is an agreement concluded in 1883 which provides for national treatment, right priority and common rules between states for patents, designs, trade marks and other forms of intellectual property.

When a patent is first applied for, that document is called the basic document and provides the priority date, country and number. The priority details are used as labels on later applications for the same invention in other countries. If applications are made within 12 months under the Paris Convention, their 'newness' counts from the priority date. The later applications are called 'equivalents' and the collection of basic and equivalents is the 'patent family'.

Each document is a national instrument, in the national language, and may describe the invention slightly differently to reflect the national approach to protection.

The Convention allows the date of invention to be frozen so that one can assess whether the market is of value and where else to apply.

The Patents Act 1977 is the main UK legislation and codifies what went before. The Patents Act 2004 introduced a number of changes that affected some procedural details of how the system works, rather than its essence.

5.2.2   Software and intellectual property law

Software is protected by copyright, and potentially it could be protected by a patent but only where it consists of something more than a computer program. For example, as was the case in Symbian Ltd v. Comptroller General of Patents [2008] EWCA Civ 1066 (www.bailii.org/ew/cases/EWCA/Civ/2008/1066.html) where it was held that a substantive technical contribution was made.

To determine whether there is a technical contribution, ask whether:

- technical means are used to produce a result or solve a problem
- the invention produces a technical result.

There is also the Aerotel/Macrossan test, which was established by the legal case Aerotel Ltd v. Telco Holdings Ltd [2006] EWCA Civ 1371 (www.bailii.org/ew/cases/EWCA/Civ/2006/1371.html). In this case it says that the court should adopt a four-stage approach:

1 Properly construe the claim.
2 Identify the actual contribution.
3 Ask whether it falls solely within the excluded subject matter.
4 Check whether the contribution is actually technical in nature.

There have been pressures for software to be protected under patent law so that computer programs can benefit from greater protection. Indeed, there have been a number of failed attempts in the European Parliament to introduce a directive allowing for software to be protected by patents. In mid 2005, for example, the European Parliament voted by a massive majority to reject the proposed software patents directive (COM(2002) 92).

Copyright protects an author's original expression in a computer program as a 'literary work' and reformulating a program in a different language as a translation. Source code can thus be viewed as a human-readable literary work, which expresses the ideas of the software engineers who authored it. Not only the human-readable instructions (source code) but also binary machine-readable instructions (object code) are considered to be literary works or 'written expressions,' and, therefore, are also protected by copyright.

The software directive (2009/24/EC which is a codified version of the 1991 directive) contains a provision that ensures contract law cannot override a requirement for lawful users of computer software to be able to make a back-up copy. The directive was implemented by SI 1992/3233 – The Copyright (Computer Programs) Regulations 1992 – which inserted section 50A into the CDPA 1988:

CDPA 1988 s50A. –

(1) It is not an infringement of copyright for a lawful user of a copy of a computer program to make any back-up copy of it which it is necessary for him to have for the purposes of his lawful use.

(2) For the purposes of this section and sections 50B and 50C a person is a lawful user of a computer program if (whether under a licence to do any acts restricted by the copyright in the program or otherwise) he has a right to use the program.

(3) Where an act is permitted under this section, it is irrelevant whether or not there exists any term or condition in an agreement which purports to prohibit or restrict the act (such terms being, by virtue of section 296A, void).

If someone tried to contract their way out of this obligation any such provision would be considered to be void by a court. It isn't clear the extent to which the making of a back-up copy would be permitted under this section. It revolves around what is meant by the word 'necessary'. Imagine, for example, a scenario in which the original version of a computer software package becomes corrupted. Having a back-up copy means that the software user is able to quickly restore the software so that it continues to work as it should.

The other acts relating to software which cannot be overridden by a contract are set out in the following sections of the CDPA 1988:

S50B   Decompilation
S50BA   Observing, studying and testing of computer programs.

5.3   Trade and service marks

Trade and service marks are for brand identity. They allow distinctions to be made between the goods and services of one company as opposed to those belonging to another company.

Trade marks fall into two types – registered and unregistered. Registered trade marks involve a formal application procedure with associated fees and renewal fees. As part of the process of registration a check is carried out in order to ensure that there are no other companies which have registered the same word, symbol or image as a trade mark in the sector of the economy nominated by the registering company. A history of use of a trade mark may establish its viability and support its subsequent legal recognition.

Trade marks, like patents, are territorial rights. They give the owner the exclusive right to use their mark for the goods or services that it covers in the country in which the mark is registered. Trade mark registration could be at a national, EU or international level. The UK Trade Marks Registry forms part of the Intellectual Property Office and successful applicants are given rights in the UK in relation to the sign that has been registered. At an EU level a single application is made to the Office for Harmonization of the Internal Market (OHIM) and it results in the granting of a single trade mark which operates throughout the EU. There is also the possibility of international registration administered by WIPO. This merely facilitates the acquisition of national trade marks, but it enables people to obtain protection in the countries where they would like protection through a single application.

A trade mark can be registered if it satisfies three main criteria:

1 It is distinctive for the goods or services for which an application is made to register.
2 It is not deceptive, or contrary to law or morality.
3 It is not similar or identical to any earlier marks for the same or similar goods or services.

The advantage of registering a trade mark is that it makes it easier to take legal action against infringers. Whilst unregistered trade marks involve no such procedures or costs, the disadvantage is that they provide far less robust protection. Trade marks are typically a symbol, image or word (though they can in some circumstances be a shape, a colour or a combination of these) that is associated with particular goods or services provided by the owner. Both types of mark can last indefinitely so long as the owner still actively uses them and, in the case of a registered trade mark, that the fees are paid.

Registering a trade mark entitles the owner of the mark to put the ® symbol next to it in order to warn others against using it. However, using this symbol for a trade mark that is not registered is an offence. Unregistered trade marks use the symbol ^{TM}.

A registered trade mark:

- may put people off using your trade mark without your permission
- allows the owner to take legal action against anyone who uses the trade mark without permission
- allows Trading Standards Officers or the police to bring criminal charges against counterfeiters if they use the trade mark
- is the 'property' of the trade mark owner and as such it can be bought or sold; or, if they so wish, the owner could let other people have a licence to use the mark.

The owner of a registered trade mark has the right to take legal action to prevent third parties from using their mark in the course of trade and this is much easier if the mark has been registered. In the case of an unregistered trade mark the owner would have to make use of the common law of passing off; but in order for a passing off action to succeed, they would have to prove that they:

- own the mark
- have built up a reputation in the mark
- have been harmed in some way by the other person's use of the mark.

It can be both difficult and costly to prove a passing off action.

Trade marks are not registrable if they:

- describe the goods or services or any characteristics of them, such as where the mark shows the quality, quantity, purpose, value or geographical origin of the goods or services
- have become customary in the line of trade for which the trade mark is being registered
- are not distinctive
- are three-dimensional shapes, if the shape is typical of the goods you are interested in (or part of them), has a function or adds value to the goods
- are specially protected emblems
- are offensive
- are against the law
- are deceptive.

It is worth saying that simply because someone has a particular company name registered at Companies House, it does not automatically mean that they also have a registered trade mark.

5.3.1 Trade mark law and practice

The laws that make up trade mark legislation in the UK are extensive, but the main ones are the Trade Marks Act 1994 and the Trade Marks Rules 2008: SI 2008/1797. The Trade Marks Act 1994 covers the registration of trade marks and the protection of registered trade marks in the United Kingdom.

⇥ Useful resource

The *Manual of Trade Marks Practice* sets out guidance on the IPO's work practices. The IPO also issues law practice directions to provide additional guidance on the conduct of adversarial proceedings brought before them. www.ipo.gov.uk/pro-types/pro-tm/t-law/t-manual.htm

5.3.2 Renewing trade marks

In order to keep a trade mark in force, the mark must be renewed on the tenth anniversary of the filing date and every ten years after that. There is no limit to how long a trade mark owner can keep their mark registered provided that the mark continues to be used and that the ten-yearly renewal fee is paid. A trade mark owner can opt not to renew the mark if they so wish, or to voluntarily surrender it at any time.

5.3.3 Trade marks and domain names

Top-level internet domain names come from the Internet Corporation for Assigned Names and Numbers (ICANN), a non-profit-making company. Within each country, licensed subsidiaries let out the names inside the highest codes.

At the very highest level are .com or .org. Country codes such as .uk are used by all countries except the US. The US codes, particularly .com, tend to be used to mean 'international'. Therefore many large enterprises in other countries don't want to use their country codes as they feel this might restrict the perception of users.

Companies using a .com or .eu domain name, or displaying international codes for phone numbers, are more likely to be 'directing' their activities at foreign consumers, and this increases their exposure to foreign lawsuits according to a ruling from the ECJ (Joined Cases C-585/08 and C-144/09, Peter Pammer v. Reederei Karl Schlüter GmbH & Co KG (C-585/08), and Hotel Alpenhof GesmbH v. Oliver Heller (C-144/09).

If a company or other institution has a trade mark, they may well wish to use it in their domain name, such as Harrods.com. But when the name is used in this way it is simply an address. It is not being used in the sense of a trade mark for a specific category of goods or services.

One group of traders who do use their web addresses as trade marks are the '.com companies' such as Amazon.com who have no other tangible presence; and for whom their name 'Amazon.com' *does* act as a trade mark.

Trade marks are registered nationally, so trying to treat domain names in the same way would, for example, require UK-based firms to use .uk (rather than .com etc.). This is not how domain names are currently chosen, so it would take a lot of international negotiation to bring the two systems together.

Treating domain names as trade marks is difficult. Firstly, because trade marks are administered by different bodies in each country. Secondly, because registering a trade mark gives the owner the exclusive right to use their mark only in relation to those goods or services for which the mark has been registered, whereas in the case of domain names there can only be the one name, no second name is possible for a different category of commercial activities.

5.3.4   Cybersquatting

Cybersquatting (also known as domain squatting) is when someone deliberately registers a domain name, knowing that it is based on a trade name used by an existing party – they do so in order to profit from the goodwill of that trade mark by offering to sell the domain name at an inflated price to the person or company who owns the trade mark contained within the name.

The courts have required that registrations be made over to the well known names because these registrations were not being used and had been made only for the purpose of extracting payments. This was not considered to be a desirable practice, and there is now a dispute resolution procedure in place to deal with it called the Uniform Domain-Name Dispute-Resolution Policy (UDRP) (McBain, 2006).

There have been numerous instances of cybersquatters who register the domain names of well-known companies intending to cash in on that name by trying to extract money from the true owner. In the case of Burger King, for example, cybersquatters offered the company the name burgerking.co.uk for £25,000 + value added tax (VAT).

British Telecommunications v. One in a Million 1998 EWCA Civ 1272

One in a Million registered a number of domain names, which contained the trade marks of well-known British companies such as Virgin and Marks & Spencer. They then tried to sell these to the companies concerned for many thousands of pounds. The High Court banned them from dealing in domain names and the Court of Appeal subsequently threw out One in a Million's appeal against that ruling, dismissing their right to appeal to the House of Lords and ordering them to surrender the collection of domain names they had amassed. In effect, the court said that the registered trade mark will usually prevail over the registered domain name.

One in a Million was ordered by the High Court to pay £65,000 legal costs and

5.3.5 Uniform Domain-Name Dispute-Resolution Policy

Assignment of names has traditionally been on a first-come, first-served basis, but, in recognition of the problems legitimate users have with cybersquatters, applicants must now certify that they know of no other claim to a name when they ask for it. If a claim for the name is then made, registration will be suspended pending agreement or action before the UDRP panel where the registration authority will fulfil the judgment and allocate the name as directed.

5.3.6 Company names and trade marks

If you are planning on registering a company in the UK and have already thought of a name for the new business it would be best to undertake a number of checks as part of a due diligence process:

1 Check that the name isn't already being used by another business.
2 Check to see if an identical name has been registered at Companies House as a UK limited company name using the Companies House name check:
   http://wck2.companieshouse.gov.uk/53b733218dab3d4d1a4c6b27aa166f93/wcframe?name=accessCompanyInfo.
3 Check to see if an identical name has been registered as a UK trade mark in relation to the type of goods or services that you sell (including those phonetically similar) using the IPO UK trade mark enquiry page: www.ipo.gov.uk/tm/t-find/t-find-text.
4 Check to see if an identical name has been registered as a Community Trade Mark (and is therefore enforceable throughout the EU) using the EU trade mark consultation service:
   http://oami.europa.eu/CTMOnline/RequestManager/de_SearchBasic?transition=start&source=Log-in.html&language=en&application=CTMOnline.
5 Check the .com and .co.uk domain name checkers (www.internic.net/whois.html and www.nominet.org.uk, respectively) to see if the name has already been registered as a domain name.

If you don't do this you could potentially end up in a costly row, a trade mark infringement or a 'passing off' action in the courts.

5.4 Design right

Designs are for product appearance of either the whole or part of a product resulting from the features of the lines, contours, colour, shape, texture and/or materials of the product itself and/or its ornamentation.

Design right can apply to industrial as well as handcrafted items. It is not concerned with how the item works but concentrates on the appearance of the product.

Registered designs offer protection throughout the UK. The protection lasts initially for five years and can be renewed every five years for up to a maximum of 25 years. The design needs to be registered at the IPO's Design Registry within a year of it first being disclosed publicly.

UK design right prevents others from copying your design. It is not a complete right as it covers only the three-dimensional aspects of the item and does not protect the surface decoration of the product or any two-dimensional pattern such as a wallpaper or carpet design.

Registered Community Design (RCD) offers like protection in all of the EU member states, and can be renewed every five years up to a maximum of 25 years. Applications are processed by OHIM to which formal representations of the design and the appropriate fees should be sent.

5.5   Further information

EC (2011) *Regulation on Enhanced Co-Operation for Creating Unitary Patent Protection*, COM(2011)215/3,
   http://ec.europa.eu/internal_market/indprop/docs/patent/20110413-proposal-enhanced-cooperation_en.pdf.

European Patent Office (2008) *Patents for Software?*
   www.epo.org/topics/issues/computer-implemented-inventions/software.html.

Hall, B.H. (2009) *The Use and Value of Patent Rights*, Intellectual Property Office,
   www.ipo.gov.uk/ipresearch-useandvalue-200906.pdf.

Hart, R. et al. (2000) *The Economic Impact of Patentability of Computer Programs*, European Commission,
   http://ec.europa.eu/internal_market/indprop/docs/comp/study_en.pdf.

IPO (2010a) *Patents: basic facts*, rev. edn,
   www.ipo.gov.uk/p-basicfacts.pdf.

IPO (2010b) *Trade Marks: application guide*, rev. edn,
   www.ipo.gov.uk/.

IPO (2010c) *Trade Marks: essential reading*, rev. edn,
   www.ipo.gov.uk/t-essentialreading.pdf.

IPO (2011) *Patents: essential reading*, rev. edn,
   www.ipo.gov.uk/p-essentialreading.pdf.

Patent and Trade Mark Group (Special interest group of CILIP):
   www.cilip.org.uk/get-involved/special-interest-groups/patent/pages/default.aspx.

Patent Information Users Group, Inc.:
   www.piug.org.

References

HM Treasury (2006), *Gowers Review of Intellectual Property*, TSO.

McBain, M. (2006) 'Appropriation of domain names and domain name blocking', dissertation, City University.

CHAPTER 6

Contracts and licensing agreements

Contents

6.1   General principles

Information professionals need to be able to negotiate licence agreements with information providers, because licences are often the means by which access to information products is controlled. Information professionals are in the business of providing access to information. They also have an obligation to respect the moral and legal rights of the creators and distributors of intellectual property.

Some would argue that copyright exceptions and limitations have been rendered practically meaningless in the digital arena. How, for example, are the limitations and exceptions to be applied in the digital environment in view of the widespread deployment of technological protection measures?

The exceptions available under the CDPA are extremely limited in their application to electronic information sources. Consider, for example, matters such as multiple copying, converting from one format to another, or storage in a central repository.

To get around these limitations, information professionals are increasingly turning to licences as the means of providing access to works. Licences are binding on both parties. They are governed by the law of contract, and enable information professionals to reach agreement with rights holders to permit their users to have access to electronic information services such as online databases, e-journals, or websites in ways that meet their users' needs.

It is important to point out that a licence does not confer ownership rights. It merely specifies the conditions upon which databases and other copyright works can be used and exploited, and by whom. There needs to be a mindshift from ownership to leasing. Licensees are merely provided with access to content for a limited period of time. Typically, the licences that information professionals negotiate are non-exclusive, granting the same rights to many different users.

Where there is a contract, a licence, or a set of terms and conditions in place this will override copyright law in all but two respects. The Hargreaves report *Digital Opportunity: a review of intellectual property and growth* (Hargreaves, 2011) makes clear that the government should legislate to ensure that the copyright exceptions are protected from override by a contract. Hargreaves says:

> At present it is possible for rights holders licensing rights to insist, through licensing contracts, that the exceptions established by law cannot be exercised in practice [...] Applying contracts in this way means a rights holder can rewrite the limits the law has set on the extent of the right conferred by copyright. It creates the risk that should Government decide that UK law will permit private copying or text mining, these permissions could be denied by contract.
>
> (Hargreaves, page 51 paragraph 5.39)

The only instances where the permitted acts cannot be overridden by a contract can be traced back to two European directives (the database directive 96/9/EC and the software directive 2009/24/EC). The Copyright and Rights in Databases Regulations 1997: SI 1997/3032, www.legislation.gov.uk/uksi/1997/3032/contents/made, implemented the database directive in the UK, and Regulation 19 says:

Avoidance of certain terms affecting lawful users
19. – (1) A lawful user of a database which has been made available to the public in any manner shall be entitled to extract or re-utilize insubstantial parts of the contents of the database for any purpose.
(2) Where under an agreement a person has a right to use a database, or part of a database, which has been made available to the public in any manner, any term or condition in the agreement shall be void in so far as it purports to prevent that person from extracting or re-utilizing insubstantial parts of the contents of the database, or of that part of the database, for any purpose.

The only other place in the legislation where copyright cannot be overridden by a contract is with regard to software. SI 1992/3233 [The Copyright (Computer Programs) Regulations 1992] implemented directive 91/250/EEC (which was subsequently codified into directive 2009/24/EC) and inserted s50A into the CDPA 1988.

Section 50A of the CDPA 1988 says:

50A.—(1) It is not an infringement of copyright for a lawful user of a copy of a computer program to make any back-up copy of it which it is necessary for him to have for the purposes of his lawful use.

(2) For the purposes of this section and sections 50B 50BA and 50C a person is a lawful user of a computer program if (whether under a licence to do any acts restricted by the copyright in the program or otherwise) he has a right to use the program.

(3) Where an act is permitted under this section, it is irrelevant whether or not there exists any term or condition in an agreement which purports to prohibit or restrict the act (such terms being, by virtue of section 296A, void).

The other acts relating to software which cannot be overridden by contract are set out in the following sections of the CDPA 1988:

S50B   Decompilation
S50BA   Observing, studying and testing of computer programs.

6.2   Negotiating licences

 It may sound trite to say it, but it is important to read the licence terms thoroughly. When one receives a licence for signature, rather than automatically signing the agreement this should be viewed as the starting point of a negotiation process.

There are some instances, though, where there is no scope for negotiation – such as 'click-through' or 'shrink-wrap' licences.

There are also instances where websites display a set of terms and conditions without requiring the user to click on an 'I agree' button before gaining access to the contents of the site. In such instances, the question arises as to whether or not the user has entered into an enforceable contract.

◆ Useful resource

The Electronic Frontier Foundation has produced *The Clicks That Bind: ways users 'agree' to online terms of service* (Bayley, 2009), which sets out best prac - tice for click-wrap agreements intending to create a contractual relationship.

Information professionals do need to be extremely careful when signing licence agreements. It would be wrong to assume that if an agreement contains terms you consider to be unfair, then the courts would overturn it. It is certainly the case that under the Unfair Contract Terms Act 1977 agreements should satisfy a test of reasonableness, but there are very limited circumstances in which the courts would overturn an unfair contract term.

Under the Unfair Contract Terms Act 1977 (www.legislation.gov.uk/ukpga/ 1977/50) a person cannot exclude or restrict their liability for death or personal injury resulting from negligence. They can exclude or restrict liability for other loss or damage resulting from negligence but only if the exclusion clauses satisfy a test of reasonableness. It would be for the party seeking to impose a contract term to demonstrate to the court that it was reasonable, should they be challenged.

In any case, the Unfair Contract Terms Act 1977 specifically excludes any form of intellectual property rights from its main provisions. Schedule 1 to the Act says that as far as the following sections are concerned, they do not apply to any contract so far as it relates to the creation or transfer of a right or interest in any patent, trade mark, copyright or design right; any registered design, technical or commercial information or other intellectual property; or the termination of any such right or interest:

- Section 2 – Negligence liability
- Section 3 – Liability arising in contract
- Section 4 – Unreasonable indemnity clauses
- Section 7 – Miscellaneous contracts under which goods pass.

In 2011 a new Consumer Rights Directive was published (2011/83/EC) whose aim is to update and consolidate parts of the European consumer law acquis especially in the light of technological changes and the increasing importance of digital markets. Recital 19 to the directive states explicitly that contracts for the supply of digital content such as the download of digital music, or the streaming of video or the provision of online games, do fall within the scope of the directive:

> Digital content means data which are produced and supplied in digital form, such as computer programs, applications, games, music, videos or texts, irrespective of whether they are accessed through downloading or streaming, from a tangible medium or through any other means. Contracts for the supply of digital content should fall within the scope of this directive.

Article 5 of the directive sets out the information which must be provided before a consumer would be considered to be bound by any contract. The information should include details of any technical protection measure used as well as any relevant details regarding the interoperability of the digital content. It would also cover other restrictive or potentially invasive technologies such as regional coding or tracking and monitoring tools. The precise wording is:

> Before the consumer is bound by a contract other than a distance or an off-premises contract, or any corresponding offer, the trader shall provide the

consumer with the following information in a clear and comprehensible manner, if that information is not already apparent from the context:

1(g) where applicable, the functionality, including applicable technical protection measures, of digital content.

1(h) where applicable, any relevant interoperability of digital content with hardware and software that the trader is aware of or can reasonably be expected to have been aware of.

The Consumer Rights Directive also includes a right to withdraw from purchases of digital content before it is actually downloaded (as opposed to when it is made available for download, for example via a link in an email).

In the Court of Appeal ruling in Watford Electronics v. Sanderson [2001] EWCA Civ 317 paragraph 55 (www.bailii.org/ew/cases/EWCA/Civ/2001/317.html), Lord Justice Chadwick said that the courts should be reluctant to interfere in contractual relationships where each party has freely entered into a contract and where each party enjoys reasonably equal bargaining power:

Where experienced businessmen representing substantial companies of equal bargaining power negotiate an agreement, they may be taken to have had regard to the matters known to them. They should, in my view, be taken to be the best judge of the commercial fairness of the agreement which they have made; including the fairness of each of the terms in that agreement. They should be taken to be the best judge on the question whether the terms of the agreement are reasonable. The court should not assume that either is likely to commit his company to an agreement which he thinks is unfair, or which he thinks includes unreasonable terms. Unless satisfied that one party has, in effect, taken unfair advantage of the other – or that a term is so unreasonable that it cannot properly have been understood or considered – the court should not interfere.

It is essential that you read and understand the whole agreement. You cannot get out of contractual terms on the basis that you didn't read that particular term.

For example, the licence agreement might be 13 pages long, but unless you spend time reading it in detail you won't spot that on page 8 it makes clear that the agreement automatically renews unless you give 3 months' notice of your intention to terminate the agreement. In these instances you might want to consider handing in the signed agreement and the cancellation notice at the same time, in order to have maximum flexibility at the time when the licence agreement is due for renewal.

You also need to be careful about signing a licence agreement if there is anything that you don't fully understand (see Figure 6.1 for a typical structure found in licence agreements, as well as some of the key legal terms used). It is no defence to say that the agreement is invalid because you didn't understand a particular clause. If there is something that you don't understand, ask the supplier for clarification or, if you have one, refer it to your in-house legal team.

Licence agreements are often written in technical language or 'legalese', and can therefore be quite intimidating and difficult for the layman to understand. It is worth reading through a few standard licence agreements (such as the ones at licensingmodels.org) in order to become familiar with the layout of licences used for online products. If you want a vendor to insert a clause, or if you want an existing clause to be reworded, it is well worth looking at:

Parties: the full contractual names of the parties to the licence.

Key definitions: essential terms are defined (e.g. Authorized Users, Licensed Materials, Library Premises, Secure Network, Term, Permitted Purpose, Licence Fee, Intellectual Property, etc.).

Services: description of the material to be licensed. This is also likely to explain how the form and content may change during the contract period, particularly if the provider is an information aggregator who is reliant on data from a range of publishers. However, you should check carefully how you will be told about any changes, and whether you are happy with those arrangements.

Usage rights and prohibited uses: sets out precisely what authorized users are entitled to do with the licensed materials such as access, use, display, download, print; and any restrictions on their use such as removing copyright notices; or altering, adapting or modifying the licensed materials.

Warranties and indemnities: it is essential that the licence contains a warranty confirming that the licensor has the legal right to license use of the copyright material, and that this does not infringe any third-party IPRs. The warranty should also be backed up by an indemnity to this effect.

Term and termination: sets out the subscription period and the conditions under which either party can terminate the licence.

Force majeure: this 'Act of God' clause excuses the supplier for circumstances beyond its reasonable control (such as riot, war, flood, etc.).

Legal jurisdiction and dispute resolution: this clause makes clear which law governs interpretation of the licence, and any arrangements for the resolution of disputes.

Fees and payment: the subscription price, payment arrangements and details of any other charges, such as taxes.

Assignment: whether or not the licence is transferable, either by the licensor or by yourself to another third party.

Schedules: there may be one or more schedules appended to the main licence agree-

---

Figure 6.1 *Contract clauses*

➡ Useful resource

'Analysis of 100 contracts offered to the British Library' (http://pressandpolicy.bl.uk/ImageLibrary/detail.aspx?MediaDetailsID=691): The BL examined 100 licences that had been offered to them and matched them against seven criteria:

1   archiving
2   printing
3   downloading and electronic copying
4   fair dealing
5   visually impaired
6   inter-library loan
7   exceptions (does the licence cross refer to any exception in UK law or that of another jurisdiction?).

What is especially useful is that where the licences did cover those topics, the precise form of words found in the contracts is reproduced in the BL document and as a result this is a valuable resource because you might be able to find a form of words which express exactly what you want to achieve on a particular issue.

Keep all documentation from the negotiation process: the negotiation process can sometimes be quite lengthy and involve discussion over very specific points. Where this is the case, there is likely to be a certain amount of correspondence in the form of letters, faxes and e-mails that relates to the licence, and this should be kept on file. You might, for example, have asked for clarification on access restrictions, service content or acceptable download limits. You might have sought clarification on whether the definition of authorized users enables you to send information from the online service to your clients; or to staff in your overseas offices. You might even have managed to negotiate a special deal with your account manager, which will give you the option of renewing the service at the same rate as for the current subscription period.

It is essential to retain all this documentation, not just the licence. Even where the clarification was given orally, you should keep a written record. You don't want to rely on staff working for the information provider being aware of what has been agreed, because having everything carefully documented will come in extremely useful if your account manager moves on to another job, or if a dispute arises.

There are several documents on licensing matters which information professionals will find particularly helpful when negotiating licences.

❧ Useful resources

In May 2001, the International Federation of Library Associations (IFLA) approved a set of licensing principles (www.ifla.org/en/publications/licensing-principles) which should prevail in the contractual relationship and written contracts between libraries and information providers. (These have subsequently been updated, and the latest version at the time of writing was for March 2010). These principles touch upon aspects such as the applicable law, access, usage, users and pricing.

The European Bureau of Library, Information and Documentation Associations (EBLIDA) has published a helpful guide entitled *Licensing Digital Resources: how to avoid the legal pitfalls* (Giavarra, 2001) which is full of practical tips and advice.

Finally, it is worth mentioning Lesley Ellen Harris's book *Licensing Digital Content: a practical guide for libraries* (2009).

There are a number of key issues that need to be considered when you negotiate a licence for an information product. These include:

1 Applicable law:
This should preferably be the national law of where your organization is located. If you were based in the UK, for example, you would not want the applicable law to be that of a state in the USA; otherwise, if there is a problem relating to the interpretation of your licence, you could end up having to travel to a US court in order to plead your case.
2 Ensure that statutory rights are recognized:

 To avoid any doubt, the licence should contain a term which explicitly acknowledges that nothing in the licence prevents the licensee from dealing with the licensed materials in ways which are expressly permitted by statute:

This agreement is without prejudice to any acts which the licensee is permitted to carry out by the terms of the Copyright, Designs and Patents Act 1988 and nothing herein shall be construed as affecting or diminishing such permitted acts in any way whatsoever.

This is particularly important in preserving the right to copy materials under the fair dealing provisions of the CDPA.
3 Perpetual access to the licensed material:
When libraries subscribe to a journal in hard copy, even if they cancel their subscription, they still have the back issues available for future reference. This

is not automatically the case with electronic products. Are there any arrangements outlined in the licence agreement for perpetual access? Does it, for example, have a clause along the lines that 'on termination of this licence, the publisher shall provide continuing access for authorized users to that part of the licensed materials which was published and paid for within the subscription period'?

Both publishers and the users of their services have tried to come up with solutions to this issue. For example: Nature Publishing amended its site licence policy to provide customers with post-cancellation rights to content associated with their licensed publications, subject to payment of an annual access fee; meanwhile the UK LOCKSS Alliance is a cooperative activity of UK libraries that are committed to identify, negotiate, and build local archives of material that librarians and academic scholars deem significant. LOCKSS (http://lockss.stanford.edu) – 'Lot of copies keep stuff safe' is a low cost system that preserves access to a library's online journals in a local 'LOCKSS box' in a manner acceptable to publishers.

4 Warranties and indemnities:
The licence should contain a clear warranty that the publisher/licensor is the owner of the intellectual property rights in the licensed material and/or that they have the authority to grant the licence. This helps to protect the library against an author who subsequently claims that they are the real owner of the intellectual property rights; or against claims from a new owner that you have to buy a fresh licence from them. It is also common to have a clause that the licence will not be assigned to a third party without the agreement of the other. Indemnities back up a warranty with a promise to insure or compensate the other party against losses and expenses arising from a breach of the warranty. The licence should indemnify the library against any action by a third party over the intellectual property rights that are being licensed. This indemnity should cover all of the losses, damages, costs and expenses that are incurred, including legal expenses, on a full indemnity basis.

Having in place warranties and indemnities relating to the information provider having the right to license your use of the intellectual property is very important. There have been a number of legal cases in which people took out a licence with the wrong person:

- Retail Systems Technology v. Mcguire [2007] IEHC 13 (2nd February 2007).
- Lady Anne Tennant v. Associated Newspapers [1979] FSR 298 (involving the *Daily Mail*'s use of photographs of Princess Margaret, although the judge said that the *Mail* should have doubted the source of the licence anyway).
- Mansell v. Valley Printing [1908] 2 Ch 441, in which a publisher relied on

permission from a person who owned no rights, and was found to have infringed.

5 End-users:

The library should not incur legal liability for each and every infringement by an authorized user. It is perfectly reasonable to ask the library to notify the publisher/licensor of any infringement that comes to the library's notice and for them to co-operate with the publisher/licensor to prevent further abuse. Of course, if the library condoned or encouraged a breach to continue after being notified of the breach by the publisher/licensor, then they would be held liable.

6 Non-cancellation clauses:

For example, there should be no penalty for cancelling the print version in order to sign up to the electronic version of an information source.

7 Non-disclosure clauses:

If the licence contains a non-disclosure clause, it needs to be clear what information is subject to the obligation of confidence; and you need to decide whether this is reasonable. There are obviously some things – most notably the price – which are in the supplier's interests to keep confidential, especially if you have negotiated a preferential rate. Public authorities should bear in mind their obligations under the FOIA; and vendors should recognize that public authorities can't simply 'contract out' of their FOIA obligations.

8 Termination clause:

Licences should always contain a clause that sets out the mechanism or circumstances in which the licence terminates.

9 'Reasonable endeavours' and 'best endeavours' clauses:

The phrases 'reasonable endeavours' and 'best endeavours' (sometimes expressed as 'reasonable efforts' and 'best efforts') are ambiguous, and should, wherever possible, be avoided. It is important that the terms in a contract provide both parties with legal certainty, especially terms dealing with price, quantity, time, obligation and performance of the contract.

An obligation to use reasonable endeavours probably requires the relevant party to take one reasonable course, not all of them, whereas an obligation to use best endeavours probably requires that party to take all the reasonable courses that they can.

If these phrases are used, it would be best if the contract expressly spells out a specific set of steps that the person subject to the obligation is required to do as part of using their reasonable or best endeavours to perform the obligation.

Both sides will usually have some things which are non-negotiable, and which could therefore be potential deal breakers. It is important for both sides to be clear about what they are trying to achieve with the licence agreement, and to be upfront about what is non-negotiable. If an issue is a deal breaker, then the party which feels so strongly about that issue needs to recognize it, and know when negotiation isn't going to resolve the issue and that it's therefore time to walk away.

6.2.1   Factors that can make or break a deal

- applicable law
- warranties and indemnities
- remote access
- price
- access by walk-in users
- inter-library loan
- fair use
- archival access/perpetual rights
- adequate definition of authorized user
- IP access
- definition of university/campus as single site.

6.3   Consortia and standard licences

Negotiating licences can be extremely time-consuming. If you have to negotiate separate licences with each information provider, this is not only going to take up a lot of time but also creates practical issues relating to compliance. Can you really be expected to know each of the licences you have signed up to inside out, especially if you have to take account of the terms and conditions in the licences for a large number of products?

Consortia purchasing and/or the use of standard licences is recognition of the amount of time and effort involved in negotiating licence terms, as well as the expertise required. There are a number of initiatives to produce a standard form of licence:

⊷ Useful resources

1   Licensingmodels.org is an initiative led by a number of subscription agents. John Cox Associates produced a number of model standard licences for use by publishers, librarians and subscription agents for electronic resources. There are licences covering the whole range of library types: single academic institutions, academic consortia, public libraries, and corporate and other special libraries; and one licence on e-books and journal archives.

2   In the academic sector, the JISC often negotiates access to digital materials on behalf of interested universities. There is also a model licence that was negotiated by JISC with the Publishers Association (PA). The 'Standard Licensing Arrangements' working party was asked by the

JISC and the PA to explore options for developing 'umbrella' licence models, which individual publishers could employ. These generic tools were intended to cover different products and different types of use and would set out the more routine conditions of use, but leave a limited number of commercial issues – such as price per access or territory – to be added by different suppliers.

3 The International Coalition of Library Consortia (ICOLC) (www.library.yale.edu/consortia/statement.html) produced a statement of current perspective and preferred practices for the selection and purchase of electronic information back in 1998. This was primarily aimed at the higher education community. There are several updates to the original statement:
   • Update No. 1: new developments in e-journal licensing, December 2001, www.library.yale.edu/consortia/2001currentpractices.htm.
   • Update No. 2: Pricing and Economics, October 2004, www.library.yale.edu/consortia/2004icolcpr.htm.

4 The JISC Model Licence for Journals (www.jisc-collections.ac.uk/nesli2/ NESLi2-Model-Licence) is based on the National Electronic Site Licence Initiative (NESLI) site licence.

The corporate sector has not tended to work together to create consortia in order to negotiate agreements with information providers. There are a number of reasons for this. The sector is quite disparate, consisting of a wide range of organizational types: media, law, property, professional services, engineering, pharmaceutical, etc. Many commercial organizations will not want their competitors to know of any specially negotiated contractual terms, especially not the price agreed; and may even be cagey about what services they subscribe to. One example of where the corporate sector has worked together is the sample licence for electronic journals produced by the Pharma Documentation Ring (www.p-d-r.com).

Some large companies have produced a standard licence agreement for the supply of online information services, and have used their buying power to persuade information providers to let them have access to their products using the standard licence agreement that they, the customer, have drafted.

6.4   Technology solutions

Compliance with the terms and conditions of licences for electronic products is a major concern for both publishers and librarians, and suppliers will increasingly look to the available technology to control access to electronic information products.

SI 2003/2498, which implements EU directive 2001/29/EC, recognizes digital rights management systems and promotes their adoption, protection and use.

Where a library purchases a journal article or book in electronic format, the supplier might require them to accept a set of terms and conditions restricting access to, and use of, the item being purchased. But they might not rely solely on a set of terms and conditions to protect their intellectual property. Rather, they might use the technology to build in a number of security settings. Examples of how this could be applied in practice might include building in settings such as:

- Any use of the file is limited to the machine on which it is downloaded.
- Printing is set to one copy only.
- Saving and viewing of the article is permitted, but for a limited period of time.
- Forwarding and copying functions are disabled.
- Annotations and conversion to speech are permitted.
- Encrypted data which ensures that the material can only be read by one person who has been given access to the software that decodes the data.

6.5   Use of passwords for licensed products

Be careful about your use of passwords for online databases, making sure that you comply with the terms of the licence agreement.

In February 2009 the *Financial Times* took legal action against one of their customers – Blackstone Group – for sharing passwords, eventually reaching a successful out-of-court settlement, rumoured to be a six-figure sum (Owen 2009a, 2009b).

In May 2010 the investment data provider Ipreo alleged that Goldman Sachs had infringed their copyright and that Goldman Sachs employees had shared log-ins intended only for a named contact. Ipreo alleged that at least two Goldman Sachs employees, and possibly more, illegally accessed its Bigdough contacts and profiles database over 200 times, downloading substantial amounts of data using log-in credentials belonging to someone else (Vijayan, 2010).

It is important to be absolutely clear what type of contract you have – whether it is for a single user or for multiple users – and to abide by the contract terms. Where it is for multiple users, you should know whether it works on the basis of a set number of nominated individuals being allocated specific user IDs and passwords; or if it is based on a set number of concurrent users.

6.5.1   Usage data

When taking out a licence for an electronic product it is important to bear in mind usage data. Does the product automatically give you, as the administrator, access to the usage data of everyone who uses the product, and does it do so in the format you require? If not, it might be necessary to include a clause in the contract requiring the vendor to supply you with usage data on a regular basis. Being able to monitor the usage levels, you are then in a position to spot if the usage for a particular user is suspiciously high and will be able to take pre-emptive action as necessary, such as changing the password if you think it might have been shared with someone else.

 Make sure that you have access to usage data for the key online resources you subscribe to. In some instances usage data will be accessible directly from within the product; sometimes it requires access to a separate module; but sometimes the only way to guarantee that you are able to see the usage data is to ensure that there is a clause in the contract requiring the information provider to supply you with the data on a regular basis.

6.6   Further information

The Association of Learned and Professional Society Publishers (ALPSP): www.alpsp.org/ngen_public/default.asp?id=373Licensing.

Bebbington, L. (2001) Managing Content: licensing, copyright and privacy issues in managing electronic resources, *Legal Information Management*, **1** (2), 4–13.

Copyright Management for Scholarship: www.surf.nl/copyright.

Durrant, Fiona (2006) *Negotiating Licences for Digital Resources*, Facet Publishing.

International Coalition of Library Consortia (ICOLC) Statement of current perspective and preferential practices for the selection and purchase of electronic information: www.library.yale.edu/consortia/statement.html.

JISC/Publishers Association Working Party Papers and Reports: www.ukoln.ac.uk/services/elib/papers/pa.

LIBLICENSE: licensing digital information: www.library.yale.edu/~llicense/index.shtml.

Licensing models as drawn up by John Cox Associates: www.licensingmodels.org.

Tilburg University Licensing Principles: http://webdoc.sub.gwdg.de/ebook/aw/prinzliz/1_lizp-e.htm.

UKSG (Serials, Serials e-news, lis-e-journals): www.uksg.org.

US principles for licensing electronic resources: www.arl.org/sc/marketplace/license/licprinciples.shtml.

References

Bayley, E. (2009) *The Clicks That Bind: ways users 'agree' to online terms of service*, Electronic Frontier Foundation, www.eff.org/wp/clicks-bind-ways-users-agree-online-terms-service.

Giavarra, E. (2001) *Licensing Digital Resources: how to avoid the legal pitfalls*, 2nd edn, EBLIDA.

Hargreaves, I. (2011) *Digital Opportunity: review of intellectual property and growth*, www.ipo.gov.uk/ipreview-finalreport.pdf.

Harris, L.E. (2009) *Licensing Digital Content: a practical guide for libraries*, American Library Association.

Owen, T.B. (2009a) FT Gets Tough on Multiple Log-ins, *VIP Magazine*, 7 February,
www.vivavip.com/go/e16109.

Owen, T.B. (2009b) Tighter DIY Policing of FT Usage? *VIP Magazine*, 22 April,
www.vivavip.com/go/e18994.

Vijayan, J. (2010) Ipreo Sues Goldman Sachs for Data Theft, *Computerworld*, 7 May,
www.computerworld.com/s/article/9176441/Ipreo_sues_Goldman_Sachs_for_data_theft.

CHAPTER 7

Data protection

Contents

7.1   Introduction

Information professionals process personal data as part of their daily work. Examples include the maintenance of user registration and circulation records, or management statistics on usage of the information service. They might be responsible for a contact database, or maintain an intranet or website through which they collect and process personal data. In addition to the need to comply with the Data Protection Act 1998, CILIP members also need to abide by the *Ethical Principles and Code of Professional Practice for Library and Information Professionals* (CILIP, 2009). The code states that information professionals should 'protect the confidentiality of all matters relating to information users, including their enquiries, any services to be provided, and any aspects of the users' personal circumstances or business'.

7.2   General principles

The Data Protection Act 1998 (DPA) came into force on 1 March 2000. It sets out how personal data should be handled. As far as the DPA is concerned, personal data means data that relates to an identified or identifiable living individual (see Figure 7.1). The data could be about anyone in the world because the DPA applies if control of the data is UK-based or if the data itself is held in the UK.

The DPA sets out the rules for the processing of personal information and it applies to personal data held on computer and in some paper records where these form part of a 'relevant filing system' (DPA 1998 s1). In essence, for manual records to be covered by the DPA, they need to fulfil three criteria:

The DPA defines personal data in section 1(1) as:
data which relate to a living individual who can be identified –
(a)   from those data, or
(b)   from those data and other information which is in the possession of, or is likely to come into the possession of, the data controller,
and includes any expression of opinion about the individual and any indication of the intentions of the data controller or any other person in respect of the individual.

The Court of Appeal judgment in Durant v. FSA [2003] EWCA Civ 1746 (paragraph 28) (www.bailii.org/ew/cases/EWCA/Civ/2003/1746.html) provides further guidance on what constitutes personal data. The Court of Appeal concluded that data would relate to an individual if it 'is information that affects [a person's] privacy, whether in his personal or family life, business or professional capacity'.

If in doubt as to whether information relates to an individual, ask yourself whether the information in question is capable of having an adverse impact upon the individual. The Court of Appeal identified two notions which will assist those who need to determine whether the information 'relates to' an individual:

1. Is the information biographical in a significant sense?
2. The information should have the individual as its focus.

Mere mention of an individual's name does not constitute 'personal data', unless its inclusion affects that individual's privacy. So the mere reference to an individual's name where that name is not associated with any other personal information; or the incidental mention in the minutes of a meeting of an individual's attendance at that meeting would not normally be personal data.

In cases where the information in question can be linked to an identifiable individual, the following are examples of personal data:

- information about the medical history of an individual
- an individual's salary details
- information concerning an individual's tax liabilities
- information comprising an individual's bank statements
- information about an individual's spending preferences.

Figure 7.1 *What constitutes 'personal data'?*

1 They are not automatically processed.
2 They are structured by reference to individuals or criteria relating to individuals.
3 They contain specific information about individuals that is readily accessible.

Some manual records are covered by the DPA regardless of whether they are part of a relevant filing system. They include records relating to health matters, educational matters, housing and social security matters. The DPA also covers other media such as tape recordings and CCTV footage.

In Durant v. Financial Services Authority [2003] EWCA Civ 1746, paragraph 48, the judge considered what is meant by a 'relevant filing system'. The Court of Appeal took the view that the Act intended to cover manual files 'only if they are of sufficient sophistication to provide the same or similar ready accessibility as a computerized filing system'.

Any manual filing system 'which, for example, requires the searcher to leaf through files to see what and whether information qualifying as personal data of the person who has made the request [for access to his personal data] is to be found there, would bear no resemblance to a computerized search' (paragraph 45). It would not, therefore, qualify as a relevant filing system.

The judgment concluded that:

A 'relevant filing system' for the purposes of the Act, is limited to a system:

1) in which the files forming part of it are structured or referenced in such a way as to clearly indicate at the outset of the search whether specific information capable of amounting to personal data of an individual requesting it under section 7 is held within the system and, if so, in which file or files it is held; and

2) which has, as part of its own structure or referencing mechanism, a sufficiently sophisticated and detailed means of readily indicating whether and where in an individual file or files specific criteria or information about the applicant can be readily located (paragraph 50).

Where manual files fall within the definition of relevant filing system, the content will either be so sub-divided as to allow the searcher to go straight to the correct category and retrieve the information requested without a manual search, or will be so indexed as to allow a searcher to go directly to the relevant page/s.

Following the Durant judgment, it is likely that very few manual files are covered by the provisions of the DPA. However, it should be borne in mind that section 69 of the FOIA amends the DPA to insert a right of access to unstructured personal data held by public authorities.

On 29 November 2005, the House of Lords rejected a petition by Michael Durant to hear an appeal against the Court of Appeal's ruling in the case which he brought against the Financial Services Authority.

Whilst the DPA 1984 wasn't prompted by legislation at an EU level, the DPA 1998 was introduced in order to ensure that UK law complied with the EU data protection directive (95/46/EC). Article 1 of the directive aims to protect the individual's rights of privacy. This principle is enshrined in Article 8 of the European Convention on Human Rights ('Everyone has the right to respect for his private and family life, his home and his correspondence.') and it is important to recognize that the UK's data protection legislation is based on these human rights foundations (see Figure 7.2).

The European Commission is currently in the process of reviewing the general EU legal framework on the protection of personal data. The main policy objectives for the Commission are to:

1980: OECD guidelines. Recommendation of the Council concerning guidelines governing the protection of privacy and transborder flows of personal data. Adopted by the Council 23 September 1980.
1981: Council of Europe Convention (108/81) for the protection of individuals with regard to automatic processing of personal data.
1984: First UK Data Protection Act (now repealed).
1990: United Nations guidelines concerning computerized personal data files adopted by the general assembly on 14 December 1990.
1995: EU Directive (95/46/EC) on the protection of individuals with regard to the processing of personal data and on the free movement of such data.
1997: EU Telecommunications Data Protection Directive (97/66/EC) (now repealed and replaced by 2002/58/EC).
1998: Data Protection Act.
1998: Human Rights Act.
2000: Data Protection Act came into force.
2000: Human Rights Act came into force.
2000: Freedom of Information Act.
2000: Regulation of Investigatory Powers Act.
2002: EU Directive (2002/58/EC) on privacy and electronic communications.
2003: The Privacy and Electronic Communications (EC Directive) Regulations 2003 (SI 2003/2426).
2004: The Privacy and Electronic Communications (EC Directive) (Amendment) Regulations 2004 (SI 2004/1039).
2005: Freedom of Information Act came into force.
2006: Data Retention Directive 2006/24/EC.
2009: Directive 2009/136/EC (known as the 'cookie directive') amending directives 2002/22/EC, 2002/58/EC and Regulation 2006/2004.
2011: Protection of Freedoms Bill.
2011: The Privacy and Electronic Communications (EC Directive) (Amendment) Regulations 2011.

Figure 7.2 *Legislative history of data protection laws*

- Modernize the EU legal system for the protection of personal data, in particular to meet the challenges resulting from globalization and the use of new technologies.
- Strengthen individuals' rights, and at the same time reduce administrative formalities to ensure a free flow of personal data within the EU and beyond.
- Improve the clarity and coherence of the EU rules for personal data protection and achieve a consistent and effective implementation and application of the fundamental right to the protection of personal data in all areas of the EU's activities.

On 4 November 2010, the Commission adopted a strategic Communication on a comprehensive approach on personal data protection in the EU (COM (2010)609).

7.3   The eight data protection principles

The DPA says that those who record and use personal information must be open about how the information is used and must follow the eight principles of 'good information handling' (see Figure 7.3). These eight principles are set out in Schedule 1 to the Act. Since the eight principles are enshrined in law, data controllers are required to ensure that their handling of personal data is in line with these principles.

Data must be:

1   fairly and lawfully processed
2   processed for limited purposes (notified to the Commissioner and to the data subject)
3   adequate, relevant and not excessive
4   accurate
5   not kept for longer than is necessary
6   processed in line with the data subject's rights
7   kept secure
8   not transferred to countries without adequate protection.

Figure 7.3 *The eight principles of 'good information handling'*

7.3.1   First principle

The first data protection principle says that personal data should be processed fairly and lawfully. The information must be processed in a way that complies with the general law and in a manner which is fair to individuals. The whole ethos of the legislation is that for processing to be fair there should be transparency. So, the data subject needs to know how to contact the data controller, the purpose for which the information is going to be processed, and any other information necessary to ensure that the processing is fair.

7.3.2   Second principle

The second data protection principle says that data must only be obtained for a specified purpose. You need to let individuals know the reason(s) why you are collecting the data. If you subsequently decide that data collected for one purpose would be useful for another purpose, you should first let the data subjects know what you are intending to do and give them an opportunity to opt out.

7.3.3   Third principle

The third data protection principle says that personal data shall be adequate, relevant and not excessive in relation to the purpose for which it is processed. So you should only collect the minimum data necessary to fulfil the purpose for which you are processing it. This principle should be borne in mind when designing forms, and in the case of online forms you might want to make some of the fields optional.

7.3.4   Fourth principle

The fourth data protection principle says that personal data shall be accurate and where necessary kept up to date. This requires data controllers to take reasonable steps to ensure the accuracy of the data. Upon a data subject's request you should correct, change or delete inaccurate details.

7.3.5   Fifth principle

The fifth principle requires that personal data should not be kept for longer than is necessary. Data controllers should have a clear policy on how long they keep data, and at the end of that period the data should be reviewed or destroyed as appropriate. But there are circumstances in which the destruction of personal data can be construed as unfair or damaging. Experian's *A Simplified Guide to the Data Protection Act 1998* (Experian, no date) uses an example to illustrate this: 'If sales records needed for the calculation of agreed retrospective discounts are destroyed, the customer can claim that their destruction is detrimental to his business.'

7.3.6   Sixth principle

The sixth data protection principle states that personal data shall be processed in accordance with the rights of data subjects under the DPA. In other words you should do nothing to undermine those rights.

7.3.7   Seventh principle

The seventh principle states that appropriate technical and organizational measures should be used to protect against unauthorized or unlawful processing of personal data and against accidental loss or destruction of, or damage to, personal data.

This principle covers not just technical measures, but also organizational measures. For example, library staff need to be careful about the positioning of computer terminals at enquiry desks, ensuring that third parties cannot see what's on the screen. They also need to be wary of speaking on the telephone about a person's record within earshot of third parties.

The interpretation of this principle in Schedule 1 of the DPA says that 'the data controller must take reasonable steps to ensure the reliability of any employees of his who have access to the personal data'. Therefore it is necessary to consider, for example, whether you should ask temporary staff who are given access to personal data to sign a confidentiality agreement; or how you might ensure that visitors to your organization are not inadvertently given access to personal data.

The Privacy and Electronic Communications (EC Directive) Regulations 2003: SI 2003/2426 take the seventh data protection principle a stage further with regard to the security of public electronic communications services. Where there is a significant risk to security, service providers are required to inform subscribers of the nature of that risk (see Figure 7.4).

7.3.8   Eighth principle

The eighth data protection principle requires that personal data shall not be transferred to a country or territory outside the European Economic Area (EEA) unless that country or territory ensures an adequate level of protection for the rights and freedoms of data subjects in relation to the processing of personal data.

The EEA consists of the 27 Member States of the EU plus Norway, Iceland and Liechtenstein. No distinction is made between transfer to others within your organization and transfer to third parties.

The eighth data protection principle causes practical difficulties for companies wishing to do business across national borders. There are, however, a number of initiatives to minimize those difficulties:

1   The EU has recognized the adequacy of the protection of personal data for the following countries:
    - Andorra
    - Argentina
    - Australia
    - Canada
    - Faeroe Islands

Regulation 5 of The Privacy and Electronic Communications (EC Directive) Regulations SI 2003/2426 (www.legislation.gov.uk/uksi/2003/2426/contents/made) says:

5. - (1) Subject to paragraph (2), a provider of a public electronic communications service ('the service provider') shall take appropriate technical and organisational measures to safeguard the security of that service.

   (2) If necessary, the measures required by paragraph (1) may be taken by the service provider in conjunction with the provider of the electronic communications network by means of which the service is provided, and that network provider shall comply with any reasonable requests made by the service provider for these purposes.

   (3) Where, notwithstanding the taking of measures as required by paragraph (1), there remains a significant risk to the security of the public electronic communications service, the service provider shall inform the subscribers concerned of -
      (a) the nature of that risk;
      (b) any appropriate measures that the subscriber may take to safeguard against that risk; and
      (c) the likely costs to the subscriber involved in the taking of such measures.

   (4) For the purposes of paragraph (1), a measure shall only be taken to be appropriate if, having regard to -
      (a) the state of technological developments, and
      (b) the cost of implementing it, it is proportionate to the risks against which it would safeguard.

   (5) Information provided for the purposes of paragraph (3) shall be provided to the subscriber free of any charge other than the cost to the subscriber of receiving or collecting the information.

Figure 7.4 *Security of public electronic communications services*

- Guernsey
- Isle of Man
- Israel
- Jersey
- Switzerland
- USA (companies signed up to the 'safe harbor' agreement)
- USA (transfer of air passenger name record to the United States Bureau of Customs and Border Protection).

⊷ Useful resource

For up-to-date information on EC decisions on the adequacy of the protection of personal data in third countries, visit
http://ec.europa.eu/justice/policies/privacy/thridcountries/index_en.htm.

2 The EC has adopted a decision setting out standard contractual clauses ensuring adequate safeguards for personal data transferred from the EU to countries outside the Union (*Safer standards for European citizens*, IP/10/130). The decision obliges Member States to recognize that companies or organizations using such standard clauses in contracts concerning personal data transfers to countries outside the EU are offering 'adequate protection' to the data. In February 2010 the EC adopted a decision updating the standard contractual clauses and the update contains specific provision to allow, under certain conditions, for the outsourcing of processing activities to sub-processors.

3 The US Department of Commerce developed a 'safe harbor' agreement, which was approved by the European Union in July 2000 (www.export.gov/safeharbor), but this only covers US companies who have agreed to abide by the 'safe harbor' principles.

There are a number of instances in which transfer of personal data to non-EEA countries is acceptable, and these are outlined in schedule 4 of the DPA. They include the following:

• Individuals have given their consent.
• It is necessary for the performance of a contract.
• It is necessary for reasons of substantial public interest.
• It is necessary for legal reasons (in connection with legal proceedings, obtaining legal advice, etc.).
• The data subject has requested it.
• It is necessary to protect the vital interests of the data subject.
• The transfer is part of the personal data on a public register.

7.4 Processing of personal data

The DPA regulates the processing of information about individuals, and it defines processing widely to cover everything that can be done with personal information such as the obtaining, recording, holding, disclosing, blocking, erasure or destruction of personal data.

The DPA requires that personal data be processed 'fairly and lawfully'. Personal data will not be considered to be processed fairly unless certain conditions are met. These conditions are set out in Schedule 2 of the Act. Processing may only be carried out where one of the following conditions has been met:

1 Individuals have given their consent to the processing.
2 The processing is necessary for the performance of a contract with the individual.
3 The processing is required under a legal obligation.

4 The processing is necessary to protect the vital interests of the individual.

5 The processing is necessary to carry out public functions.

6 The processing is necessary in order to pursue the legitimate interests of the data controller or third parties (unless it could prejudice the interests of the individual).

The DPA treats 'sensitive personal data' differently, giving it added protection. Figure 7.5 outlines what is meant by 'sensitive personal data'. The added protections state that it is necessary not only to comply with the fair processing conditions, but also to comply with further conditions, which are set out in Schedule 3 of the Act. So, one of the conditions in Schedule 2 must apply plus one of the following conditions from Schedule 3:

1 Data subjects have given their explicit consent.

2 They are required by law to process the data for employment purposes.

3 It is necessary to protect the vital interests of the data subject or another person.

4 Processing is carried out in the course of its legitimate activities by any body which exists for political, philosophical, religious or trade union purposes, and which is not established or conducted for profit.

5 The information has been made public by the data subject.

6 It is necessary for the administration of justice or legal proceedings.

7 It is necessary for defending legal rights.

8 The processing is necessary for medical purposes and is undertaken by a health professional or someone with an equivalent duty of confidentiality.

9 It is necessary for equal opportunities monitoring.

Sensitive personal data refers to personal data about an individual's:

- racial or ethnic origin
- religious or political beliefs
- trade union membership
- physical or mental health
- sex life
- criminal record

Figure 7.5 *Sensitive personal data*

7.5   Notification

The DPA says that those who record and use personal information must notify the Information Commissioner's Office (ICO) that they process personal data.

Single v. BNP

Matt Single pleaded guilty to leaking the British National Party's (BNP) membership list on the internet in 2008. He was a disgruntled former official of the party. He was sentenced to a derisory £300 fine by a court in Nottingham after accepting full responsibility for leaking the list. The court heard that there were 160 complaints from people who had been threatened or had had their property vandalized as a result of the leaked list. There were examples of people losing their jobs as a result of their membership of the BNP becoming known.

Sentencing Mr Single, Judge John Stobart said he was 'frustrated' at the fact that he could not fine Mr Single more. Mr Single was on Job Seeker's Allowance, and this restricted the amount by which he could be fined. The £300 fine consisted of £200 for the criminal offence and £100 towards the prosecution and investigation costs, which, the judge said, amounted to many thousands of pounds.

Judge Stobart told Single: 'Anything that is posted on the internet has the effect of opening a Pandora's box. What you put on the internet can never be taken from it and while there may be some members in this organization who do not deserve to be protected by the law, they should be able to expect that officers within the organization will not abuse the information provided to them. The law exists to save people from such revenge attacks.'

Judge Stobart added: 'It came as a surprise to me, as it will to many members of the party, that to do something as foolish and as criminally dangerous as you did will only incur a financial penalty.' He went on to state that it was because Single was on Job Seeker's Allowance that 'the fine is so low as to be ridiculous'.

⊷ Useful resource

A register of data controllers is available on the website www.ico.gov.uk/ESDWebPages/search.asp. Each entry consists of:

- the data controller's name and address
- a description of the personal data being processed
- the categories of data subject to which they relate
- data classes such as employment details
- a description of the purpose(s) for which data is or may be processed
- a description of the recipient(s) to whom the data will be disclosed
- the names of countries or territories outside the EEA to which the data is or might be transferred either directly or indirectly by the data controller.

Those who process personal data must provide access to the data that they hold on a person in order for the data subject to check and correct their records and prevent certain types of processing.

A data controller may only have one register entry. Therefore, even in the case of large organizations, there should only be a single entry per organization on the register. Data controllers register for one year at a time. In the case of data controllers with either a turnover of £25.9 million and over 250 members of staff, or if they are a public authority with over 250 members of staff, then the notification fee is £500. Otherwise the notification fee is £35 for the year. They must ensure that the register entry for their organization is up to date and any changes must be notified to the ICO within 28 days. Changes to the register entry can be made at any time free of charge. There is a notification helpline (08456 306060) and an e-mail address (notification@ico.gsi.gov.uk) for any questions about the notification process.

It should be noted that there are a number of people posing as data protection 'agencies' who offer to register your company on your behalf. They send out notices on headed notepaper requesting sums of at least £95. Indeed, some people are even posing as collectors of data protection and are attending business premises requesting payment for Data Protection Registration. These 'collectors' produce identification cards and receipt books. They have no connection with the ICO, and anyone approached in this way is advised not to make any payment and to notify the local police. In fact, notification is relatively simple and it can be done by companies themselves following the guidelines that are available on the website of the ICO (www.ico.gov.uk).

If you process personal data, then you need to ensure that you are registered with the ICO and that your register entry adequately covers the scope of your operations.

It is important to be clear who within the organization has ultimate responsibility for data protection matters, as well as who would handle access requests, who would handle contractual or data transfer issues, or who would deal with complaints by customers about issues relating to their personal data.

7.6   How to protect your information

Personal information is a valuable commodity. Think before supplying anyone with your personal data, and always ask yourself why an organization is asking for information about you. Do they need this information or are they asking for more information than is necessary? You may not have to provide it. They may, for example, be asking about your income, hobbies, interests or family life for possible future marketing campaigns. If someone wants to use your information for a purpose other than the reason for which the data is being collected, you should be told about it and given a choice. Of course, there will be times when you will need to give your personal information for legal reasons. If this is the case, this should be clearly explained. It is important to read the data protection clauses at the end of documents very carefully and to ensure that you make full use of the 'opt-out' or 'opt-in' choices. Sometimes an organization will put several tick boxes at the end of a document and they may use a mixture of opt-ins and opt-outs. It is well worth taking the time to read through the wording of such documents to ensure that you have made the right choices. Figure 7.6 outlines the steps you should take

1	Limit the disclosure of your personal information.
2	Set up a separate e-mail account for e-commerce activities.
3	Reject cookies planted in your computer by intrusive businesses.
4	Use tools to protect privacy and enable you to surf anonymously (see http://epic.org/privacy/tools.html).
5	Learn about your legal rights and be prepared to use them.

Figure 7.6 *Five steps to protecting your privacy online (Source: Privacy@net, Consumers International, 2001)*

to protect your privacy online.

There are a number of different 'preference services' which are available if, for example, you want to stop unwanted marketing material being sent to you, or if you want to stop receiving uninvited telesales calls or telemarketing faxes (see

Mailing Preference Service (MPS): DMA House, 70 Margaret Street, London W1W 8SS; 020 77291 3310.
Telephone Preference Service: 0845 070 0707.
Fax Preference Service: 0845 070 0702.
Green Preference Service: www.greenpreferenceservice.com/ (operates as a commercial business).

Figure 7.7 *Preference services*

Figure 7.7).

The Privacy and Electronic Communications (EC Directive) (Amendment) Regulations 2004: SI 2004/1039 enable corporate subscribers to register their telephone numbers with the Telephone Preference Service (TPS). This means that anyone making promotional and/or fundraising calls to any business is required to ensure that they are not calling a business number registered on the TPS. If a business wants to register its number(s) on the TPS list, it must do so in writing. Registration is renewable annually.

Since May 2011, as a result of The Privacy and Electronic Communications (EC Directive) (Amendment) Regulations 2011: SI 2011/1208, the Information Commissioner has had new powers to serve monetary penalties of up to £500,000 for the most serious incidents of businesses and other organizations making unwanted marketing e-mails and texts, as well as unwanted live and automated marketing phone calls to consumers.

7.7   Identity theft

Identity theft takes place when an individual's personal information is used fraudulently, without their knowledge or permission, by someone else. It might then be used in order to open a bank account or set up a number of credit cards in the name of the victim. The victims of identity theft have to spend a considerable amount of time contacting each of the separate companies against which there are bad debts. It is not simply a case of calling up a credit reference company and asking for the bad debts to be removed from your credit record on the grounds that they were undertaken without your knowledge. If you become a victim of identity theft, you could find yourself being refused a credit card, a mortgage, or being prevented from setting up a bank account. Indeed, it may only be when you apply for a credit card, bank account or mortgage that you realize that someone has stolen your identity.

In order to avoid becoming a victim of identity theft, the best advice would be to look after your personal information very carefully (see Figure 7.8). As the saying goes, 'prevention is better than cure'. In order to do this, you need to be extremely cautious about giving out information such as your mother's maiden name or your date of birth. If you undertake electronic commerce transactions – such as buying books, music or DVDs online; booking rail tickets, a flight or a holiday on the web – the companies may ask you first to register your details. If the registration process requires you to divulge your mother's maiden name or your date of birth, think very carefully before giving out the correct information. Are you confident that the information is secure?

One of the most effective ways of looking after your personal information is to ensure that you have internet security software on your PC, and that you update

---

- Think before giving out key information such as your mother's maiden name or your date of birth.
- Password-protect your computer.
- Use passwords to protect documents.
- Invest in a shredder.
- Check your credit record on a regular basis – if your identity has been stolen, the record may show details of bad debts you may otherwise have no knowledge of.
- Don't put anything in your household waste that could be of use to identity thieves.
- Set up your computer to lock itself after a period of inactivity.
- Encrypt sensitive data.
- Keep your computer's anti-virus/internet security software up to date.

Figure 7.8 *Tips for avoiding becoming a victim of identity theft*

it on a regular basis. This can help protect you against viruses, malware and phishing attempts, and can also block undesirable websites.

Another way of safeguarding your personal information is to invest in a shredder. Thieves often steal household waste with the aim of gathering useful snippets of information which can then be used to steal a person's identity. To minimize the risks involved, it is advisable to shred documents such as bank statements or council tax bills, as well as marketing literature from financial institutions trying to sell you a particular product in which they have very usefully printed your personal details on the application form.

 If anyone becomes a victim of identity theft, and is having difficulty resolving matters, it is worth investigating membership of the CIFAS protective registration service (www.cifas.org.uk). This enables a person who is at greater risk of being (or already is) a victim of identity theft to place a protective warning on their credit file. It introduces added precautions for ensuring that any use of a person's details is genuine.

7.8 Rights of the data subject

The DPA gives certain rights to individuals. They are allowed to find out what information is held about them on computer and in some paper records. This is known as the 'right of subject access'. To assert this right the individual will need to write to the data controller at the organization which they believe holds the information. They should ask for a copy of all the information held about themself to which the DPA applies (see Figure 7.9). If they are not sure who to write to within an organization, it is best to address it to the Company Secretary, Chief Executive or the contact job title given on the register of data controllers (via the

---

Your address
The date

Dear Sir/Madam,

Please send me the information I am entitled to under section 7(1) of the Data Protection Act 1998.

If you need further information from me, or a fee, please let me know as soon as possible.

If you do not normally handle these requests for your organization, please pass this letter to your Data Protection Officer or another appropriate official.

Yours faithfully,

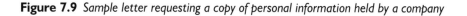

Figure 7.9 *Sample letter requesting a copy of personal information held by a company*

website www.ico.gov.uk), which is kept by the ICO.

Some decisions are made by an automatic process. If the requester wishes to be informed of the logic involved in certain types of automated decisions which the controller may take (for example, their performance at work or credit-worthiness), after 'section 7(1)' in their letter, they should add 'including information under section 7(1)(d)'.

In response, the data subject should receive a copy of the information held about them. The DPA (s8) says that the information should be in permanent form unless (a) the supply of such a copy is not possible or would involve disproportionate effort or (b) the data subject agrees otherwise. This means that the information will usually be provided on paper and may therefore be sent as a computer printout, in a letter or on a form. The data subject should also receive a description of why their information is processed, anyone it may be passed to or seen by, and the logic involved in any automated decisions. The DPA requires that the information should be in an intelligible form, and thus any codes used should be explained.

Data controllers are obliged to reply. If the data subject does not receive a reply to their request within 40 calendar days, they should send the organization a reminder by recorded delivery. If they still don't receive a reply fairly quickly, or if the inform-ation they receive is wrong or incomplete, then they should contact the ICO. The Commissioner can help the data subject to get a reply, and if one of the principles has been broken, they can take enforcement action against the data controller.

It is best for data subjects to send their request by recorded delivery in the first instance, and it is important for them to keep a copy of the letter and any further correspondence. In many cases they will be asked to provide further detail in order to confirm their identity. It will obviously help if the data subject provides the data controller with these details as quickly as possible. They are generally entitled to receive a reply within 40 calendar days of providing these details, as long as they have paid the required fee. There are different periods for copies of credit files (seven working days) and for school pupil records (15 school days). Many organizations choose not to charge a fee at all, but where a fee for access to information held about a data subject is levied, this cannot normally be more than £10. However, in the case of certain medical or educational records the amount can be up to £50; and in the case of credit records the fee is normally £2.

Usually the data subject can see all the personal data held about them. However, there are some exemptions (see Figure 7.10) – for example, if providing the information would affect the way crime is detected or prevented, affect catching or prosecuting offenders or affect assessing or collecting taxes or duty. It should also be noted that material which infringes the privacy of third parties might be withheld. In some cases their right to see certain health and social work details may also be limited. If a data subject thinks that information is being unreasonably held

Personal data collected for:

- national security (s.28)
- crime and taxation (s.29)
- health, school education and social work (s.30)
- certain types of regulatory activity (s.31)
- journalism, literature, art (s.32)
- research, history and statistics (s.33)
- legal proceedings (s.35)
- parliamentary privilege (s.35A)

Figure 7.10 *Exemptions to the right of inspection*

back, they should contact the ICO.

The rights that a data subject has are:

1 Right of access to personal data. Individuals have a right to know the identity of the data controller, the purposes for which their data will be used, where the data has come from and gone to, and to be given any other information that is necessary to make the processing 'fair', such as details of likely disclosures (i.e. who is likely to have seen the data) or transfers.

2 Right to prevent processing that is causing, or likely to cause, unwarranted and substantial damage or distress to the individual, or to anyone else – according to Experian (no date), examples of causing substantial damage or distress would include sending letters to dead people or to their family relating to the deceased; or revealing payment details to a third party without consent.

3 Right to prevent processing for the purposes of direct marketing.

4 Right to be given an explanation as to how any automated decisions taken about you have been made.

5 Right to compensation. Data subjects are entitled to claim compensation through the courts if damage has been caused as a result of a data controller not meeting any requirements of the DPA, and in particular if they have broken any of the data protection principles. If damage is proved, the court may also order compensation for any associated distress. Data subjects can claim compensation for distress alone in very limited circumstances, e.g. because of intrusion by the media.

6 Right to correction, blocking, erasure or destruction of inaccurate data.

7 Right to request an assessment by the Information Commissioner of the legality of processing that is occurring (s42).

7.8.1 Credit reference agencies

Credit reference agencies hold information to enable credit grantors to exchange information with each other about their customers. They also have access to the electoral roll and publicly available financial information which will have a bearing on an individual's credit-worthiness, including County Court judgments and Scottish decrees. If an individual wants to see the information that the credit reference agencies hold about their financial standing – their 'credit file' – the main credit reference agencies are:

- Equifax plc, Credit File Advice Service, PO Box 1140, Bradford BD1 5US.
- Experian Ltd, Consumer Help Service, PO Box 8000, Nottingham NG80 7WF.
- Callcredit plc, Customer Services Team, PO Box 491, Leeds LS3 1WZ.

The data subject should send a fee of £2 and provide their full name and address, including postcode, any other addresses they have lived at during the last six years, and details of any other names they have used/been known by in that time. Unless the agencies require any further information to locate the file, they have seven working days from the receipt of the letter in which to supply the individual with a copy of their credit file.

The credit reference agency will only send a data subject information about their financial situation, unless they specifically request other information, such as that outlined in Figure 7.9.

7.9   Data protection and employment

The ICO has published a four-part Employment Practices Data Protection Code:

- Part 1: Recruitment and Selection
- Part 2: Records Management
- Part 3: Monitoring at Work
- Part 4: Medical Information.

The aim of the Employment Code is to strike a balance between a worker's legitimate right to respect for their private life and an employer's legitimate need to run its business. Compliance with the code will: increase trust in the workplace; protect organizations from legal action; encourage workers to respect personal data; aid organizations in meeting other legal requirements such as the Human Rights Act 1998 and the Regulation of Investigatory Powers Act 2000; assist global business in complying with similar legislation in other countries; and help to prevent illegal use of information by workers. By contrast, a failure to comply with the code will lead to prosecution of both the company and/or the individual. Many companies would regard a serious breach of data protection rules as being a disciplinary offence.

As aforementioned, data protection covers personal data held on computer and in some paper records where these form part of a relevant filing system. In respect of the employment code, this would include information such as salary details, e-mails, notebooks and application forms of applicants, former applicants, employees, agency workers, casual workers, contract workers, volunteers and work experience placements.

Before an employer can store and process sensitive personal data (see Figure 7.5), at least one of the conditions set out in Schedule 3 must be met. For example:

- It is necessary for the purposes of exercising any right or obligation – for example, to ensure health and safety, to avoid discrimination or to check immigration status.
- The data subject has freely given explicit consent to the processing.

Employees are entitled to see their data. The request must be in writing and the company must respond within 40 calendar days and can charge up to £10. There are exemptions from disclosure in areas such as criminal investigations or management planning (promotions, transfers or redundancies).

7.9.1   Recruitment and selection

The section of the Employment Code relating to recruitment and selection covers any data on applicants, employees, agency workers and casual workers (current and former) which is stored on a computer or on paper in a relevant filing system. It relates to the processing of data – that is, obtaining, keeping, using, accessing, disclosing or destroying it. This also applies to sensitive personal data, which includes information about racial or ethnic origin, political opinions, religious beliefs, physical or mental health, or sex life. Figure 7.11 gives a checklist for employers to follow in order to make sure that they are in compliance with the Employment Code.

7.9.2   Employment records and references

Part 2 of the Employment Practices Data Protection Code covers records management issues relating to personal data stored on computer or on paper in a relevant filing system. References are subject to the DPA. The *writer* of a confidential reference is not obliged to provide the data subject with access to its contents, but the *recipient* of a reference is obliged to show the data subject the reference if a subject access request is received. The employee is therefore able to obtain a copy of the reference from their new employer or would-be employer. It makes no difference whether the reference is marked 'confidential' or not. If the reference was fraudulent or negligent, the writer of the reference might be sued

Recruitment and selection
- If possible, use the company name in recruitment advertisements.
- Only ask for information that is relevant to the selection process.
- When shortlisting, use objective methods such as selection matrices and interview guides in order to avoid subjective decisions.
- Check that your selection criteria do not discriminate in terms of race, age, gender, etc.
- Keep CVs locked away. Only give access to those involved in the recruitment process.
- Explain what information will be checked, and how. For example, reference and qualification checks. If these checks suggest discrepancies, allow the applicant the opportunity to explain the inconsistencies.
- Take interview notes. Store them securely and shred after six months. Ensure the notes are relevant and justifiable for the process, e.g. make no assumptions based on age, appearance, etc. Candidates have the right to see these notes.
- Advise unsuccessful applicants if you intend to keep their details on file for future vacancies. Give them the opportunity to ask to have their details removed.
- Only transfer information from recruitment records to employment files where this information is relevant to ongoing employment.
- Remember that workers have the right to see their personal files.
- Keep personal data on staff securely.
- Include a privacy statement when seeking to capture personal data.

Employment records
- Ensure that new joiners are aware of any information kept about them, how it will be used, and to whom it will be disclosed.
- Only collect necessary information and destroy it when no longer required.
- Ask the individual to check the accuracy of information.
- Put systems in place to avoid accidental loss or unauthorized access.
- Place confidentiality clauses in contracts.
- For discrimination reasons, keep sickness and accident records separate from absence records. Only disclose information for legal reasons or if the individual has given consent.
- Make sure the information is secure when sending it. Use passwords where possible.
- Anonymize any information where practical, for example the author of an employment reference.
- Establish the identity of the person making the request for information. Only dis-

Figure 7.11 *Employment Code compliance checklist*

for compensation.

According to the Institute of Management's *Guidelines for Managers on the Human Rights Act 1998* (2001), an employer does not have the right to demand an employee's home telephone number, unless it is specified in the contract that the employee has a duty to be available outside normal working hours. Telephone calls made by a manager to an employee at home could be held to be an invasion of privacy under the Human Rights Act 1998. Even when an employee has indicated a willingness to be called at home, managers should respect privacy and not make unnecessary or inappropriate calls.

7.9.3   Employee monitoring

One of the most controversial parts of the Employment Code relates to monitoring at work of such things as e-mail, internet usage, telephone calls or CCTV footage. The DPA does not prevent monitoring. However, employers should ensure that the introduction of monitoring is a proportionate response to the problem that it seeks to address. Staff should also be made aware that such monitoring might occur. In making that decision, employers should be absolutely clear about the benefits that monitoring will bring; whether there will be an adverse impact upon workers; whether comparable benefits can be obtained with a lesser impact; and the techniques available for carrying out monitoring.

The monitoring of employees' electronic communications such as telephone calls, fax messages, e-mails and internet access is governed by the RIPA, the HRA and the Telecommunications (Lawful Business Practice) (Interception of Communications) Regulations 2000: SI 2000/2699.

While RIPA covers the *content* of communications, Part 11 of The Anti-Terrorism, Crime and Security Act 2001 covers the retention of *communications data*. Communications data is information about a communication, but does not include the contents of the communication. It includes:

* Traffic data: information such as a telephone number you call, when you made the call, where you were when you made the call and the location of the person you call.
* Service data: information about what telecommunications services you use, and when.
* Subscriber data: information about you that is held by your service provider, such as your name and address.

In April 2009, the government published a consultation called *Protecting the Public in a Changing Communications Environment* (Home Office, Cm 7586). It looked at the importance of communications data in helping to protect and safeguard the public. The Regulation of Investigatory Powers (Communications Data) Order 2010: SI 2010/480 deals with access to and use of communications data.

In December 2005, the EU passed a directive on data retention (2006/24/EC) which was implemented in the UK through the Data Retention (EC Directive) Regulations 2007 SI: 2007/2199 for fixed network and mobile telephony and the Data Retention (EC Directive) Regulations 2009: SI 2009/859 for data relating to internet access, internet telephony and internet e-mail. It imposes data retention obligations on the telecommunications service and network providers operating within the UK and requires all telephone and internet traffic data to be retained for 12 months by ISPs, telecommunications companies and mobile operators for use by police authorities. The purpose of the measure is the prevention, investigation and prosecution of criminal and terrorist activity.

The simple listening-in, in real time, on telephone calls without recording them, does not involve the processing of personal data and therefore falls outside the scope of the DPA. However, if an employer carries out monitoring involving an interception which results in the recording of personal data, then they will need to ensure that they comply with the DPA, and that they have also taken account of other relevant statute law such as the RIPA and the HRA.

Monitoring of employees should only be undertaken if there are specific business benefits, and when an impact assessment has concluded that the impact of monitoring on workers is justified by the likely benefits. In making that assessment employers should consult trade unions or other workers' representatives. Where employers undertake monitoring in order to ensure compliance with regulatory requirements or to ensure that the company's policies are not breached, it is important to make sure that the rules and standards are clearly set out and that workers are fully aware of them. Workers should be told what monitoring is taking place and the reasons for it, and they should be periodically reminded that monitoring is undertaken unless covert monitoring can be justified. There should be proper safeguards in place to ensure that information obtained through monitoring is kept securely. One aspect of this would be to strictly limit those who have access to the information, and to include in their contracts a confidentiality clause. Another point would be to take care if sensitive personal data (see Section 7.4) is collected, so that the requirements of Schedule 3 are complied with. It may be that where an organization undertakes monitoring, this results in the employer gleaning information which might be interesting, but not strictly relevant to the purpose for which the monitoring was originally put in place. If this happens, the employer must avoid using that information unless it is quite clearly in the employee's interest to do so or it reveals activity which no reasonable employer could be expected to ignore. Figure 7.12 contains guidance for employers on monitoring at work, taken from the Employment Practices Data Protection Code.

Whilst employees of a company might know that monitoring of phone conversations is routinely undertaken, that will not automatically be true of those making calls to or receiving calls from employees of the company. They should therefore be made aware that the telephone call might be monitored.

E-mail is subject to the DPA. The ability of employees to send messages around the world at the touch of a button has its own problems, such as attracting negative publicity, as was demonstrated in December 2000 by the case of Claire Swire. Swire became a household name after an e-mail reached thousands of people

- Covert monitoring should not normally be considered. It will be rare for covert monitoring of workers to be justified. It should therefore only be used in exceptional circumstances.
- Deploy covert monitoring only as part of a specific investigation and cease once the investigation has been completed.
- If embarking on covert monitoring with audio or video equipment, ensure that this is not used in places such as toilets or private offices.
- There may be exceptions to this in cases of suspicion of serious crime, but there should be an intention to involve the police.
- Check any arrangements for employing private investigators to ensure your contracts with them impose requirements on the investigator to collect and use information on workers in accordance with your instructions and to keep the information secure.
- In a covert monitoring exercise, limit the number of people involved in the investigation.
- Prior to the investigation, set up clear rules limiting the disclosure and access to information obtained.
- If information is revealed in the course of covert monitoring that is tangential to the original investigation, delete it from the records unless it concerns other criminal activity or equivalent malpractice.
- Where private use of a vehicle is allowed, monitoring its movements when used privately, without the freely given consent of the user, will rarely be justified.
- If the vehicle is for both private and business use, it ought to be possible to provide a 'privacy button' or similar arrangement to enable the monitoring to be disabled.
- Where an employer is under a legal obligation to monitor the use of vehicles, even if used privately, for example by fitting a tachograph to a lorry, then the legal obligation will take precedence.
- Make sure, either in the policy or separately, that details of the nature and extent of monitoring are set out.
- Check that workers using vehicles are aware of the policy.
- Where there is any doubt seek legal advice.

Source: Chapter 3 of The Employment Practices Code (Office of the Information Commissioner, 2005) on monitoring at work.

Figure 7.12 *Guidance on covert monitoring*

around the world in a matter of minutes (BBC News, 2000)). Other potential problems are that e-mail might increase an employer's liability to actions for defamation, racial or sexual harassment, and increase the chance of employees unintentionally creating contractual commitments for which their employers may be responsible. Figure 7.13 provides a checklist for the monitoring of electronic communications, while Figure 7.14 offers the employer a checklist for monitoring e-mail and internet access.

- If your organization does not have a policy on the use of electronic communications, decide whether you should establish one.
- Review any existing policy to ensure that it reflects data protection principles.
- Review any existing policies and actual practices to ensure that they are not out of line, e.g. whether private calls are banned in the policy but generally accepted in practice.
- Check that workers are aware of the policy and if not bring it to their attention.
- Interception occurs when, in the course of its transmission, the contents of a communication are made available to someone other than the sender or intended recipient. It does not include access to stored e-mails that have been opened.
- The intended recipient may be the business, but it could be a specified individual.
- Check whether any interception is allowed under the Lawful Business Practice Regulations (SI 2000/2699).
- Take any necessary action to bring such monitoring in line with RIPA and the Lawful Business Practice Regulations (SI 2000/2699).
- Automated systems can be used to provide protection from intrusion, malicious code such as viruses and Trojans, and to prevent password misuse. Such systems may be less intrusive than monitoring of communications to or from workers.
- If telephone calls or voicemails are monitored, or will be monitored in the future, consider carrying out an impact assessment.
- If voicemails need to be checked for business calls when workers are away, make sure they know this may happen and that it may be unavoidable that some personal messages are heard.
- In other cases, assess whether it is essential to monitor the content of calls and consider the use of itemized call records instead.
- Ensure that workers are aware of the nature and extent of telephone monitoring.
- Remember that expectations of privacy are likely to be significantly greater at home than in the workplace.
- If any workers using mobiles or home telephone lines, for which you pay, are currently subjected to monitoring, ensure that they are aware of the nature and the reasons for monitoring.
- If e-mails and/or internet access are presently monitored, or will be monitored in the future, consider carrying out an impact assessment.
- Check that workers are aware of the nature and extent of e-mail and internet access monitoring.
- Ensure that e-mail monitoring is confined to address/heading unless it is essential for a valid and defined reason to examine content.
- Encourage workers to mark any personal e-mails as such and encourage them to tell those who write to them to do the same.
- If workers are allowed to access personal e-mail accounts from the workplace, such e-mails should only be monitored in exceptional circumstances.
- It may be practicable – for example, when soliciting e-mail job applications – to provide information about the nature and extent of monitoring.
- In some cases, those sending e-mails to a workplace address will be aware that monitoring takes place without the need for specific information.
- If e-mail accounts need to be checked in the absence of workers, make sure they

Figure 7.13 *Monitoring electronic communications checklist*

know this will happen.
- Encourage the use of a marking system to help protect private or personal communications.
- Avoid, where possible, opening e-mails that clearly show they are private or personal communications.
- Check whether workers are currently aware of the retention period of e-mail and internet usage.
- If not already in place, set up a system (e.g. displaying information online or in a communication pack) that informs workers of retention periods.

Source: Chapter 3 of *The Employment Practices Code* (Office of the Information

Figure 7.13 *Continued*

- Use simple, clear disclaimers on e-mails and web pages where necessary.
- The policies on authorized access and acceptable use should be available at the log-in screen.
- Inform workers of the extent to which information about their internet access and e-mails is retained in the system and for what length of time.
- Do not retain data for any longer than you need to.
- Make sure that sensitive data is adequately secured.
- Take into account the possibility of unintentional access of websites by workers when you are reviewing the results of any monitoring.
- Train staff to exercise caution when using e-mail, just as much as with other written documents.
- Handle complaints in a fair, consistent and sensible manner, as they arise.
- Ensure that any precautions taken are proportionate to the level of risk.
- Where there is any doubt seek legal advice.

Source: Chapter 3 of *The Employment Practices Code* (Office of the Information Commissioner, 2005) on monitoring at work

Figure 7.14 *E-mail and internet access monitoring checklist*

7.10   The business case

Ensuring that your organization processes data in accordance with policies and procedures that meet the requirements of the DPA makes sound business sense. It is important that, in their dealings with users of their information services, information professionals build up a relationship of trust with them. Having a well-thought-out data protection policy and a privacy statement will go a long way to inspiring confidence in users.

Privacy is a strategic business issue that needs to be applied enterprise-wide. Many organizations recognize that they need to take privacy and data protection issues seriously, and that a failure to do so ultimately has the potential to harm their relationships with customers, business partners or employees. The consequences of not keeping data secure can manifest themselves in a number of different ways, such as security breaches, hacking, or credit card details getting into the wrong hands. These problems can be compounded where an individual is in the habit of using the same log-in ID and password for a wide variety of services, since a hacking incident affecting a large number of users of a highly popular website can result in the log-in credentials being tested against other websites to see just how many work on those as well. In December 2010, for example, BBC News Online reported that Yahoo!, Twitter and LinkedIn were asking users to change their details days after the gossip site Gawker had been hacked (BBC News, 2010).

Where companies fail to protect the personal data of customers, clients, employees or partners, the consequence might be that a fine is imposed. Whilst the ICO only issued fines relating to four of the 2,565 suspected data security breaches that had been reported to them between 6 April 2010 and 22 March 2011, it should be remembered that since April 2010 the ICO has had the power to issue civil penalties of up to £500,000 to organizations who are found to have breached the DPA in a serious way, where it is likely to cause substantial damage or distress (see Section 7.13). Where monetary penalties have been imposed this is often where unencrypted laptops containing large amounts of customer or client personal data have been lost.

Once news of an incident of poor management of personal data gets out, it can have a dramatic impact upon the organization's reputation, and it might even have a negative impact on the company's share price and result in a loss of clients.

In cases where the ICO issues an enforcement notice and this is then breached, the company risks potential criminal prosecution.

In 2008 the ICO commissioned a report on privacy by design (ICO, 2010) to help articulate the business case for investing in proactive privacy protection. The report's key conclusions were:

• Personal information has a value and protecting it makes good business sense.
• It brings real and significant benefits that far outweigh the effort privacy protection requires.
• Ignoring privacy and not protecting personal information has significant downsides.

In 2009, the BSI conducted a survey of senior decision-makers in small and medium businesses. The survey sought to reflect the way in which British businesses manage the personal information that they hold on both staff and customers (BSI, 2009). Findings from the survey include:

• 65% of businesses provide no data protection training for their staff.
• Nearly half of those surveyed admit that there is no one in their business with specific responsibility for data protection.

- 15% of businesses are not confident that their data sharing practices conform to the DPA and, worryingly, almost 5% of these frequently share data regardless.
- 18% of businesses said that data protection is less of a priority in the current economic climate.

7.11 Data protection compliance audits

A data protection compliance audit is a systematic and independent examination to determine whether activities involving the processing of personal data are carried out in accordance with an organization's data protection policies and procedures, and whether this processing meets the requirements of the DPA.

The key factors involved in data protection audits are that they should: involve a systematic approach; where possible, be carried out by independent auditors; be conducted in accordance with a documented audit procedure; have a documented audit report as an outcome.

There are a number of reasons why data protection audits should be carried out:

- To assess the level of compliance with the DPA.
- To assess the level of compliance with the organization's own data protection system.
- To identify potential gaps and weaknesses in the data protection system.
- To provide information for a data protection system review.

The audit is a mechanism for ensuring that personal data is obtained and processed fairly, lawfully and on a proper basis. When carrying out a data protection audit in any area of an organization there are three clear objectives:

- To verify that there is a formal documented and up-to-date data protection system in place in the area.
- To verify that all the staff in the area involved in data protection are aware of the existence of the data protection system, and that they understand and use that system.
- To verify that the data protection system in the area actually works and is effective.

Undertaking a data protection audit facilitates compliance with the DPA. The very fact that an audit is taking place serves to raise awareness of data protection issues amongst both management and staff, and can act as a training tool. Additionally, where weaknesses are identified and then addressed, this can lead to improved customer satisfaction because it proactively tackles areas that might otherwise have led to complaints.

The auditor needs to check that the data protection procedures in place comply with the data protection legislation in the context of other pieces of legislation such as the Human Rights Act; that they comply with the data subject's rights; that there are clear policies, codes of practice, guidelines and procedures in place; that where personal data is processed there are proper quality assurance safeguards to ensure that the information is accurate, complete, up to date, adequate, relevant and not excessive; and that there are formal retention policies in place to ensure that appropriate weeding and deletion of information occurs automatically.

➥ Useful resource

The ICO has produced a *Data Protection Audit Manual* (2001), a useful guide to data protection compliance auditing which contains a step-by-step guide with a series of forms, checklists and basic guidance to help ensure that even small organizations with limited auditing experience are able to undertake compliance audits.

7.12   Issues concerning websites and intranets

Anyone who hosts a website which processes personal data needs to ensure that users of that site are aware of:

- The identity of the person or organization responsible for operating the website.
- The purposes for which the data collected is processed.
- Any other information that is needed in order to ensure the fairness of the processing of the data, such as whether the site uses cookies.

An amendment to the Privacy and Electronic Communications Regulations which implements the e-Privacy directive 2009/136/EC came into force on 25 May 2011 and it requires websites which run in the UK to get consent in order to store or access information on consumers' computers. The ICO has issued advice on the new requirements entitled *Changes to the Rules on using Cookies and Similar Technologies for Storing Information* (2011). Essentially, the new requirement says that cookies can only be placed on machines where the user or subscriber has given their consent. The only exception to this is where what you are doing is 'strictly necessary' for a service requested by the user. This exception is intended to be interpreted very narrowly, where the service is 'explicitly requested' by the user. The ICO's guidance gives the example of where you use a cookie to ensure that when a user of your site has chosen the goods they wish to buy and clicks the 'add to basket' or 'proceed to checkout' button, your site 'remembers' what they chose on a previous page. You would not need to get consent for this type of activity (ICO, 2011).

The more privacy-intrusive your activity, the greater the priority that you should give to getting the explicit consent of the user. For example, building up a detailed profile of an individual's browsing activity is quite intrusive. The information gleaned from gathering the data could potentially be sensitive personal data (it could, for example, show what someone's political affiliations were, or their sexual orientation).

The DCMS issued some advice on the topic in the form of an open letter from Ed Vaizey (the Minister for Culture, Communications and Creative Industries), published on 24 May 2011, in which the government suggests that 'browser settings may give consumers a way to indicate their consent to cookies' (Vaizey, 2011). It led the Open Rights Group to comment that the UK has no intention of implementing any form of meaningful consent for tracking from advertising companies (Killock, 2011).

The requirement to process data fairly and lawfully can be achieved by developing a privacy policy statement (see Figure 7.15), which covers information about the data that you collect, the reasons for collecting it, and details of who it is passed on to. It is important that the statement provides the user with information that enables them to ensure that the processing of the data is fair.

- Your company's name and address, so that customers can contact you if they need to.
- The information that is gathered about a customer.
- What you will do with this information.
- If cookies are used to track a customer's movements, then this must be specifically drawn to their attention.
- Details of how the customer will be contacted.
- If your company is planning on sharing or disclosing personal information to any of its group companies or third parties, the customer must be informed of this.
- The customer must have the opportunity to object to being marketed to.
- Details of the rights of customers to access their personal data and rectify any inaccuracies.
- How long you intend to hold the data on your system.
- The choices available to customers about the processing of their personal information.
- How data security is managed.
- You must give the notice to your customers before they are asked to complete their

---

Figure 7.15 *What should be in a data protection/privacy statement?*

 It is well worth investing time in developing a privacy statement, because it will govern what you are able to do with the data that you collect.

Consumers are likely to have real concerns about giving out personal data through a website. They may be reluctant to engage in electronic transactions unless they can be reassured about the privacy of their personal data. Privacy policies are therefore a vital step towards encouraging openness and trust in electronic commerce among visitors to websites. Where an individual uses a website and looks up the data protection or privacy statement, they are then able to make an informed choice about whether or not to entrust their personal data to that organization, and whether or not they are willing to do business with that company.

❧ Useful resource

To assist in the process of putting together a data protection statement there is an Organization for Economic Co-operation and Development (OECD) privacy statement generator, which can be found at www.oecd.org/sti/privacygenerator.

The data protection statement should be placed in a prominent position on the organization's website and should recognize the fact that people can get to pages within a website by a number of different routes. Wherever personal data is being collected, the data subject should always have the option to click on a link to see the privacy statement or at least an outline of the basic messages and choices, even where a more detailed explanation is provided elsewhere by means of a privacy statement. As well as having a privacy statement on the organization's website, a data protection statement could also be placed onto the intranet or the library catalogue, depending on whether or not these are used to collect, process or hold personal data.

Websites and intranets might be used to collect or process personal data in a number of ways. For example, they might have a directory of employees, clients or business partners; or they might have a series of biographical information pages about members of staff, including photographs. Websites or intranets can also be used in order to collect data by means of online registration forms, requests for information or online research surveys. They might make use of invisible tracking devices such as cookies or web bugs. A key question that needs to be considered is whether or not any of the categories of data being collected fall within the definition of sensitive personal data (see Section 7.4), in which case there are stricter safeguards to be considered.

7.12.1 Privacy and Electronic Communications (EC Directive) Regulations

Directive 2002/58/EC, concerning the processing of personal data and the protection of privacy in the electronic communications sector, was implemented in the UK by The Privacy and Electronic Communications (EC Directive) Regulations: SI 2003/2426. These were subsequently amended by The Privacy and Electronic Communications (EC Directive) (Amendment) Regulations 2004: SI 2004/1039 and, as a result of directive 2009/136/EC, The Privacy and Electronic Communications (EC Directive) (Amendment) Regulations 2011: SI 2011/1208.

The Directive set an important precedent by adopting a harmonized opt-in approach to unsolicited commercial e-mail across the EU (see Figure 7.16).

- Citizens have the right to determine whether their phone numbers for mobile or fixed lines, their e-mail addresses and physical addresses figure in public directories.
- The use of privacy-sensitive location data indicating the exact whereabouts of mobile users is subject to explicit consent by the user. Moreover, users should have the possibility to temporarily block the processing of these location data such as 'cell of origin' data at any time.
- Invisible tracking devices, such as cookies that may collect information on users of the internet, can only be placed on machines where the user or subscriber has given their consent.
- Regulates the use of unsolicited commercial e-mail, and also covers SMS messages and other electronic messages received on any mobile or fixed terminal.

Figure 7.16 *Key features of the Privacy and Electronic Communications (EC Directive) Regulations*

7.12.2 Spam

Spamming is the practice of bulk-sending unsolicited commercial e-mails in order to market and promote products and services. The e-Commerce directive (2000/31/EC), which was implemented in the UK in August 2002 through The Electronic Commerce (EC Directive) Regulations 2002: SI 2002/2013, requires unsolicited commercial e-mail to be clearly identified as such in the title. This makes it easier for addressees to delete or filter out messages that they do not want to read. The Privacy and Electronic Communications (EC Directive) Regulations 2003 brought in further rules on the sending of spam, which require the prior consent of an individual before unsolicited commercial e-mail is sent unless there is an existing customer relationship. It also makes it unlawful to send junk mail anonymously or by using a false identity. In the UK this only applies to 'individual subscribers', by which the directive means a residential subscriber, a sole trader or an unincorporated partnership in England, Wales or Northern Ireland.

According to Symantec's *MessageLabs Intelligence: 2010 Annual Security Report* (2010), 89.1% of all e-mails sent are spam. So even if only a tiny percentage of people reply to spam messages, the potential for criminal scams, including the sale of counterfeit drugs, is enormous.

The European Commission undertook a study entitled *Unsolicited Commercial*

Communications and Data Protection (2001), which found that junk mail costs internet users 10 billion EUR a year, worldwide. This study identified a number of steps that can be taken to minimize junk mail:

1   Use the e-mail filters employed by your ISP (for example, to say that you only wish to receive e-mails from a list of people that you specify).
2   Contact one of the associations devoted to preventing junk e-mail such as CAUCE (www.cauce.org) or EuroCAUCE (www.euro.cauce.org/en).
3   Use e-mail checking software such as Mailwasher (www.mailwasher.net).

 If you have a problem with spam, it is good advice not to reply or request to unsubscribe unless you recognize the sender. Doing so only confirms that you are a real recipient. If you receive unsolicited e-mail and you can tell from the subject or sender that it is spam, you should delete it without opening it. In many cases, the senders track the opening of e-mails and use this to confirm that the recipient is real. They then send more.

7.13   Fines and prosecutions

Section 144 of The Criminal Justice and Immigration Act 2008 added section 55A to the DPA. It introduced new powers to impose fines of up to £500,000 for serious breaches of the DPA, which are likely to cause substantial damage or distress, and which are committed deliberately or recklessly. The new powers came into force on 6 April 2010 through The Data Protection (Monetary Penalties) (Maximum Penalty and Notices) Regulations 2010: SI 2010/31, and the first monetary penalties for serious breaches of data protection were served in November 2010 (see Section 10.1.1).

↦ Useful resource

The ICO has published statutory guidance about how it intends to use these powers: www.ico.gov.uk/upload/documents/library/data_protection/detailed_specialist_guides/ico_guidance_monetary_penalties.pdf.

In October 2009, the Ministry of Justice published a consultation paper: *The Knowing or Reckless Misuse of Personal Data: introducing custodial sentences*. It proposed the introduction of increased maximum penalties available to the courts for those guilty of offences under section 55 of the DPA. At the time of writing, custodial sentences for misuse of personal data had not been introduced. If the proposals were to be introduced it would mean that those convicted could be imprisoned for up to two years on indictment, and up to 12 months on summary conviction. This would be in addition to the fines already available to the courts.

In October 2011 the Justice Committee published a report on referral fees and the theft of personal data (House of Commons Justice Committee, 2011). Sir Alan Beith, chair of the Justice Committee said: 'Magistrates and judges need to be able to hand out custodial sentences when serious misuses of personal information come to light. Parliament has provided that power, but Ministers have not yet brought it into force. They must do so'.

In an ICO press release dated 23 April 2008 (ICO, 2008), it is mentioned that some 50% of the data security breaches notified to the Information Commissioner were breaches by financial institutions. Well before the Information Commissioner was given the power to fine companies up to £500,000 for serious breaches of the DPA, the Financial Services Authority (FSA) was exercising its powers to hold financial institutions to account for failing to properly look after personal data relating to their customers. Examples of enforcement action include:

- The FSA fined Norwich Union Life £1.26 million for exposing its customers to the risk of fraud.
- Merchant Securities Group Limited were fined £77,000 for poor data security. This did in fact represent a discount of 30%, which they qualified for by agreeing to settle at an early stage. Otherwise the penalty would have been £110,000.
- In July 2009, three companies within the HSBC banking group were fined a combined total of over £3 million by the FSA (UK) for customer data protection lapses (HSBC Life: £1,610,000; HSBC Actuaries: £875,000; HSBC Insurance Brokers: £700,000). Because of agreeing to pay promptly, HSBC were given a substantial discount; otherwise the combined total would have been around £4.5 million. The fines followed an investigation by the FSA, which revealed that HSBC's customer data was sent without encryption to third parties and via couriers, and left in unlocked cabinets and on open shelves.

7.14 The implications for librarians

Library and information services are likely to process personal data as part of their day-to-day operations. Examples might include:

- user registration records containing user names and addresses
- circulation records
- contact databases containing names, job titles, e-mail addresses and direct phone numbers
- staff records
- payroll and pension records
- management statistics on usage of the information service.

CILIP's *Ethical Principles and Code of Professional Practice for Library and Information Professionals* (2009) in no way affects legal obligations under the DPA, but it does supplement them with professional principles, which apply to user information. The CILIP guidelines state that information professionals are required to 'protect the confidentiality of all matters relating to information users, including their enquiries, any services to be provided, and any aspects of the users' personal circumstances or business'; and it also says that the conduct of members should be characterized by 'respect for confidentiality and privacy in dealing with information users'. See Figure 7.17 for police and security powers to scrutinize library records.

In 2005, CILIP obtained legal advice on rights of access to confidential information on library users following a number of instances where police had sought information from CILIP members on library users' activities.

The advice, which was provided by public law and human rights specialist James Eadie of Blackstone Chambers, on instructions from Bates Wells Solicitors, confirms that:

- All library sectors can be investigated.
- Police and security services investigating serious crime or terrorism in England and Wales have the right to seek information on books borrowed or internet sites accessed by certain library users.
- Police and security services can also mount surveillance operations in libraries if they believe that national security is at risk, to prevent or detect crime, or in the interests of public safety.

Although the position is not clear-cut, the powers are probably broad enough to permit the agencies concerned to insist on the installation of spyware in an appropriate case, the advice says.

According to the legal advice obtained by CILIP, the police could apply for an order authorizing access to library records under the Police and Criminal Evidence Act 1984, where an indictable offence has been committed, or under the Terrorism Act 2000, where they believed that the material was likely to be of substantial value to a terrorist investigation. Surveillance operations in libraries are also possible under the Regulation of Investigatory Powers Act 2000. This could include monitoring persons' activities or communications, recording anything monitored with a surveillance device, and engaging in covert surveillance to obtain private information about a person. Finally, under the Intelligence Services Act 1994, the Secretary of State can issue a warrant authorizing the security services to take action to protect national security against threats such as terrorism or to support the police.

The CILIP Ethical Principles (2009) make clear that librarians and information professionals have a duty of client confidentiality. So, they cannot collude with 'fishing expeditions' by the authorities. Nevertheless, they obviously have to respect the law of the land.

Figure 7.17 *Police and security services powers to scrutinize library records*

⤏ Useful resource

In 2009, CILIP issued a set of guidelines entitled *User Privacy in Libraries – guidelines for the reflective practitioner* (www.cilip.org.uk/get-involved/ advocacy/information-society/privacy/pages/privacy-guidelines.aspx), which were produced in order to support CILIP members in adhering to the Ethical Principles and Code of Professional Practice with regard to user privacy, and these were revised in May 2011.

7.14.1 E-books – privacy concerns

In 2010, the Electronic Frontier Foundation put together an *E-Book Buyer's Guide to E-Book Privacy*. It is a helpful side-by-side comparison of the privacy policies of device manufacturers and e-book distributors. It covers policies regarding searches, purchases, tracking of what you've read and annotated, and sharing of information externally, for Google Books, Amazon Kindle, iPad, Sony Reader, B&N Nook, and Adobe Content server. It looks at the following aspects of a user's privacy with regard to each of these e-book providers:

- Can they monitor what you're reading?
- Can they keep track of book searches?
- Can they keep track of book purchases?
- With whom can they share the information collected?
- Do customers have any control over the information?
- Can customers access, correct, or delete the information?

7.14.2 Electoral roll information in libraries

The Representation of the People Act 2000, along with The Representation of the People (England and Wales) (Amendment) Regulations 2002: SI 2002/1871, established a framework whereby there are two versions of the electoral register. The full register, containing everyone's details, which is available only for electoral and a limited range of other purposes, and the edited register, which continues to be available for sale for any purpose but which does not include the details of those who have chosen to 'opt out'.

In R. v. City of Wakefield Metropolitan Council & another ex parte Robertson (16 November 2001), an elector brought a case to court against his local electoral registration officer (ERO) in Wakefield. Mr Robertson was concerned that if he registered to vote he would have no right to object to the sale of his details for marketing purposes. In finding in Mr Robertson's favour the court ruled that the use of the electoral register for commercial purposes without an individual right of objection was in breach of the DPA.

Following the Robertson case, public librarians wanted clarification about how this would affect the making available of the registers in public libraries for inspection and consultation. The judge did say that EROs must consider and anticipate the purposes for which personal data are intended to be processed. If commercial data collection companies are allowed to access and copy the data in public libraries for free, then EROs are likely to be forced to clamp down on this as well.

 Staffordshire Libraries and Information Services have produced a poster entitled 'Electoral Registers Clarification', which can be accessed via the LACA website at www.cilip.org.uk/get-involved/advocacy/copyright/advice/Pages/er2.aspx.

In his 2002 annual report, the Information Commissioner expressed concerns over other public registers such as the Register of Members ('Shareholders Register'), the Register of Directors and Secretaries, the Register of County Court Judgments and the Register of Medical Practitioners. Those who own shares, take on company directorships, get into debt or practise certain professions similarly have no choice but to have their details made available for marketing and other commercial purposes. Another potential danger is that the registers can also provide the basis for those wishing to establish false identities.

Having directors' home addresses on the public record at Companies House is a key part of making sure business activity remains transparent and accountable. But when threats were made against the directors of the Cambridgeshire-based Huntingdon Life Sciences biotechnology firm by animal rights protesters, who had tracked down the directors using the information lodged at Companies House, the government decided that action needed to be taken to prevent such cases of intimidation. This is governed by the Companies (Disclosure of Address) Regulations 2009: SI 2009/214, which specifies the conditions for the disclosure of directors' usual residential addresses to public authorities and credit reference agencies under section 243 of the Companies Act 2006.

7.14.3 Radio Frequency Identification

RFID or Radio Frequency Identification refers to tiny devices that can be fitted to any goods. They comprise a microchip and an antenna, which are capable of transmitting messages to 'readers'. The readers use the message in accordance with their programmers' instructions.

Libraries use RFID for a number of reasons:

- annual stocktaking
- rapid checking that books are shelved in the correct area

- searching for specific items using a scanner
- self check-out of items
- self-return of items
- security
- library membership cards.

RFID can be employed as an electronic article surveillance system. A tag is applied to the items that are being monitored, and a detection corridor is set up at the exit to the library. If someone attempts to remove an item from the library illicitly, an alarm is triggered and a member of the library staff can check out why the alarm went off. With RFID technology in place, it is also possible to undertake a stock check extremely quickly.

However, the use of RFID tags in libraries and elsewhere has raised fears over civil liberties. The main concern is that if an item can be monitored then so can the movements of the person carrying the item, as well as their reading habits. Privacy campaigners are concerned that tags could be used for more sinister purposes, such as monitoring the whereabouts of customers and building profiles of customers' shopping preferences (or indeed their reading tastes), without their knowledge.

Taking into account the requirements of the UK's data protection laws, RFID technology should not be misused in order to collect information on library users' reading habits and other activities without their consent or knowledge. Adequate and proper security measures should be in place in order to avoid the information being read by an unauthorized third party; and it is essential to ensure compliance both with data protection law as well as industry best practice.

The Article 29 Working Party (the main body advising EU governments on data protection) has warned that RFID tags could 'violate human dignity'. The committee says that RFID systems are 'very susceptible to attacks', and that it would be possible for people owning a radar to detect passports, banknotes, books, medicines or personal belongings of people in a crowd should those objects have microchips. Under most scenarios, the committee says that consent from individuals will be the only legal ground available to data controllers justifying the use of RFID technology (EC, 2011).

The EC has published guidelines that companies can follow if they want to assess the privacy implications of their use of RFID chips (ebizlaw, 2011).

7.14.3.1 Further information on RFID

Privacy Rights Clearinghouse (2011) *RFID Implementation in Libraries: some recommendations for best practices*,
    www.privacyrights.org/ar/RFID-ALA.htm.
European Commission (2011) *Privacy and Data Protection Impact Assessment*

Framework for RFID Applications,
http://ec.europa.eu/information_society/policy/rfid/documents/
infso-2011-00068.pdf.
ebizlaw (2011) Commission Guidelines on the Use of RFID tags, 12 April,
www.ebizlaw.co.uk/legal-guidance/display.aspx?M=News&NewsID=218.

7.15   British Standard on data protection

In May 2009, the British Standards Institution published the first-ever standard to
focus on the management of personal information. BS 10012 enables
organizations, from both the public and private sectors in the UK, to put in place
an infrastructure for maintaining and improving compliance with the DPA.

BS 10012 is not a prescriptive Standard but rather it adopts a 'framework'
approach within which organizations can more effectively manage personal information. Organizations can create bespoke management systems, which include
processes to address risk assessment, training and awareness as well as key data protection issues such as the sharing, retention, disposal and disclosure of information.

Organizations are encouraged to ensure sufficient guidance and resources are
allocated to data protection and that a positive culture exists in which data
protection can occur. The Standard follows the classic 'Plan-Do-Check-Act'
model of continuous improvement as utilized by standards such as ISO 27001 and
BS 25999.

7.16   Further information

British Standards Institution
389 Chiswick High Road, London W4 4AL
Tel.: 020 8996 9000
Website: www.bsigroup.com.

Ministry of Justice
102 Petty France, London, SW1H 9AJ
Tel.: 020 3334 3555
Website: www.justice.gov.uk.

Europa – Justice and Home Affairs – Data Protection
Website: http://ec.europa.eu/justice/policies/privacy/index_en.htm.

JISC Legal Information Service
The JISC Legal Information Service, Learning Services, University of
Strathclyde, Alexander Turnbull Building, 155 George Street, Glasgow
G1 1RD
Tel.: 0141 548 4939

Fax: 0141 548 4216

E-mail: info@jisclegal.ac.uk

Website: www.jisclegal.ac.uk.

OECD privacy statement generator

Website: www.oecd.org/sti/privacygenerator.

Information Commissioner's Office

Wycliffe House, Water Lane, Wilmslow, Cheshire SK9 5AF

Tel.: 0303 123 1113

Fax: 01625 524 510

Website: www.ico.gov.uk.

References

BBC News (2000) Email Woman in Hiding, 16 December, http://news.bbc.co.uk/1/hi/uk/1072391.stm.

BBC News (2010) Gawker Hack Triggers Password Resets at Major Sites, 15 December, www.bbc.co.uk/news/technology-11998648.

BSI (2009) *Data Dilemma: one in five businesses admit breaching the Data Protection Act*, www.bsigroup.com/About-BSI/News-Room/BSI-News-Content/Disciplines/Information-Management/BS-10012-publication.

CILIP (2009) *Ethical Principles and Code of Professional Practice for Library and Information Professionals*, www.cilip.org.uk/get-involved/policy/ethics/pages/principles.aspx.

Consumers International (2001) *Privacy@net: international comparative study of consumer privacy on the internet*, www.consumersinternational.org/news-and-media/publications/privacy@net-an-international-comparative-study-of-consumer-privacy-on-the-internet.

ebizlaw (2011) Commission Guidelines on the Use of RFID Tags, April, www.ebizlaw.co.uk/legal-guidance/display.aspx?M=News&NewsID=218.

EC (2001) *Unsolicited Commercial Communications and Data Protection*, http://ec.europa.eu/justice/policies/privacy/docs/studies/spamsum_en.pdf.

EC (2011) *Art.29 Data Protection Working Party*, http://ec.europa.eu/justice/policies/privacy/workinggroup/index_en.htm.

Experian (no date) *A Simplified Guide to the Data Protection Act 1998*, www.uk.experian.com/e-consumerview/samples/databk.pdf.

House of Commons Justice Committee (2011) *Referral Fees and the Theft of Personal Data: evidence from the Information Commissioner*, HC1473.

ICO (2001) *Data Protection Audit Manual*, www.privacylaws.com/.../data_protection_complete_audit_guide.pdf.

ICO (2008) *Roll Call of Data Breaches Grows*,
www.ico.gov.uk/upload/documents/.../2008/data_security_220408_2.pdf.

ICO (2010) *The Privacy Dividend: the business case for investing in proactive privacy
protection*, www.ico.gov.uk/news/current_topics/privacy_dividend.aspx.

ICO (2011) *Changes to the Rules on using Cookies and Similar Technologies for Storing
Information*,
www.ico.gov.uk/~/media/documents/library/Privacy_and_electronic/Practical
_application/advice_on_the_new_cookies_regulations.pdf.

Institute of Management (2001) *Guidelines for Managers on the Human Rights Act
1998*.

Killock, J. (2011) Ed Vaizey says cookie directive is in effect meaningless, Open
Rights Group, May 25,
www.openrightsgroup.org/blog/2011/ed-vaizey-says-cookie-directive-is-
meaningless.

Ministry of Justice (2009) *The Knowing or Reckless Misuse of Personal Data:
introducing custodial sentences*,
www.justice.gov.uk/consultations/docs/data-misuse-increased-penalties.pdf.

Office of the Information Commissioner (2005) *The Employment Practices Code*,
www.ico.gov.uk/upload/documents/library/data_protection/practical_applicati
on/coi_html/english/employment_practices_code/part_3-
monitoring_at_work_1.htm.

Symantec (2010) *MessageLabs Intelligence: 2010 Annual Security Report*,
www.symantec.com/about/news/release/article.jsp?prid=20101207_01.

Vaizey, E. (2011) Open letter on the UK implementation of article 5(3) of the
e-privacy directive on cookies, DCMS, 24 May.

CHAPTER 8

Privacy

Contents

8.1   General principles

There has never been an absolute 'right to privacy' in English or Scots law. The coming into force of the HRA in October 2000 marked the implementation of the ECHR in the UK. The ECHR states that 'everyone has the right to respect for his private and family life, his home and his correspondence'. A number of the rights enshrined in the ECHR conflict with one another, and there will always be a tension between them. In particular, the right to privacy (Article 8) and the right to freedom of expression (Article 10) often conflict (see Figure 8.1). In every situation, a balance needs to be struck between those two rights; and courts need to consider the issues on a case-by-case basis.

Since the HRA came into force, the courts have had to interpret existing law in ways that secure these rights. The existing law, however, remains piecemeal, and privacy complaints can be found in actions for breach of confidence, harassment, trespass, malicious falsehood and data protection legislation or pursued under regulatory codes of practice (see Section 8.6).

8.2   Obligation of confidence v. breach of privacy

An obligation of confidence, by definition, arises firstly from the circumstances in which the information is given. By contrast, a right of privacy in respect of information would arise from the nature of the information itself; it would be based on the principle that certain kinds of information are categorized as private

---

Article 8 – Right to respect for private and family life

1   Everyone has the right to respect for his private and family life, his home and his correspondence.

2   There shall be no interference by a public authority with the exercise of this right except such as is in accordance with the law and is necessary in a democratic society in the interests of national security, public safety or the economic well being of the country, for the prevention of disorder or crime, for the protection of health or morals, or for the protection of the rights and freedoms of others.

Article 10 – Freedom of expression

1   Everyone has the right to freedom of expression. This right shall include freedom to hold opinions and to receive and impart information and ideas without interference by public authority and regardless of frontiers. This article shall not prevent States from requiring the licensing of broadcasting, television or cinema enterprises.

2   The exercise of these freedoms, since it carries with it duties and responsibilities, may be subject to such formalities, conditions, restrictions or penalties as are pre-scribed by law and are necessary in a democratic society, in the interests of national security, territorial integrity or public safety, for the prevention of disorder or crime, for the protection of health or morals, for the protection of the reputation or rights of others, for preventing the disclosure of information received in confidence, or for

---

Figure 8.1 *Articles 8 and 10 of the European Convention on Human Rights*

and for that reason alone ought not to be disclosed. In many cases where privacy is infringed, this is not the result of a breach of confidence.

8.3   Codes of practice

There are a number of codes of practice governing the media, and, in any cases relating to privacy or breach of confidence, the courts have regard to any relevant privacy code. These codes include:

- For newspaper and magazine publishing in the UK: The Editors' Code of Practice (2011), www.pcc.org.uk/cop/practice.html (known more commonly as the Press Complaints Commission code).
- BBC editorial guidelines (2010): www.bbc.co.uk/guidelines/editorialguidelines.
- The Ofcom Broadcasting Code (2010): http://stakeholders.ofcom.org.uk/broadcasting/broadcast-codes/broadcast-code. Ofcom has a duty to apply adequate protection for audiences against unfairness or the infringement of privacy. The Broadcasting Code came into force on 20 December 2010. It covers matters relating to taste, decency, fairness and privacy.

In considering whether to grant an injunction (interdict in Scotland), courts would have regard to the standards the press has itself set in voluntary codes of practice. Under The Editors' Code of Practice (as above) a publication would be expected to justify intrusions into any individual's private life, which had been made without consent.

In September 2010, the 12th edition of The UK Code of Non-Broadcast Advertising, Sales Promotion and Direct Marketing (the Committee of Advertising Practice or CAP Code) was published. The code applies to non-broadcast marketing communications in the UK and is endorsed and administered independently by the Advertising Standards Authority (ASA).

The CAP Code takes account of the UK's Consumer Protection (Distance Selling) Regulations 2000: SI 2000/2334 and the EU's Privacy and Electronic Communications Directive (directive 2002/58/EC as amended by directive 2009/136/EC). As far as the obligation of confidence is concerned, the code states that 'the ASA and CAP will on request treat in confidence any genuinely private or secret material supplied unless the courts or officials acting within their statutory powers compel its disclosure'.

In September 2010, the first edition of the UK Code of Broadcast Advertising (the BCAP Code) was launched. It replaces the four previous separate BCAP Codes. The Code applies to all advertisements (including teleshopping, content on self-promotional television channels, television text, and interactive television advertisements) and programme sponsorship credits on radio and television services licensed by Ofcom.

8.4   Injunctions

When an individual seeks to prevent publication of material about themself, they sometimes go to court to seek an injunction to prevent the information being published. An injunction is a court order requiring a party to do or to refrain from doing certain acts. However, the use of an injunction to prevent publication is a legal remedy which only works if the individual about whom the problematic information relates is aware in advance that someone is intending to publish that information so that they have adequate time to seek a court order to prevent publication from going ahead.

If, for example, a tabloid newspaper kept secret its intention to publish the details of a sex scandal involving a premiership footballer, and then goes ahead and publishes the material, the footballer would have to decide whether it was worth initiating a full privacy trial, given the huge legal costs that would be involved. Getting a super-injunction could cost between £50,000 and £100,000. It begs the question as to where this leaves the protection of the privacy of those who aren't as wealthy as premiership footballers, film stars or other high-profile celebrities.

Max Mosley took a case to the European Court of Human Rights (Mosley v.

United Kingdom [2011] ECHR 774) in which he argued that the privacy of individuals cannot be fully assured without the introduction of a new law on prior notification in which newspapers would be required to notify subjects before publishing details about their private lives.

Whilst the judges at the European Court of Human Rights ruled that the publication of the story about Mr Mosley by the *News of the World* did result in a flagrant and unjustified invasion of his private life, they also ruled that the media were not required to give prior notice of publication.

There has been a recent trend by the rich and famous to use superinjunctions to gag the press. The term 'superinjunction' is used to refer to a gagging order by which the press are prevented from reporting even the very existence of the injunction, let alone any details of the nature of the case in question, such as the name of the person or the company seeking the injunction.

In 2009, *The Guardian* was prohibited from reporting the contents of an internal report by the oil trader Trafigura into the 2006 Ivory Coast toxic waste dump scandal. In the same year, Barclays Bank obtained a court order banning *The Guardian* from publishing a number of leaked memos, which showed how the bank had avoided paying hundreds of millions of pounds in tax (The Guardian, 2009).

In April 2011, Andrew Marr let it be known that back in 2008 he had taken out a superinjunction in order to suppress reports of an affair that he had had with a fellow journalist. He had done so in order to protect his family's privacy, but as a journalist himself, Mr Marr said that he now felt embarrassed and uneasy about the use of the super-injunction, telling the *Daily Mail*, 'I did not come into journalism to go around gagging journalists.' (*The Scotsman*, 2011).

In April 2011, Mr Justice Eady issued a *contra mundum* order in the case of a man who was determined to ban the publication of material about his private life. A *contra mundum* order is, in effect, a perpetual worldwide ban on the reporting of information. Such a sweeping privacy injunction sets a worrying precedent as this type of order is normally reserved for situations where evidence before the court shows that a failure to make such an order would be life-threatening.

In a legal case in May 2011, High Court judge Mr Justice Baker specifically banned publishing information on any 'social network or media including Twitter or Facebook' as well as in other media, thus making it more likely that in future injunctions and super-injunctions these outlets would be explicitly named (BBC News Online, 2011).

The use of super-injunctions has been the cause of disquiet from a number of quarters. In April 2011, David Cameron said that he was uneasy about the way in which judges, rather than Parliament, were creating a new law of privacy. Meanwhile, Liberal Democrat MP John Hemming has tried to force an inquiry into the use of super-injunctions. In an article in *The Guardian* (2011), Mr Hemming expresses concern regarding three types of injunctions:

1 Super-injunctions are those whose existence is secret. Without an article 6 compliant judgment these are unlawful (article 6 of the ECHR is the right to a fair trial).
2 Hyper-injunctions are those whereby there is an attempt to prevent people talking to MPs.
3 Quaero-injunctions are those where investigation is prevented, stopping people from seeking information about a case.

In 2010, a committee of judges was set up, headed by the Master of the Rolls, Lord Neuberger, to inquire into the use of super-injunctions. Its findings (Master of the Rolls, 2011) provide guidance to lawyers and journalists of the steps to be followed before a super-injunction or an anonymized injunction is applied for. The report says that judges who are asked to grant injunctions should make sure that the media know about the application in advance, and as a result gives the media a greater opportunity to contest orders before they happen.

8.5   Privacy and libraries

The professions are subject to obligations of confidentiality. The CILIP *Ethical Principles* (2009) addresses the question of confidentiality from several different perspectives:

1 One of the general principles states that the conduct of information professionals should be characterized by respect for confidentiality and privacy in dealing with information users.
2 One of the specific responsibilities to information users says that information professionals should protect the confidentiality of all matters relating to information users, including their enquiries, any services to be provided, and any aspects of the users' personal circumstances or business.
3 In the list of responsibilities to society it says that information professionals should strive to achieve an appropriate balance within the law between demands from information users, the need to respect confidentiality, the terms of their employment, the public good and the responsibilities outlined in the Code.

Section A.3 of the EIRENE *Code of Practice for Information Brokers* (1993) says that a broker shall:

• Hold the affairs of the client in the strictest confidence, except where the law requires disclosure.
• Declare any conflicts of interest if they are likely to undermine confidentiality.
• Undertake not to reuse or misuse information gained as part of the client contract for personal or professional gain.

CILIP's *User Privacy in Libraries* guidelines (2011) include a useful set of web links to relevant legislation, guidance and good practice covering topics such as data sharing, personal data security, children and privacy, closed-circuit television (CCTV) in libraries, use of the internet, photography and filming in libraries, and how to handle requests for data. There is also a section on the use of the internet in prison libraries, and the paramount importance of prison security.

8.6   Case law

MGN Limited v. the United Kingdom application no. 39401/04

In 2001, the *Daily Mirror* carried an article entitled: 'Naomi: I am a drug addict.' The article reported that:
- Naomi Campbell had a drug addiction
- she was receiving treatment
- part of the treatment involved attending Narcotics Anonymous meetings
- details of the treatment, including frequency of attendance at meetings and information of that kind.

The article was accompanied by a photograph, taken surreptitiously with a long lens, of her leaving a Narcotics Anonymous meeting in London. Prior to the publication of the article, Naomi Campbell had always maintained that she did not take drugs and had made public statements to that effect.

Naomi Campbell sued the *Daily Mirror* and claimed damages for breach of confidence and for misuse of personal data under the Data Protection Act 1998 in respect of articles and photographs which showed that she was attending meetings of Narcotics Anonymous. The case was about confidentiality, privacy, the Human Rights Act and data protection. She won in the High Court and was awarded damages of £3,500 (the damages being so low in part because the judge took the view that Naomi Campbell had not been entirely frank and truthful).

The *Daily Mirror* appealed to the Court of Appeal, which overturned the judgment of the High Court and found in the newspaper's favour. In this case, the Court of Appeal applied the practical test for what information or conduct is to be considered private and confidential – the common law test of offensiveness – whether disclosure or observation of the information would be highly offensive to a reasonable person of ordinary sensibilities.

When the case reached the House of Lords, Lord Carswell said it was not necessary in this case to ask whether disclosure of the information would be highly offensive to a reasonable person of ordinary sensibilities because it was sufficiently established by the nature of the material that it was private information which attracted the duty of observing the confidence in which it was imparted to the respondents. Publication of the details about Naomi Campbell's attendance at therapy carried out by Narcotics Anonymous, highlighted by the photographs printed, constituted in the judgment of Lord Carswell a considerable intrusion into her private affairs, which was capable of causing substantial distress, and on her evidence did cause it to her. It is difficult to assess how much, if any, actual harm it may have done to her progress in therapy. In her evidence she said that she had not gone back to the World's End centre of Narcotics Anonymous since the article was published and that she had only attended about four meetings in other centres in England, though she had gone to meetings abroad and met privately at her home with other Narcotics Anonymous attendees. Lord Carswell concluded that the publication of the article did create a risk of causing a significant setback to her recovery.

Outcome: By a three-to-two majority, the House of Lords upheld Naomi Campbell's appeal in her claim against the *Daily Mirror* (Naomi Campbell v. Mirror Group Newspapers [2004] UKHL 22). The Lords' decision reinstated the damages awarded in the High Court decision, and reversed the Court of Appeal's award of expenses in favour of the *Daily Mirror* against Campbell. It was decided that the publication of detailed information about the treatment she was undergoing for drug addiction was a breach of her right to keep her personal information private.

The House of Lords observed that photographs of people in circumstances in which the person has a reasonable expectation of privacy can be particularly intrusive. Unless there is a compelling public interest justification for publication of such photographs, there is likely to be an invasion of privacy. The House of Lords roundly endorsed the part of the Press Complaints Commission guidelines that states that long-lens surreptitious photography is not acceptable.

The case subsequently went to the European Court of Human Rights (MGN Limited v. the United Kingdom application no. 39401/04) who ruled in January 2011 that the *Daily Mirror*'s freedom of expression was violated by the £1 million legal costs it had to pay when it lost the case.

(Ms Campbell's solicitors had served three bills of costs on the applicant in the total sum of pounds sterling, £1,086,295.47: £377,070.07 for the High Court; £114,755.40 for the Court of Appeal; and £594,470.00 for the House of Lords. The latter figure comprised 'base costs' of £288,468, success fees of £279,981.35 as well as £26,020.65 disbursements.)

Naomi Campbell had taken out her case on a no-win, no-fee basis, and a big part of the legal costs which Mirror Group Newspapers were required to pay were the 'success fees', which are paid out in 'no-win, no-fee' civil cases as well as damages. The ECHR judges considered it to be an 'excessive' obligation on the *Daily Mirror* to pay the 'success fees', concluding that 'the requirement on Mirror Group Newspapers to pay the 'success fees', which had been agreed by Ms Campbell and her solicitors, was disproportionate to the aim sought to be achieved by the introduction of the success fee system' and that as such there had been a violation of Article 10 of the Convention (the right to freedom of expression). But the Court did find that the UK courts had correctly backed Ms Campbell's claim for her breach of right to respect for her private life.

The footballers case A v. B & another [2002] EWCA Civ 337

The claimant was a Premier League footballer who was granted an interim injunction restraining the first defendant B from publishing stories about his extra-marital affairs with two women C and D.

The court considered the balance between Article 8 of the ECHR on the right to respect for private life and Article 10 on the right to freedom of expression. The Court of Appeal said that the judge had been wrong to reject any element of public interest in the publication of the proposed stories.

The Lord Chief Justice, Lord Woolf, said that the more stable the relationship, the greater would be the significance attached to it by the court. But the court should not protect brief affairs of the sort the footballer enjoyed with the two women, when the women wanted to talk about them. Banning the two women from telling their stories for publication was an interference with their freedom of

Theakston v. MGN Ltd [2002] EWHC 137

Television presenter Jamie Theakston sought an injunction to prevent publication of photographs and an article relating to his visit to a brothel. He relied on the grounds of breach of confidentiality and breach of his right to privacy as reflected in the Press Complaints Commission Code, and as contained in Article 8 of the ECHR. Mr Theakston claimed that he had been in a private place with friends, that the events were private and confidential and that he had never discussed the details of his private life or sex life in public.

The judge stated that he did not consider the brothel to be a private place. Mr Theakston had courted publicity regarding his private life, which led to his enhanced fame and popularity.

Mr Theakston was successful in obtaining an injunction preventing publication of the photographs, but was unsuccessful in preventing publication of the article.

Douglas and others v. Hello! Ltd [2005] EWCA Civ 595 (18 May 2005)

Background: Catherine Zeta Jones and Michael Douglas had signed an exclusive deal with magazine *Hello!*'s rival *OK!* to publish photographs of their wedding. The couple applied to the Court of Appeal for an injunction to prevent publication by *Hello!*, but this was rejected. *Hello!* magazine went ahead and published photographs of the wedding. Jones and Douglas sought damages for both breach of confidence and breach of privacy.

Outcome: The court held that the publication of wedding photographs of Michael Douglas and Catherine Zeta Jones was a breach of commercial confidence in circumstances where photography was explicitly prohibited after their wedding. The celebrity couple succeeded in their claims for both breach of confidence and breach of privacy and the appeals against them were dismissed.

Key points from the case:

1 As a general rule (although it is not always the case), once information is in the public domain, it will no longer be protected by the law of confidence; and this also applies to private information of a personal nature. Once intimate information about a celebrity's private life has been widely published, it is not likely to serve any useful purpose to prevent further publication. It is important to distinguish between textual articles and photographs; because this is not necessarily true with respect to photographs. A photograph enables the viewer to focus on intimate personal detail and, as such, there may be a fresh invasion of privacy every time the photograph is viewed. This is true even if precisely the same photograph has been published before; and it is also true even if it is the same person or people who have seen the picture before.

2 In addition to their right to keep private information about their wedding private, Michael Douglas and Catherine Zeta Jones also had a right to protect their opportunity to profit from confidential information about themselves. This is similar to the right of a company to protect its potential to profit from information amounting to a trade secret.

3 With regard to the right to privacy, photographs are in a different category to verbal information and special considerations apply to them. In short, the courts will apply stricter standards to photographs than to their verbal equivalent. This is because a photograph is a particularly intrusive means of invading privacy. A camera could potentially be used to gain access to scenes, which those being photographed could reasonably expect would not be brought to the notice of the public.

4 The right to privacy is something that can only be enforced by the person to whom the private information relates. It isn't akin to a property right which can be assigned to someone else.

The case subsequently went to the House of Lords where a three-to-two majority found in favour of *OK!*. They found that publication of the unauthorized photographs by *Hello!* breached *OK!*'s right of confidentiality in the authorized pictures and simultaneous publication by *OK!* of the authorized photographs had

Mosley v. The United Kingdom – 48009/08 [2011] ECHR 774 (10 May 2011)

Max Mosley was the president of the motorsports organization, Fédération Internationale de l'Automobile (FIA), which is also the governing body for Formula One. In 2008, during his tenure of the FIA, the *News of the World* published a story and posted a video on its website about him paying five women to take part in a sado-masochistic orgy, suggesting also that there were Nazi overtones to the orgy. (Mosley is the son of Oswald Mosley, the leader of the British fascists in the 1930s and 1940s.)

The edited video footage was viewed over 1.4 million times over 30 and 31 March 2008. The online version of the article was visited over 400,000 times during the same period. The print version of the *News of the World* had an average circulation of over three million copies, before its demise in July 2011, following the phone-hacking scandals.

Max Mosley won his High Court battle against the *News of the World*, with the paper ordered to pay him £60,000 in damages (Max Mosley v. News Group Newspapers Limited [2008] EWHC 1777). www.bailii.org/ew/cases/EWHC/QB/2008/1777.html. The amount was the highest in recent legal history for a privacy action.

For Max Mosley, the case wasn't purely about money. Even though he was awarded £60,000 damages, he maintained that money alone could not restore his reputation. He therefore took his case to the ECHR. He hadn't been made aware of the newspaper's intention to publish, and therefore didn't have an opportunity to seek a court injunction to prevent the story from being published. At the ECHR he argued that there should be a system of 'prior notification', whereby the media would be required to inform the subject of a proposed exposé that they were intending to publish about them. If that were the case, Mr Mosley argues, it would give the subject the chance to seek an injunction in order to prevent publication of a story that might potentially be an infringement of privacy.

In May 2011, the ECHR published its judgment, rejecting Mr Mosley's proposal that there should be a system of pre-notification. The judgment said:

> The court has consistently emphasized the need to look beyond the facts of the present case and to consider the broader impact of a pre-notification requirement. The limited scope under Article 10 for restrictions on the freedom of the press to publish material which contributes to debate on matters of general public interest must be borne in mind. Thus, having regard to the chilling effect to which a pre-notification requirement risks giving rise, to the significant doubts as to the effectiveness of any pre-notification requirement and to the wide margin of appreciation in this area, the court is of the view that Article 8 does not require a legally binding pre-notification requirement. Accordingly, the court con-

cludes that there has been no violation of Article 8 of the Convention by the absence of such a requirement in domestic law.

(www.bailii.org/eu/cases/ECHR/2011/774.html, paragraph 132)

Nevertheless, the ECHR was highly critical of the *News of the World*. They noted that the publication of photographs and of video footage, which had been obtained through clandestine recording, had a far greater impact than the articles themselves. The use of a video obtained by using long-lens photography didn't really add anything to the story, apart from titillating the newspaper's readership and adding to Mr Mosley's embarrassment.

Further information

American Library Association (2011) Privacy Toolkit,
   www.ala.org/ala/aboutala/offices/oif/iftoolkits/toolkitsprivacy/default.cfm.
Magi, T.J. (2006) *Protecting Library Patron Confidentiality: checklist of best practices*,
   www.aallnet.org/products/pub_sp0709/pub_sp0709_Handout.pdf.

References

BBC News Online (2011) *"Twitter Ban" issued by High Court Judge*, BBC News
   Online, 13 May 2011,
   www.bbc.co.uk/news/uk-13392712.
CILIP (2009) *Ethical Principles and Code of Professional Practice for Library and
   Information Professionals*,
   www.cilip.org.uk/get-involved/policy/ethics/pages/principles.aspx.
CILIP (2011) *User Privacy in Libraries: guidelines for the reflective practitioner*,
   www.cilip.org.uk/get-involved/advocacy/information-society/privacy/pages/
   privacy-guidelines.aspx.
The Guardian (2009) Barclays Gags Guardian Over Tax, 19 March,
   www.guardian.co.uk/business/2009/mar/17/barclays-guardian-injunction-tax.
The Guardian (2011) The Gag That Stops You Talking to an MP, 29 April,
   www.guardian.co.uk/commentisfree/libertycentral/2011/apr/29/
   mp-superinjunctions-hyperinjunctions.
Master of the Rolls (2011) *Report of the Committee on Super-injunctions: super-
   injunctions, anonymized injunctions and open justice*, Judiciary of England and
   Wales,
   www.judiciary.gov.uk/media/media-releases/2011/committee-reports-findings-
   super-injunctions-20052011.
The Scotsman (2011) Andrew Marr 'Embarrassed' After Revealing Super-
   injunction, 22 August,
   http://news.scotsman.com/news/Andrew-Marr-39embarrassed39-after-

CHAPTER 9

Freedom of information

Contents

9.1   General principles of freedom of information

United Nations General Assembly Resolution 59(i), which was passed at its first session on 14 December 1946, states that: 'Freedom of information is a fundamental human right and is the touchstone of all the freedoms to which the United Nations is consecrated.'

The legal right to information is not limited to access to information laws, because each country has its own mix of legislation covering areas such as public records/archives, environmental protection, data protection and privacy, state secrets, and media.

Openness and transparency is now considered to be an essential part of any modern government, and nearly 90 countries around the world have adopted comprehensive access to information laws, with around 50 countries having laws on both the right to privacy and the right to information (World Bank, 2011). An open government backed by a properly implemented and working freedom of information regime provides many benefits both to government bodies as well as to citizens.

Freedom of information regimes exist in order to promote transparency and accountability. The public sector, by definition, is funded from the public purse, and as such has a responsibility to demonstrate that it is held to account for that expenditure. Key benefits of a fully fledged freedom of information system are:

- participation in public debate
- improved administration and decision-making
- accountability in the spending of public money
- allowing the public to understand decisions made about them
- promoting public health and safety.

In addition to transparency and openness, freedom of information promotes a sense of accountability across the public sector. For example, details of expenditure on taxis, which were released as a result of an FOI request by Paul Hutcheon (Scottish political editor of the *Sunday Herald*), ultimately led to the resignation of the leader of the Scottish Conservative Party, David McLetchie. The information showed the MSP to have claimed unusually high travel expenses for an Edinburgh-based MSP. In the Westminster Parliament, the 'expenses scandal' of 2009 continues to have repercussions. This came about as a result of an FOI request made by Heather Brooke for details of a number of high-profile MPs' expenses. Ms Brooke took the matter to the Information Tribunal and also to the High Court. It ultimately led to the resignation of the Speaker, Michael Martin, and to the convictions and/or imprisonment of a number of ex-MPs and members of the House of Lords:

- The former Labour MP David Chaytor was jailed for 18 months for fraudulently claiming more than £20,000 in expenses, but was released after serving only a quarter of his sentence.
- Former labour MP Eric Illsley was sentenced to a year in jail after pleading guilty to £14,000 of expenses fraud.
- Former Labour MP Jim Devine was jailed for 16 months for expenses fraud.
- Elliott Morley, a former Labour MP, was sentenced to 16 months in jail, having pleaded guilty to fraudulently claiming £32,000 in expenses, which included payments for a mortgage on his home in Scunthorpe that had already been paid off.
- Lord Taylor of Warwick was convicted of dishonestly claiming over £11,000 in allowances by an 11 to 1 majority verdict and jailed for 12 months.
- Lord Hanningfield was found guilty on all six counts of false accounting relating to nearly £14,000 of Parliamentary expenses and jailed for nine

months. The trial heard that he had claimed for non-existent journeys and overnight stays in London.

The FOIA and the Freedom of Information (Scotland) Act 2002 (FOI(S)A) give citizens the right to see all kinds of information held by the government and other public authorities. Citizens can use this legislation to: find out about a problem affecting their community and to check whether an authority is doing enough to deal with it; see how effective a policy has been; find out about the authority's spending; check whether an authority is doing what it says it is; and learn more about the real reasons for decisions. Public authorities can only withhold information if an exemption in the Act allows them to do so. Even exempt information may have to be disclosed in the public interest. If a member of the public thinks that information has been improperly withheld they can complain to the independent Information Commissioner (or the Scottish Information Commissioner), who can then order disclosure.

9.2   The Freedom of Information Act 2000 (FOIA)

The FOIA gives a general right of access to all types of 'recorded' information held by public authorities; it sets out a number of exemptions from that right and it also places a number of obligations on public authorities (Legislation.gov.uk, 2011).

Around 100,000 public bodies are covered by the FOIA. The list is set out in Schedule 1 of the Act, and it has been amended by a number of Statutory Instruments (see Figure 9.1).

The FOIA does not apply to information held by the Security Service, the Secret Intelligence Service (SIS), the Government Communications Headquarters (GCHQ), the Special Forces or any unit or part-unit assisting GCHQ.

- central government and government departments
- local authorities
- non-departmental public bodies
- National Health Service (NHS) bodies (hospitals, doctors' surgeries, dentists, pharmacists and opticians)
- state schools
- colleges
- universities
- police forces
- prison services
- House of Commons
- House of Lords
- Northern Ireland Assembly
- National Assembly of Wales.

Figure 9.1 *Public authorities covered by the FOIA*

As far as libraries are concerned, relevant organizations covered by the FOIA include the British Library, National Library of Wales and Arts Council England; and, in Scotland, the National Library of Scotland comes within the remit of the FOI(S)A.

The FOIA is enforced by the Information Commissioner whose role is to: promote good practice; approve and advise on the preparation of publication schemes; provide information as to the public's rights under the FOIA; and enforce compliance with the FOIA. He is also required to report annually to Parliament (Chapter 10 gives a more comprehensive overview of the role of the Information Commissioner). In 2002, the Scottish Executive passed the FOI(S)A, which is overseen by a Scottish Information Commissioner (see Section 10.3). Responsibility for freedom of information and data protection comes within the remit of the Ministry of Justice.

There are three codes of practice issued under the FOIA and the Environmental Information Regulations (EIR), which provide guidance to public authorities:

1   On responding to requests for information and associated matters, this code (Ministry of Justice, 2009a) provides guidance on the:

  • provision of advice by public authorities to those making requests for information
  • transfer of requests from one public authority to another
  • consultation with third parties to whom the information requested relates or who may be affected by its disclosure
  • inclusion in contracts entered into by public authorities of terms relating to the disclosure of information
  • development of procedures for handling complaints from applicants.

2   On the management of records, this code (Ministry of Justice, 2009b) aims to give advice to public authorities subject to the Public Records Act 1958 and the Public Records (Northern Ireland) Act 1923, as to desirable practice in record keeping, and also advise on the practices to be followed when transferring records to the National Archives or the Public Records Office of Northern Ireland, in the context of the FOIA. One of the most significant amendments to the DPA by the FOIA is that the definition of 'data' is extended to cover *all* personal information held, as far as public authorities are concerned. This includes both 'structured' and 'unstructured' manual records.

3   This code of practice (ICO, 2005), on the discharge of the obligations of public authorities under the EIR, covers:

- training
- proactive dissemination of information
- provision of advice and assistance to persons making requests for information
- timeliness in dealing with requests for information
- charges
- transferring requests for information
- consultation with third parties
- EIR and public sector contracts
- accepting information in confidence from third parties
- consultation with devolved administrations
- refusal of requests
- review and complaints procedures.

Figure 9.2 shows the two main obligations public authorities have under the FOIA.

---

1. Public authorities have to produce a 'publication scheme' as a guide to the information that they hold which is publicly available.

Figure 9.2 *Obligations of public authorities under the FOIA*

9.2.1 Local authorities

A draft *Code of Recommended Practice for Local Government Data Transparency* was published by the Department for Communities and Local Government on 7 February 2011, for consultation, providing a clear outline of what will additionally be expected of local authorities.

In the push for transparency, councils are being asked to publish an organizational chart including the names and responsibilities of staff paid over £58,200 (equivalent to the lowest Senior Civil Service pay band). Ministers believe this will give the public the full picture of a council's management composition.

Councils will also be expected to respond to public demand for more information, where residents decide what data is important, so they can see exactly where their taxes go and how their council is performing.

The code also recommends a public inventory should be registered at the government's central information hub (www.data.gov.uk), in an accessible format so that it is easy to locate or reuse.

The code proposes the minimum datasets that should be released, openly and for reuse, by local authorities as:

- expenditure over £500 (including costs, and supplier and transaction information)
- grants and payments under contract to the voluntary community and social enterprise sector
- names, budgets and responsibilities of staff paid over £58,200
- an organizational chart
- councillor allowances and expenses
- copies of contracts and tenders to businesses and to the voluntary community and social enterprise sector
- policies, performance, audits and key indicators on the authority's fiscal and financial position
- data on democratic running of the local authority including the constitution, election results, committee minutes, decision-making processes and records of decisions.

9.3   Publication schemes

The FOIA places a duty on public authorities to adopt and maintain publication schemes, which must be approved by the Information Commissioner. A publication scheme is essentially a guide to information that a public authority routinely publishes or intends to publish; and the word 'publication' should be defined widely enough to cover not just items to be found in bound or printed form, but also computer printouts, website downloads, etc. The emphasis is on information rather than documents. Such schemes must set out the types of information the authority publishes, the format, and the details of any charges.

A model publication scheme was introduced on 1 January 2009, which all public authorities have to adopt. The scheme lists information under seven broad classes (Figure 9.3). Each authority is required to prepare a guide to information for the public, which gives details of what the authority will provide under the scheme.

The ICO has a set of definition documents and template guides which set out the types of information they would expect particular kinds of authority to publish and list in their guide.

The FOIA has provided a tremendous opportunity for information professionals to play a key part in the development of the guide to information that the public authority will provide under their publication scheme. Information professionals have considerable information management expertise that can be utilized by carrying out information audits so that public authorities can produce a detailed inventory of what they produce.

The FOIA increased pressure for public authorities to have effective records management systems in place because only by managing their records in a professional manner can public authorities be confident that they have a

Who we are and what we do:
Organizational information, locations and contacts, constitutional and legal governance.

What we spend and how we spend it:
Financial information relating to projected and actual income and expenditure, tendering, procurement and contracts.

What our priorities are and how we are doing:
Strategy and performance information, plans, assessments, inspections and reviews.

How we make decisions:
Policy proposals and decisions, decision-making processes, internal criteria and procedures, consultations.

Our policies and procedures:
Current written protocols for delivering our functions and responsibilities.

Lists and registers:
Information held in registers required by law and other lists and registers relating to the functions of the authority.

The services we offer:
Advice and guidance, booklets and leaflets, transactions and media releases. A

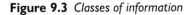

Figure 9.3 *Classes of information*

comprehensive overview of the information that they hold. Such knowledge can then assist those authorities to respond to requests effectively and to speedily identify cases where an exemption might be relied upon. Public authorities need to have formal records management procedures in place, including the development of proper retention, destruction and archiving policies. Sound principles of information handling and retrieval are the foundation of freedom of information.

The code of practice on records management (Ministry of Justice, 2009b) recognizes that any freedom of information legislation is only as good as the quality of the records to which it provides access. Records management can exist without freedom of information but freedom of information cannot exist without records management.

Public authorities should be monitoring the access requests that they receive in order to determine whether information that is regularly being requested should be made available routinely. Indeed, it is good practice for authorities to keep a log of requests made for information that is not already included in their publication schemes.

It is left to the public authority to decide how to publish its scheme. The Information Commissioner's original guidance from 2002 does make clear, though, that making the publication scheme available on the web is not sufficiently universal to render it the sole means by which a scheme is delivered (ICO, 2002). Public authorities must cater for the needs of those who do not have web access, and they must also pay due attention to the needs of people with disabilities. They need to take account of their obligations under the Equality Act 2010. The information guide should be available to all who request it and, in normal circumstances, public authorities should not charge users for copies of it.

The model publication scheme specifies the 'classes' of information that the public authority publishes or intends to publish (Figure 9.3). These classes might be described as groupings of information having one or more common characteristics. The ICO publishes a set of definition documents and template guides for a number of different types of organization, which sets out the types of information that the ICO would expect those organizations to publish and list within their guide to information.

Each class of information within the scheme commits the public authority to publishing the information that falls within it. It is therefore important that a public authority, and its staff, understand what material is covered and that the coverage is clear to the user. Where it is intended that certain information is not included, this must also be clear to users.

9.4   Copyright implications of the FOIA

Most documents disclosed under freedom of information, whether they are covered by a publication scheme or sent to an individual in response to a freedom of information request, will be subject to copyright protection. Section 50 of the Copyright Designs and Patents Act 1988 (CDPA) says:

Acts done under statutory authority
50.—(1) Where the doing of a particular act is specifically authorized by an Act of Parliament, whenever passed, then, unless the Act provides otherwise, the doing of that act does not infringe copyright.
(2) Subsection (1) applies in relation to an enactment contained in Northern Ireland legislation as it applies in relation to an Act of Parliament.
(3) Nothing in this section shall be construed as excluding any defence of statutory authority otherwise available under or by virtue of any enactment.

The FOIA does not, however, explicitly 'authorize' the *copying* of material that is used in order to respond to an FOIA request. What the FOIA authorizes is that the public authority provides *access* to the material, and this need not necessarily be done by copying the information. The requirement set out in the FOIA could, for example, be achieved by the public authority making the item available for inspection at their premises, or by providing a summary.

The Code of Practice under s45 of the FOIA says:

In some cases, it may […] be appropriate to consult […] third parties about such matters as whether any further explanatory material or advice should be given to the applicant together with the information in question. Such advice may, for example, refer to any restrictions (including copyright restrictions) which may exist as to the subsequent use which may be made of such information. Ministry of Justice (2009a)

What is clear is that the recipient of the information requested under the FOIA is not free to further reproduce the material in ways that would breach a third party's copyright. Under copyright law, the enquirer cannot make further copies of the documents without obtaining the permission of the copyright owner.

The National Archives have issued guidance on Crown Copyright and FOI (National Archives, 2008). This guidance draws a distinction between the supply of information held by public authorities under freedom of information legislation and the reuse of that information, and explains those circumstances where formal licensing is required. The guidance includes a sample form of words which can be used in order to explain who owns copyright in the information and contact details for obtaining a copyright licence.

Chapter 8 of the Ministry of Justice's *Procedural Guidance* on the FOIA sets out the guidance relating to the interface between freedom of information and copyright:

Use of Crown Copyright

Public authorities should be aware that information which is disclosed under the Act may be subject to copyright protection. If an applicant wishes to use any information in a way that would infringe copyright, for example by making multiple copies, or issuing copies to the public, he or she would require a licence from the copyright holder.

Third Party Copyright

Public authorities complying with their statutory duty under sections 1 and 11 of the Freedom of Information Act to release information to an applicant are not breaching the Copyright, Designs and Patents Act 1988. The FOIA specifically authorises release of the information to an applicant, even if it is in such a form as would otherwise breach the copyright interests of a third party. However, the Copyright Designs and Patents Act 1988 will continue to protect the rights of the copyright holder once the information is received by the applicant. Ministry of Justice (2011)

Both section 50 of the CDPA and Schedule 1 of the Database Regulations (SI 1997/3032) Reg. 20(2)(6) allow the supply of documents under the exceptions of Acts done under statutory authority.

It is also worth mentioning that in the EIR a public authority is entitled to refuse to disclose information to the extent that its disclosure would adversely affect IPRs (Reg. 12(5)(c)). Any IPRs, including copyright-protected material, a patented design or the constituents of a chemical that has yet to be marketed, or other trade secret, may be protected by this exception where a potentially adverse effect can be reasonably anticipated and where the public interest in disclosure does not outweigh the adverse effects.

In the case of Scotland, the question of how copyright affects FOI is covered by Regulation 3 of the FOI(S)A (Consequential Modifications) Order 2004 SI 2004/3089. The Regulations insert the following as subsection (3) to section 80 of the CDPA 1988: 'Section 50 of the Copyright, Designs and Patents Act 1988[8] and paragraph 6 of Schedule 1 to the Copyright and Rights in Databases Regulations 1997 apply in relation to the Freedom of Information (Scotland) Act 2002 as they apply in relation to this Act.'

9.5   Freedom of information and library and information professionals

Library and information professionals are uniquely placed and skilled to defend and deliver freedom of information. Representing its membership of around 17,500 information staff, the CILIP attaches a high value to freedom of information, which is considered to be a core responsibility of its members. CILIP's position statement on information access states that:

> CILIP is committed to promoting a society where intellectual activity and creativity, freedom of expression and debate, and access to information are encouraged and nurtured as vital elements underpinning individual and community fulfilment in all aspects of human life. It is the role of a library and information service that is funded from the public purse to provide, as far as resources allow, access to all publicly available information, whether factual or fiction and regardless of media or format, in which its users claim legitimate interest. [In some cases this will be limited to those areas reflecting the primary purpose of a parent institution; in others it will be generalist in nature.]
>
> Access should not be restricted on any grounds except that of the law. If publicly available material has not incurred legal penalties then it should not be excluded on moral, political, religious, racial or gender grounds, to satisfy the demands of sectional interest. The legal basis of any restriction on access should always be stated.   CILIP (2005)

CILIP's *Ethical Principles and Code of Professional Practice for Library and Information Professionals* (2009) binds its members to uphold its policy on access to information:

'The conduct of information professionals should be characterized by commitment to the defence, and the advancement, of access to information, ideas and works of the imagination.'

Information professionals have a key role to play in facilitating freedom of access to information. Libraries, information and advice centres of public authorities can provide citizens with details of what freedom of information means to them, they can guide enquirers towards the information which their authority makes routinely available through the publication schemes, and they can also alert people to their rights of access to information not covered by the publication schemes.

CILIP's position statement, which affirms the role of librarians as guardians of the unfettered right to information as CILIP policy, establishes the principle that access to information should not be restricted on any grounds except that of the law (CILIP, 2005). If publicly available material has not incurred legal penalties then it should not be excluded on moral, political, religious, racial or gender grounds, to satisfy the demands of sectional interest.

The same holds true for the emerging networked society, where the opportunities provided by information and communications technologies have revolutionized the way information is made available, but where the fundamental principle remains constant. CILIP's Council have also endorsed the Council of Europe Guidelines on Public Access to and Freedom of Expression in Networked Information (CILIP, 2011).

The Council of Europe Guidelines detail a seven-point approach to the practical issues of enabling and managing access to information in the era of the internet and e-mail. In addition to emphasizing the right to unfettered access, they also stress the obligation to support information users in making their choices of information sources and services freely and confidently.

Employers of library and information staff are urged to embed these guidelines into their practice and to support the principle of uninhibited access to information, recognizing the discretion that library and information staff will need to exercise in meeting the legitimate interests of their users.

CILIP Scotland have clearly set out the impact of freedom of information on library and information professionals (Figure 9.4).

◦• Useful resource

The Scottish Information Commissioner's website has guidance in the form of a set of FAQs on the relationship between libraries, archives and access to information through the FOI(S)A:
www.itspublicknowledge.info/FAQ/PublicAuthorityFAQ/
LibrariesArchivesFAQ.asp.

It is also worth mentioning the report to the CILIP Council produced by the now-disbanded CILIP Freedom of Information Panel, dated 10 December 2003: www.fustian.co.uk/foi.pdf.

Library and information professionals will be required to:

- help those who wish to get information from public sector bodies by suggesting how best to frame enquiries
- inform people about their right to appeal if information is withheld
- provide information on who deals with what: i.e. where to go for a particular topic
- signpost websites and helplines with further information.

Those in the public sector must also:

- help to answer enquiries from external audiences
- provide a physical location for enquirers to consult material held by their organization
- create guides and indexes to publications and other material that is released by the organization
- facilitate links via websites and other means with material issued by related bodies in terms of function or subject coverage
- be involved in ongoing development of publication schemes, encouraging growth to match interests of external audiences and lobbying for more proactive publishing
- take an active part in organizing information more effectively through improved information architecture and collection procedures.

Source: CILIP Scotland, 2004. Reproduced with the kind permission of CILIP Scotland,

Figure 9.4 *FOI and the role of the information professional*

9.6 Freedom of information rights and request procedures

The individual's right of access to information means that anyone, anywhere can make a request for information from a public authority provided that the request satisfies all the relevant conditions (for procedure see Figure 9.5). The request must include sufficient information to enable the authority to identify the information requested. You do not have to live in the UK or be a British citizen in order to ask for information, and you do not have to say why you want the information. There are no limits on the kinds of information you can ask for, although there are limits on the information that the authority has to provide. Applicants have the right to be told what information the public authority holds and they also have the right to receive the information (unless one of the exemptions disqualifies that right). The right of access is fully retrospective. It covers information recorded both before and after the FOIA was passed. Applicants do not have to mention the FOIA or the DPA when requesting information. When making a request under the FOIA, you can specify how you want the information to be given to you, and the public authority should give you the information in the form you prefer, if it is reasonably practicable to do this. The FOIA lists three ways in which you might ask for the information to be provided:

- as a copy, in permanent form or some other form acceptable to you
- by an opportunity to inspect the information
- as a summary or digest.

The authority can consider the cost when deciding how practical your preference is.

Public authorities have 20 working days within which to respond to requests, and in certain circumstances they can charge a fee, which has to be calculated according to The Freedom of Information and Data Protection (Appropriate Limit and Fees) Regulations 2004: SI 2004/3244. Where a fee is required, the 20 working days is extended by up to three months until the fee is paid.

➽ Useful resource

For further information on the time limit for responding to requests see the *Information Commissioner Freedom of Information Awareness Guidance number 11 – Time for Compliance*:
www.ico.gov.uk/upload/documents/library/freedom_of_information/detailed_specialist_guides/timeforcompliance.pdf.

In the case of the EIR, regulation 7 says:

> Where a request is made under regulation 5, the public authority may extend the period of 20 working days [...] to 40 working days if it reasonably believes that the complexity and volume of the information requested means that it is impracticable either to comply with the request within the earlier period or to make a decision to refuse to do so.

Figure 9.5 summarizes the freedom of information requests procedure.

9.7 Exemptions and appeals

Whilst the FOIA creates a general right of access to information held by public bodies, it also sets out 23 exemptions where that right is either disapplied or qualified (see Figures 9.6 and 9.7). The exemptions relate to information held for functions such as national security, law enforcement, commercial interests and personal data.

When making a request, you must:
- ask for the information in writing, which includes fax and e-mail
- give your real name
- give an address to which the authority can reply. This can be a postal or email address
- describe the information you would like.

When responding to requests, public authorities:
- must respond to requests promptly and, in any event, within 20 working days
- may charge a fee which has to be calculated according to the Fees Regulations, and if a fee is required, the 20 working days will be extended by up to three months until the fee is paid
- must tell the requester whether they hold the information that is being requested
- must give reasons for their decision where the authority has grounds not to release the information requested, and must tell the applicant of their right to complain.

Figure 9.5 *Freedom of information requests procedure*

s22 Information intended for future publication
s24 National security (other than information supplied by or relating to named security organizations, where the duty to consider disclosure in the public interest does not arise – see section 23)
s26 Defence
s27 International relations
s28 Relations between administrations in the United Kingdom
s29 The economy
s30 Investigations and proceedings conducted by public authorities
s31 Law enforcement
s33 Audit functions
s35 Formulation of government policy
s36 Prejudice to effective conduct of public affairs (except information held by the House of Commons or the House of Lords)
s37 Communications with Her Majesty and honours, etc. (NB an absolute exemption now applies for information relating to communications with the sovereign, heir to the throne or second in line to the throne or those acting on their behalf)
s38 Health and safety
s39 Environmental information (Regulations covering environmental information may be made under section 74)
s42 Legal professional privilege

Figure 9.6 *Exemptions where the public interest test applies*

Most of the exemptions require a public authority to consider a test of prejudice *and* a public interest test:

1 There is a 'test of prejudice'. For example, in the case of the s31 exemption, where a public authority considers the information to be exempt because it is

held in connection with law enforcement, they can only withhold that information if its release would prejudice the prevention or detection of a crime.

2 In the case of the 'public interest test', this requires a public authority to consider whether the public interest in withholding the exempt information outweighs the public interest in releasing it; and the balance lies in favour of disclosure, in that information may only be withheld if the public interest in withholding it is greater than the public interest in releasing it.

Public authorities do need to take care when applying the exemptions. Where a requested document contains some exempt information, only those specific pieces of exempt information can be withheld and the remainder of the document must be released.

Usually, the public authority will give you a special notice explaining why it is not providing the information you have asked for. A public authority is not required to give you a full explanation if this would involve giving you information that is itself exempt. So, in some circumstances, you will only be given a partial explanation. However, the notice will explain:

- how you can complain to the particular authority about the way your request has been handled, or explain that the authority has no complaints procedure
- your right to ask the Information Commissioner to decide whether your request has been properly dealt with.

These are the exemptions where, if the exemption applies, there is no duty to consider where the public interest lies:

s21 Information accessible to the applicant by other means
s23 Information supplied by or relating to bodies dealing with security matters
s32 Court records
s34 Parliamentary privilege
s36 Prejudice to effective conduct of public affairs (absolute for information held by House of Commons or House of Lords; for all other information covered by this section the public interest test applies)
s40 Personal information (access is given in accordance with the rules in the DPA)
s41 Information provided in confidence
s44 Prohibition on disclosure where a disclosure is prohibited by an enactment or would constitute contempt of court

---

Figure 9.7 *Absolute exemptions*

9.8   Enforcement

A person who has made a request for information and is unhappy with the response that they have received should first go through the public authority's own complaints procedure. However, if they are still unhappy, they may apply to the Information Commissioner for a decision as to whether the request has been dealt with according to the FOIA. In response, the Information Commissioner may serve a decision notice on the public authority and applicant setting out any steps that are required in order to comply.

The Information Commissioner has the power to serve information notices and enforcement notices on public authorities. In certain circumstances the Information Commissioner may issue a decision or enforcement notice requiring disclosure of information in the public interest. All notices may be appealed to the independent First-Tier Tribunal (Information Rights). However, where the Information Commissioner issues a notice requiring disclosure of the information this may be subject to an 'executive override'. In such a case the public authority has 20 days from receipt of the notice to obtain a signed certificate from a Cabinet Minister overriding the Information Commissioner's notice. There is no right of appeal against the ministerial certificate. The Information Commissioner may issue a practice recommendation in respect of non-conformity with either code of practice.

The Information Commissioner has made it clear that the ministerial override should only be used in exceptional circumstances; and if it is ever used, this will be reported to Parliament.

The ministerial veto was used by Jack Straw in 2009 when the Information Commissioner cited the public interest when ordering the release of the Cabinet minutes of the meetings which authorized the war in Iraq, including the Attorney General's advice. The information has now been released but only by means of extreme political pressure and in the form of a public inquiry.

On another occasion Jack Straw exercised the ministerial veto to prevent the disclosure of 1997 Cabinet Committee minutes on devolution. The matter had been due to be heard at the Information Tribunal on 25 January 2010 but in exercising the ministerial veto ahead of that date, the Tribunal's role was completely disregarded.

9.9   The Environmental Information Regulations 2004 (EIR)

The EIR came into force on 1 January 2005, coinciding with the implementation of the right of access to information under the FOIA. The regulations clarify and extend previous rights of access to environmental information held by public authorities. The rights in the EIR stem from Council directive 2003/4/EC of the 28 January 2003 on public access to environmental information and repealing council directive 90/313/EEC.

On 25 June 1998, the European Community signed the United Nations Economic Commission for Europe (UN/ECE) Convention on Access to Information, Public Participation in Decision-making and Access to Justice in

Environmental Matters (the Aarhus Convention), and the provisions of Community law must be consistent with the Convention.

The First-Tier Tribunal (Information Rights) considers appeals from notices issued by the Information Commissioner under the EIR.

The Environmental Information (Scotland) Regulations 2004 (SSI 2004/520) (EI(S)R) provide for the making available of environmental information held by Scottish authorities. There is also a code of practice on the discharge of functions by public authorities under the EI(S)R, and this is enforced by the Scottish Information Commissioner.

Destroying information with the intention of preventing disclosure is an offence under the FOIA (section 77), the DPA, and the EIR (regulation 19).

9.9.1   What is environmental information?

Information in written, visual, oral, electronic or other material form about:

1 The state of the elements of the environment (such as air, atmosphere, water, soil, land, landscape and natural sites, GMOs, biological diversity) and the interactions between them.
2 Substances, energy, noise, radiation or waste including radioactive waste, emissions and discharges into the environment affecting or likely to affect the elements in (1).
3 Measures (including administrative measures, policies, legislation, plans, programmes and environmental agreements) and activities affecting or likely to affect the elements and factors in (1) and (2).
4 Reports on the implementation of environmental legislation.
5 Cost benefit and other economic analyses used within the measures and activities covered in (3).
6 The state of human health and safety, conditions of human life, contamination of the food chain, cultural sites and built structures in as much as they are or may be affected by (1), (2) or (3).

There are a number of similarities as well as a number of differences between the UK's freedom of information regime and the EIR. To put this into context, it should be borne in mind that the FOIA was initiated by the Westminster Parliament; whereas the EIR derives from European legislation (see directives 313/90/EC and 2003/4/EC which subsequently replaced it).

There are two types of exception under the EIR – a group of exceptions based on the category of information and another group of exceptions where they would have an adverse effect on xyz. *All* of the EIR exceptions are subject to a public interest test. Refusals can be made if:

- information is not held (refer request on)
- request is manifestly unreasonable
- request is too general
- request is for unfinished documents or data (in which case estimated time for completion must be given)
- request is for an internal communication.

Refusals may be made if disclosure would adversely affect:

- international relations/public security/defence
- the course of justice and right to fair trial
- IPRs
- confidentiality of proceedings
- commercial confidentiality
- the interests of the person who provided the data
- protection of the environment.

Information on emissions cannot be refused under the last four points.

Both the EIR and FOIA regimes encourage the proactive dissemination of information and the use of publication schemes; they have the same time limit of 20 working days; and both require public authorities to provide advice and assistance and to provide information in the form and format requested where possible.

In terms of the differences between the two regimes, EIR requests do not have to be in writing and can be made orally; they cannot be refused solely on the grounds of cost. Whilst the FOIA does have a public interest test, in the case of the EIR *all* of the exceptions are subject to the public interest test.

9.10   Freedom of information in Scotland

The Scottish Executive's objectives in passing the FOI(S)A 2002 were to:

- establish a legal right of access to information held by a broad range of Scottish public authorities
- balance this right with provisions protecting sensitive information
- establish a fully independent Scottish Information Commissioner to promote and enforce the freedom of information regime
- encourage the proactive disclosure of information by Scottish public authorities through a requirement to maintain a publication scheme
- make provision for the application of the freedom of information regime to historical records.

The FOI(S)A came into force in January 2005, in line with the rest of the UK. A detailed list of the public authorities covered by the Act is contained in Schedule 1. It includes:

- the Scottish Executive and its agencies
- local authorities
- NHS Scotland
- schools, colleges and universities
- the police
- the Scottish Parliament.

The Act provides for other authorities to be added later, and for organizations to be designated as public authorities if they exercise functions of a public nature or provide a service under contract, which is a function of a public authority. This provision would enable private companies to be brought within the scope of the Act should they be involved in significant work of a public nature such as major private finance initiative (PFI) contracts. In such cases, only the company's involvement in work of a public nature would come within the freedom of information remit.

As part of the devolution settlement, UK government departments operating in Scotland and cross-border public authorities such as the Ministry of Defence are not covered by Scottish freedom of information legislation, but instead by the UK FOIA.

Scottish public authorities are required to respond to requests within 20 working days, as is the case with the FOIA. But in certain circumstances the Keeper of the Records of Scotland has 30 working days to respond to requests.

Most requests under the FOI(S)A should be dealt with free of charge and where a fee is charged it is likely to be small. If someone has a disability and because of that wants the information in a particular format, an authority cannot pass on to them any extra costs it has to pay in order to provide it in that format. If the cost to the authority is more than £100 but less than £600, the authority can charge the requester 10% of the cost of providing the information, but the first £100 is always free. So the maximum it can charge you in most situations is £50 (this would be where the cost to the authority is £600). For example:

If the cost to the authority is £200, it can only charge you £10: 10% x (£200 –£100).
If the cost to the authority is £600, it can charge you £50: 10% x £600 –£100).

If the total cost to the authority is more than £600 the authority can refuse your request. If, however, it decides to deal with your request, the authority can charge you the full cost (i.e. up to £15 an hour for staff time plus reasonable photocopying costs) over and above this £600 limit. The authority may be able to advise you how to reduce the costs by making changes to your request.

As far as the exemptions are concerned (Figure 9.8), a key difference is that the test is whether the information would *prejudice substantially* the purpose to which the exemption relates. In other words, the exemptions are harder to justify in Scotland than in England and Wales.

FOI(S)A Part 2 – Exempt information (ss25–41)

Exemptions to which the public interest test *does not* apply:

25 information otherwise accessible

26 prohibitions on disclosure

36(2) confidentiality

37 court records etc.

38 personal information.

Exemptions to which the public interest test *does* apply:

27 information intended for future publication

28 relations within the United Kingdom

29 formulation of Scottish Administration policy etc.

30 prejudice to effective conduct of public affairs

31 national security and defence

32 international relations

33 commercial interests and the economy

34 investigations by Scottish public authorities and proceedings arising out of such investigations

35 law enforcement

36(1) confidentiality

39 health, safety and the environment

40 audit functions

41 communications with Her Majesty etc. and honours.

Figure 9.8 *Exemptions under the FOI(S)A*

9.11   Freedom of information and data protection

The DPA gives individuals the right to find out what structured information is held about them by organizations in both the public and the private sectors, and to obtain a copy of that information. But in the case of public authorities, section 69 of the FOIA extends this to give individuals a right of access to *all* the personal data held about them. Manual records only fall within the remit of the DPA where they are structured; but the FOIA says that for public authorities individuals have a right of access to all personal data held, whether structured or unstructured (see Section 9.2).

9.11.1 Fees and charges

9.11.1.1 Data protection fees

Organizations can charge people who make subject access requests under the data protection legislation. Many organizations do not make a charge, but where they do, this can be up to a maximum of £10. In the case of credit records the fee would be £2, and in the case of medical and educational records the maximum fee is £50.

9.11.1.2 Freedom of information fees

In the case of freedom of information requests, many are free of charge. Calculation of fees is undertaken in accordance with The Freedom of Information and Data Protection (Appropriate Limit and Fees) Regulations 2004: SI 2004/3244. The regulations state that where the prescribed costs are over £600 in the case of government departments and £450 in the case of other public bodies they are not required to provide the information; but, with the agreement of the enquirer, they can charge the full, prescribed costs for any costs above that threshold. In addition, the full costs for disbursements such as photocopying and postage and packing can be charged back to the enquirer.

With the FOIA it is important to make a clear distinction between costs associated with answering freedom of information requests and costs for items within the publication scheme. The publication scheme should set out what is free and what is chargeable.

9.11.2 The time limit for responding to requests

Under data protection legislation, data controllers have 40 days to respond to requests, and this means 40 calendar days rather than 40 working days. There are different periods for copies of credit files (seven working days) and school pupil records (15 school days).

Under the freedom of information legislation, public bodies have 20 working days following receipt of the request within which to provide the information to the enquirer.

9.11.3 The exemptions

The third key area where the data protection and freedom of information legislative regimes differ is in the list of exemptions. Even if the government wanted to harmonize the two systems, they wouldn't have a completely free hand because in the case of data protection they are obliged to follow EC directive 95/46/EC. The exemptions under the FOIA are set out in Figures 9.6 (exemptions where the public interest applies) and 9.7 (absolute exemptions); and the exemptions under the FOI(S)A are set out in Figure 9.8. Figure 9.9 lists subject access exemptions under the DPA.

Section 28:   Provides an exemption to protect national security.

Section 29[*]:   Covers personal data processed for:
(a) the prevention or detection of crime;
(b) the apprehension or prosecution of offenders, or
(c) the assessment or collection of any tax or duty or of any imposition of a similar nature.

Section 30[*]:   Provides powers for the Lord Chancellor to make orders providing exemptions in relation to health, education and social work records. Orders relating to all three categories of record have been made.

Section 31[*]:   Covers personal data processed for the purposes of discharging a wide range of regulatory functions.

Section 32:   Covers personal data processed for journalistic, literary or artistic purposes.

Section 33:   Covers personal data processed only for research, statistical or historical purposes, subject to certain conditions.

Section 34:   Covers personal data which are statutorily made available to the public.

Section 38:   Provides a power for the Lord Chancellor to make orders providing exemptions where disclosure of information is statutorily prohibited or restricted, subject to certain conditions.

Schedule 7
Paragraph 1:   Covers confidential references given by data controllers in relation to education, employment or the provision of services.

Paragraph 2[*]:   Provides an exemption to protect the combat effectiveness of the armed forces.

Paragraph 3:   Covers personal data processed for the purposes of making appointments of judges and QCs, and the conferring of honours or dignities.

Paragraph 4:   Provides a power for the Lord Chancellor to make orders providing exemptions in relation to Crown appointments. An order designating a limited number of appointments has been made.

Paragraph 5[*]:   Covers personal data processed for the purposes of management forecasting or management planning.

Paragraph 6[*]:   Provides an exemption for personal data processed for corporate finance services.

Paragraph 7[*]:   Covers personal data consisting of records of the data controller's intentions in relation to negotiations with the data subject.

Paragraph 8:   Modifies the 40-day maximum period for dealing with subject access requests in relation to examination marks.

Paragraph 9:   Covers examination scripts.

Paragraph 10:   Covers personal data in respect of which legal professional privilege could be claimed. Legal advice is that this exemption covers legal advice given by Departments' in-house lawyers.

Paragraph 11:   Provides an exemption for circumstances in which by granting access a person would incriminate himself in respect of an offence other than one under the 1998 Act.

Figure 9.9 *Data Protection Act 1998: subject access exemptions*

9.12 European Union documents

The Amsterdam Treaty introduced new Article 255, which gives citizens a right of access to European Parliament, Council and Commission documents. It was under this article on 30 May 2001 that Regulation (EC) No 1049/2001 was passed on access to European Parliament, Council and Commission documents. The procedure was reviewed in 2007 (European Commission, 2007).

People can request access to any unpublished documents (subject to exemptions) as in Figure 9.10. This covers documents which have not been finalized or which are not intended for publication. It also includes documents from third parties, received and kept by the Commission.

- Make the request in writing and send it by post, fax or e-mail.
- Check to see if the document you want is listed in the document register on the Europa server (http://ec.europa.eu/transparency/regdoc/registre.cfm?CL=en).
- If it is there, quote the reference number of the document you require.
- If it is not, make your request as detailed as possible to help the Commission to be able to identify the document you want.
- The request can be made in any one of the official EU languages.
- Send the request to the Commission's Secretariat General or directly to the department responsible.
- Receipt of applications will be acknowledged.
- Within 15 working days from registration of your application, you will either be sent the document you requested or you will be given the reasons for its total or partial refusal.

Figure 9.10 *How to access European Union information*

↝ Useful resource

Europe Direct was set up to answer questions of a general nature from the public:
http://europa.eu/europedirect/index_en.htm
Freephone number: 00800 67891011.

9.13 Datasets

The government intends to legislate to require public authorities to proactively release data in a way that allows businesses, non-profit organizations, and others, to reuse the data for social and commercial purposes. In the Protection of Freedoms Bill 2011 (HL Bill 99 [2010-11]), clause 100 contains proposals to require all public authorities to release datasets in a reuseable electronic format. As a result, a new section 11(1A) will require that in the case of datasets, so far as is reasonably practicable, a public authority must provide the information in an electronic format which is capable of being reused, thereby preventing authorities from deliberately releasing the information in a format that makes data manipulation impossible (such as releasing the data in Adobe PDF format when it was originally a spreadsheet). Under a new section 19(2A) of the FOIA, publication schemes would have to include a requirement for the public authority to publish any dataset it holds which is requested by an applicant, and any updated version of the dataset (Act Now, 2011).

9.14   CCTV

The Protection of Freedoms Bill includes proposals for improved regulation of CCTV and surveillance cameras. Whilst the failure of an authority to act in accordance with the code would not of itself make that person liable to criminal or civil proceedings, the surveillance camera code will nevertheless be admissible as evidence in any such proceedings.

The ICO has produced a *CCTV Code of Practice* (2008) which provides guidance and advice for CCTV users on how to comply with the DPA.

9.15   Further information and keeping up to date
9.15.1 Organizations

The Campaign for Freedom of Information
    Suite 102, 16 Baldwins Gardens, London EC1N 7RJ
    Tel.: 020 7831 7477
    Fax: 020 7831 7461
    E-mail: admin@cfoi.demon.co.uk
    Website: www.cfoi.org.uk.

Ministry of Justice
    102 Petty France, London, SW1H 9AJ
    Tel.: 020 3334 3555
    Website: www.justice.gov.uk.

Office of the Information Commissioner
    Wycliffe House, Water Lane, Wilmslow, Cheshire SK9 5AF
    Tel.: 0303 123 1113
    Fax: 01625 524 510
    Website: www.ico.gov.uk.

Scottish Executive. Freedom of Information Unit
G-A North, Victoria Quay, Edinburgh EH6 6QQ
Tel.: 0131 244 2410
E-mail: foi@scotland.gsi.gov.uk
Website: www.scotland.gov.uk/Topics/government/foi.

Scottish Information Commissioner
Kinburn Castle, Doubledykes Road, St Andrews, Fife KY16 9DS
Tel.: 01334 464 610
Fax: 01334 464 611
E-mail: enquiries@itspublicknowledge.info
Website: www.itspublicknowledge.info.

Whatdotheyknow.com
A forum for making and/or exploring FOI requests.

9.15.2 Journals

Freedom of Information
ISSN 1745-1825
www.foij.com.

Open Government: a journal on freedom of information
ISSN 1745-8293
www.opengovjournal.org.

9.15.3 Weblogs and newsfeeds

Heather Brooke: http://heatherbrooke.org.
Out-law.com, RSS feed on freedom of information:
www.out-law.com/feeds/out-law_foi.aspx.
UK Freedom of Information Blog: http://foia.blogspot.com.

References

Act Now (2011) Datasets: the new law, May,
www.actnow.org.uk/media/newsletters/May_2011.pdf, pp. 2–3.
CILIP (2005) *Intellectual Freedom, Access to Information and Censorship (CILIP position statement)*,
www.cilip.org.uk/get-involved/advocacy/information-society/foi/pages/intellfreedom.aspx.
CILIP (2009) *Ethical Principles and Code of Professional Practice for Library and Information Professionals*

CILIP (2011) *CILIP Statement on Intellectual Freedom, Access to Information and Censorship*,
    www.cilip.org.uk/get-involved/advocacy/information-society/foi/Pages/
    intellfreedom.aspx.
CILIP Scotland (2004) *Freedom of Information (Scotland) Act 2002: a guide for the information professional*,
    www.slainte.org.uk/files/pdf/foi/foisa04.pdf.
European Commission (2007) *Review of the Rules on Access to Documents*,
    http://ec.europa.eu/transparency/revision/index_en.htm.
ICO (2002) *Freedom of Information Act 2000: preparing for implementation – publication schemes methodology: p4, v1.0.*
ICO (2005) *Code of Practice on the Discharge of the Obligations of Public Authorities Under the Environmental Information Regulations 2004*,
    www.ico.gov.uk/upload/documents/library/environmental_info_reg/
    detailed_specialist_guides/environmental_information_regulations_code_of_
    practice.pdf (SI 2004 No. 3391).
ICO (2008) *CCTV Code of Practice*,
    www.ico.gov.uk/for_organisations/data_protection/topic_guides/cctv.aspx.
Legislation.gov.uk (2011) *Freedom of Information Act 2000: Chapter 36*,
    www.legislation.gov.uk/ukpga/2000/36/contents.
Ministry of Justice (2009a) *Codes of Practice*,
    http://webarchive.nationalarchives.gov.uk/+/www.justice.gov.uk/
    guidance/foi-guidance-codes-practice.htm.
Ministry of Justice (2009b) Lord Chancellor's Code of Practice on the Management of Records Issued Under Section 46 of the Freedom of Information Act 2000,
    www.justice.gov.uk/guidance/docs/foi-section-46-code-of-practice.pdf.
Ministry of Justice (2011) *Procedural Guidance*,
    www.justice.gov.uk/guidance/freedom-and-rights/freedom-of-
    information/procedural-guidance.htm.
World Bank (2011) *The Right to Information and Privacy: balancing rights and managing conflicts*,
    http://wbi.worldbank.org/wbi/Data/wbi/wbicms/files/drupal-acquia/wbi/
    Right%20to%20Information%20and%20Privacy.pdf.

CHAPTER 10

The Information Commissioner

Contents

10.1   The role of the Information Commissioner

The ICO is not a typical non-departmental public body. Such bodies usually have a relationship with ministers based on the delegation of ministerial powers. In the case of the Commissioner, it is a UK independent supervisory authority reporting directly to the UK Parliament, and it has an international role as well as a national one: 'The ICO's mission is to uphold information rights in the public interest, promoting openness by public bodies and data privacy for individuals.' (ICO, 2011a, 6.) The ICO does this by providing guidance to individuals and organizations, solving problems where possible, and taking appropriate action when the law is broken.

Although the Commissioner operates independently in the exercise of his statutory functions, some issues do require the approval of the Secretary of State such as funding, the level of certain fees charged by the ICO, as well as the issuing of codes of practice, although the Protection of Freedoms Bill (HL Bill 99 [2010–2011]) contains provisions which will give the Commissioner greater independence.

The Information Commissioner enforces and oversees the DPA and the FOIA, using only the powers which these pieces of legislation set out. The ICO also has specific responsibilities set out in the EIR and the Privacy and Electronic Communications Regulations 2003. In addition, the Infrastructure for Spatial Information in the European Community (INSPIRE) Regulations 2009 SI 2009/3157 give the Information Commissioner enforcement powers in relation to the proactive provision by public authorities of geographical or location-based information. Decisions of the Information Commissioner are subject to the supervision of the courts and the First-Tier Tribunal (Information Rights).

The Information Commissioner is responsible for setting priorities for the ICO and deciding how they should be achieved. The ICO Corporate Plan 2011–14 says:

> Our aim is to reduce the number of times organizations get information rights wrong in the first place (under either the data protection or freedom of information regimes). The ICO will be proactive and imaginative in communicating with organizations about their responsibilities under legislation.   (ICO, 2011b, 5)

The ICO therefore has an educational role to ensure that the FOI and DP regimes work well. But they also have an enforcement role where things go wrong. The Corporate Plan (ICO, 2011b, 5) says: 'We shall make effective use of our data protection powers to undertake audits and to impose civil monetary penalties on data controllers who get things seriously wrong.'

The plan (page 3) also acknowledges that it will be 'even busier with the government's drive for transparency and openness. This includes changes to the freedom of information regime, and the right to access open and re-usable data'.

The 2010/11 annual report sets out the ICO's vision:

> To be recognized by our stakeholders as the authoritative arbiter of information rights, delivering high-quality, relevant and timely outcomes, responsive and outward-looking in our approach and with committed and high-performing staff – a model of good regulation, and a great place to work and develop.
>   (ICO, 2011a)

The ICO produces guidance for data protection and freedom of information practitioners in order to promote compliance with the law and the following of good practice. The ICO helpline gives guidance and advice to organizations and members of the public. They investigate complaints from people who believe that they have been affected by those breaking the law and, if necessary, the ICO takes legal action in order to ensure that the law does not continue to be broken.

The Information Commissioner participates in, and contributes to, European and international developments in the fields of data protection and freedom of information.

10.1.1 Data protection

The Information Commissioner's role in relation to data protection is set out in sections 51–54A of the DPA. Key elements of the role are:

- to promote good practice
- to make assessments
- to serve information notices
- to serve enforcement notices
- to use its powers of entry and inspection
- to commence proceedings for offences under the DPA
- to prepare and disseminate codes of practice for guidance on good practice
- to prepare a code of practice on data sharing.

The Commissioner also has powers of inspection of overseas information systems, being entitled to inspect any personal data recorded in the Schengen information system, the Europol information system or the Customs information system.

⊷ Useful resource

The ICO maintains a public register of organizations that hold information about people, known as the register of data controllers. This can be accessed through the website of the Information Commissioner: www.ico.gov.uk/ESDWebPages/search.asp.

The aim of the ICO is to take a practical, down-to-earth approach, to make data protection easier for the majority of organizations who seek to handle information well, and to be tough on the minority who don't.

The Information Commissioner has obligations to assess alleged breaches of the DPA. His office may serve information notices requiring data controllers to supply them with the information they need to assess compliance. Where there has been a breach, they can also serve an enforcement notice requiring data controllers to take specified steps (or to stop taking steps) in order to comply with the law. Such notices can be, and often are, appealed to the First-Tier Tribunal (Information Rights), and whilst they are subject to appeal their application is suspended. Therefore, when a notice has been appealed it has no application until either the appeal is withdrawn or the Tribunal has adjudicated on the matter. Once a notice is in force, further contravention will, subject to a defence of reasonable diligence, be an offence. The whole enforcement process is time-consuming and makes significant demands upon the resources of the ICO. This means that, where a business chooses to ignore the requirements of the law, it can be many months before the ICO are in a position to seek a criminal prosecution by the courts. In England, Wales and Northern Ireland, the Commissioner or the Director of Public Prosecutions may institute proceedings. In the case of Scotland, all prosecutions must be brought by the Procurator Fiscal.

If an individual believes that one of the data protection principles (or any other requirements of the DPA) has been breached, and they are unable or unwilling to sort the problem out themselves, they can ask the Information Commissioner to assess whether the requirements of the DPA have been met. The Commissioner will always try to deal with matters informally. However, if the Commissioner's assessment is that the requirements of the DPA have not been met and the matter cannot be settled informally, then his office may decide to take enforcement action against the data controller in question.

If the Commissioner takes enforcement action against a data controller, the controller can appeal to the independent First-Tier Tribunal (Information Rights). However, if the Tribunal agrees with the Commissioner's enforcement action and the data controller continues to break the principles, a criminal offence can result for which the data controller can be prosecuted.

The number of freedom of information complaints received during 2010–11 was 4374; while the ICO received 26,227 individual requests for advice and complaints relating to data protection and the Privacy and Electronic Communications Regulations (ICO, 2011a). Figure 10.1 shows an example.

According to the Information Commissioner's Annual Report and Financial Statements 2010/11 (ICO, 2011a), in 2010-11 there were around 302,000 notifications renewed and over 42,000 new notifications received, which makes a total of 344,000 entries on the public register of data controllers.

Consulting Association

In 2008 the Information Commissioner's Office investigated suspicions that The Consulting Association were operating a covert blacklist of people that were considered to be unsuitable to work in the construction industry, for reasons such as that they were active trade unionists or spoke out about concerns over health and safety.

The ICO's investigation did reveal that the Association were custodians of such a database. Ian Kerr (on behalf of The Consulting Association) was sentenced to a £5,000

Figure 10.1 *The Consulting Association*

On 6 April 2010 new powers came into force enabling the Information Commissioner to impose civil monetary penalties up to a maximum of £500,000 for serious breaches of the data protection principles. One of the first few penalties to be imposed was a penalty of £100,000 on Hertfordshire County Council for two serious incidents where council employees faxed highly sensitive personal information to the wrong recipients. The first incident, involving child sexual abuse, was before the courts, and the second involved details of care proceedings. Another of the first few penalties to be imposed was of £60,000, issued to employment services company A4e for the loss of an unencrypted laptop which contained personal information relating to 24,000 people who had used community legal advice centres in Hull and Leicester (ICO, 2010).

Ealing Council provides an out-of-hours service on behalf of Hounslow Council. In February 2011, the ICO served Ealing Council with a monetary penalty of £80,000 for breaching the DPA by issuing an unencrypted laptop to a member of staff in breach of its own policies. This method of working has been in place for several years and there were insufficient checks that relevant policies were being followed or understood by staff.

The ICO also served Hounslow Council with a monetary penalty of £70,000 because they breached the Act by failing to have a written contract in place with Ealing Council. Hounslow also did not monitor Ealing Council's procedures for operating the service securely.

10.1.2 Freedom of information

The Information Commissioner is also responsible for freedom of information in England, Wales and Northern Ireland, and the general functions of the Commissioner are set out in section 47 of the FOIA. With respect to freedom of information, the Commissioner's duties are to:

- approve or revoke publication schemes, including model schemes
- promote the following of good practice by public authorities
- promote public authorities' compliance with the FOIA and the provisions of the codes of practice made under sections 45 and 46, which relate respectively to dealing with requests for information and desirable practice in connection with the keeping, management and destruction of records
- disseminate information to the public about the operation of the FOIA and give advice about it
- assess whether a public authority is following good practice
- arrange for the dissemination of information about any other matters within the scope of their functions under the FOIA (he may give advice to any person about any of those matters)
- consider complaints about any alleged failure to comply with the Act
- issue decision notices and exercise enforcement powers to ensure compliance
- report annually to Parliament.

As independent referee, the Information Commissioner ensures information is released where it is required under the law. The approach is to be reasonable, responsible and robust, recognizing that greater openness should strengthen, not undermine, effective government.

⇢ Useful resource

Freedom of Information decision notices are published on the website of the Office of the Information Commissioner:

www.ico.gov.uk/tools_and_resources/decision_notices.aspx. A decision notice outlines the Information Commissioner's final assessment as to whether or not a public authority has complied with the Freedom of Information Act 2000, or the Environmental Information Regulations 2004, with regard to specific complaints.

At the same time as issuing a decision notice the ICO informs both parties of their right to appeal to the First-Tier Tribunal (Information Rights). Decisions of the First-Tier Tribunal (Information Rights) can be found at www.informationtribunal.gov.uk/Public/search.aspx .

The Information Commissioner reports to Parliament if there are any instances where a Ministerial veto has been imposed preventing the release of information (as happened in the case of proceedings of a Cabinet Committee considering devolution in Scotland and Wales; and as also happened in the case of the publication of the minutes of key Cabinet meetings held in the run-up to the 2003 war in Iraq).

The Protection of Freedoms Bill (HL 99 [2010–2011]) includes a number of provisions relating to the Information Commissioner:

1 The Information Commissioner will only be able to serve a maximum term of seven years.
2 Certain types of guidance issued by the Information Commissioner will no longer require consent from the Secretary of State for Justice.
3 The provision requiring the Secretary of State to give approval regarding the number of staff appointed to the Information Commissioner's Office, their terms and conditions is to be removed.

10.1.3 Environmental Information Regulations

The Information Commissioner has been given powers to promote and enforce The Environmental Information Regulations 2004. As with the Freedom of Information Act, the role of the Commissioner is to ensure that information is released where it is required under the law.

Regulation 16 of the Environmental Information Regulations 2004 which covers the issuing of a code of practice on the EIR and the functions of the Commissioner says:

16. – (1) The Secretary of State may issue, and may from time to time revise, a code of practice providing guidance to public authorities as to the practice which it would, in the Secretary of State's opinion, be desirable for them to follow in connection with the discharge of their functions under these Regulations.

(2) The code may make different provision for different public authorities.

(3) Before issuing or revising any code under this regulation, the Secretary of State shall consult the Commissioner.

(4) The Secretary of State shall lay before each House of Parliament any code issued or revised under this regulation.

(5) The general functions of the Commissioner under section 47 of the Act and the power of the Commissioner to give a practice recommendation under section 48 of the Act shall apply for the purposes of these Regulations as they apply for the purposes of the Act but with the modifications specified in paragraph (6).

(6) For the purposes of the application of sections 47 and 48 of the Act to these Regulations, any reference to –

(a) a public authority is a reference to a public authority within the meaning of these Regulations;

(b) the requirements or operation of the Act, or functions under the Act, includes a reference to the requirements or operation of these Regulations, or functions under these Regulations; and

(c) a code of practice made under section 45 of the Act includes a reference to a code of practice made under this regulation.

10.2   The Information Commissioner and devolved government

Data protection is a reserved matter. This means that the UK Parliament is responsible for data protection throughout the UK, and the legislation applies in England, Scotland, Northern Ireland and Wales. Freedom of information is not similarly reserved, and it can therefore be devolved to national legislatures. Consequently, the Information Commissioner is responsible for both data protection and freedom of information in England, Wales and Northern Ireland, but in Scotland is only responsible for data protection.

The ICO decided that, in view of the new constitutional arrangements for devolved government, they would establish an office presence in Scotland, Wales and Northern Ireland. Assistant Commissioners for Scotland, Northern Ireland, and Wales were appointed with offices in Belfast, Edinburgh and Cardiff, and this is a recognition that local issues and sensitivities need to be fully understood and integrated into the promotion of good information handling across the UK.

The Assistant Commissioners all report directly to the Information Commissioner. They are responsible for taking forward the Commissioner's work in promoting and enforcing both the DPA and the FOIA. In Scotland, Scottish public authorities are subject to the FOI(S)A, enforced by the Scottish Information Commissioner. The Assistant Commissioner (Scotland) liaises closely with the Scottish Commissioner's office to uphold access to information rights under UK and Scottish legislation.

In England and Wales, proceedings for a criminal offence under the FOIA can be commenced by the Information Commissioner, or by or with the consent of the Director of Public Prosecutions; in Scotland, criminal proceedings will normally be brought by the Procurator Fiscal; whilst in Northern Ireland, proceedings for an offence under the FOIA can be begun by the Information Commissioner, or by or with the consent of the Director of Public Prosecutions for Northern Ireland.

10.3   Scottish Information Commissioner

The FOI(S)A was passed by the Scottish Parliament on 24 April 2002 and received Royal Assent on 28 May 2002. It established the freedom of information regime for devolved Scotland. The FOI(S)A created the post of Scottish Information Commissioner. The Commissioner is appointed by the Queen on the nomination of the Scottish Parliament. Section 43 of the FOI(S)A sets out the Scottish Information Commissioner's general functions. It places a duty on the Commissioner to promote good practice and Scottish public authorities' compliance with the FOI(S)A, their publication schemes and codes of practice. The Scottish Information Commissioner is also obliged, where he considers it expedient, to disseminate information to the public about the operation of the freedom of information regime. The Commissioner can also make 'practice recommendations' specifying what a Scottish public authority should do to comply with the codes of practice, and is required to lay annual reports before the Scottish Parliament.

The key functions of the Scottish Information Commissioner are to:

• promote good practice by Scottish public authorities in relation to the Scottish freedom of information regime
• raise public awareness of the Scottish freedom of information regime
• consider appeals from people seeking the disclosure of information.

The statutory rights under the FOI(S)A and the Scottish Information Commissioner's regulatory powers extend to information contained in historical public records, such as those held by the National Archives of Scotland.

The main role of the Commissioner is to promote observance by public authorities of the Act, by which a person who requests information from a Scottish public authority is entitled to be given it by the authority.

The main task for the Scottish Information Commissioner is to enforce the right to access public information created by the Freedom of Information (Scotland) Act. The Act came into force on 1 January 2005, giving anyone, anywhere in the world, the right to access information held by more than 10,000 public authorities in Scotland.

If one of these authorities refuses a request for information, members of the public have the right to appeal against the decision to the Commissioner. He will then investigate whether the information should or should not be released. The Commissioner has powers to force an authority to release information if he decides that it has acted wrongly in refusing a request.

Alongside the job of enforcing freedom of information the Commissioner is responsible for ensuring that as many people as possible are aware of their right to access information. He and his staff organize and speak at events around Scotland to promote the Act and to raise public awareness.

The Scottish Information Commissioner's Office has a promotion strategy which sets out the Commissioner's proposals to deliver a clear and effective public promotion campaign to raise awareness of the new right to information held by public authorities and how to use it. In addition to a widespread public campaign, the strategy aims to ensure the message is received as widely as possible, particularly by target groups through:

- working with other organizations to communicate the new right to traditionally hard-to-reach groups
- directly promoting the Act to groups most likely to use it.

10.4   Charging for services

The Information Commissioner can charge for certain services, with regard to both their data protection and their freedom of information responsibilities. This is set out in the legislation and the wording used is: 'The Commissioner may charge such sums as he may with the consent of the Secretary of State determine for any services provided by the Commissioner' (DPA, section 51(8)), and a similar form of words is used in the FOIA (s47(4)).

This is also true of the Scottish Information Commissioner, who also has the right to charge for services, as outlined in the FOI(S)A section 43(5), where it states that 'the Commissioner may determine and charge sums for services provided under this section'.

10.5   Further information

Ministry of Justice

102 Petty France, London, SW1H 9AJ
Tel.: 020 3334 3555
Website: www.justice.gov.uk.

Office of the Information Commissioner

Wycliffe House, Water Lane, Wilmslow, Cheshire SK9 5AF
Tel.: 0303 123 1113

Fax: 01625 524 510
Website: www.ico.gov.uk.

JISC Legal Information Service
Learning Services, University of Strathclyde, Alexander Turnbull Building,
155 George Street, Glasgow G1 1RD
Tel.: 0141 548 4939
Fax: 0141 548 4216
Website: www.jisclegal.ac.uk.

Scottish Executive, Freedom of Information Unit
St Andrew's House, Regent Road, Edinburgh EH1 3DG
Tel.: 0131 244 4615
Fax: 0131 244 2582
E-mail: foi@scotland.gsi.gov.uk
Website: www.scotland.gov.uk/About/FOI.

Scottish Information Commissioner
Kinburn Castle, Doubledykes Road, St Andrews, Fife KY16 9DS
Tel.: 01334 464610
Fax: 01334 464611
E-mail: enquiries@itspublicknowledge.info
Website: www.itspublicknowledge.info.

References

ICO (2010) *First Monetary Penalties Served for Serious Data Protection Breaches*, ICO
    press release, 24 November,
    www.ico.gov.uk/news/latest_news/2010.aspx.
ICO (2011a) *Information Commissioner's Annual Report and Financial Statements
    2010/11*, www.ico.gov.uk/about_us/performance/annual_reports.aspx.
ICO (2011b) *ICO Corporate Plan 2011–14*,
    www.ico.gov.uk/about_us/plans_and_priorities/corporate_and_business_plan.
    aspx.

Human rights

Contents

11.1   General principles

The coming into force of the HRA in October 2000 marked the implementation of the European Convention on Human Rights (ECHR) in the UK. In the UK people cannot sue, or be sued by, another individual for breaking the Convention rights. But they may benefit indirectly because the Human Rights Act means that all laws have to be given a meaning and effect which is as close as possible to the Convention rights. Public authorities such as courts and tribunals need to interpret legislation and develop case law in a way which is compatible with the rights set out in the Convention. Since the HRA came into force there have been cases in areas like copyright and data protection where the significance of human rights such as freedom of expression and the right to privacy has been explored. UK courts have to take decisions of the European Court of Human Rights in Strasbourg into account, but are not required to follow them.

The passing of the HRA has been described as one of the biggest constitutional changes to British law for centuries. Most of the rights in the ECHR have been included in the HRA.

The ECHR was established in the aftermath of World War II by the Council of Europe. It guarantees largely civil and political rights rather than social and economic ones. The Council of Europe is quite separate from the European Union. It has its own Court of Human Rights in Strasbourg. Before the implementation of the Human Rights Act people were already able to go to the

Strasbourg court to claim their rights under the ECHR. However the ECHR was not previously part of the UK's domestic law. So our courts were not normally able to deal with claims.

The HRA represents a unique model for implementing the ECHR. It preserves a subtle compromise between incorporating the European Convention rights whilst retaining parliamentary sovereignty. It does this by creating a general requirement that all legislation must be read and given effect in a way which is compatible with the Convention. It also requires all public authorities to act in compliance with the Convention unless prevented from doing so by statute.

The Act does not make the Convention directly enforceable. It does not allow the Convention to override primary legislation, even if there is incompatibility, thus retaining the sovereignty of Parliament. If incompatibility occurs, then the higher courts, on appeal, may issue a 'declaration of incompatibility', which will then be fast tracked to Parliament for amendment.

The HRA does three key things:

1 It makes it unlawful for a public authority, like a government department, local authority or the police, to breach the Convention rights, unless an Act of Parliament means it couldn't have acted differently.
2 It means that cases can be dealt with in a UK court or tribunal. Previously, anyone who felt that their rights under the Convention had been breached had to go to the European Court of Human Rights in Strasbourg.
3 It says that all UK legislation must be given a meaning that fits with the Convention rights, if that's possible. If a court decides that this is not possible it will be up to Parliament to decide what to do.

Particularly relevant to library and information professionals are Articles 8 and 10 of the ECHR (see Figure 11.1). Article 8 on the right to respect for private and family life is relevant in areas such as data protection and breach of confidence; whilst Article 10 on the right to freedom of expression is relevant in areas such as copyright, freedom of information and libel.

It is important to recognize that a number of the rights which are set out in the Convention are not absolute rights, and that restrictions to those rights may be necessary and can be justified in certain circumstances. Article 10 on freedom of expression must always be balanced against Article 8, which protects the right to respect for a person's private and family life.

In May 2005, The Council of Europe's Committee of Ministers adopted a declaration which sets standards for human rights and the rule of law in the information society of mobile phones, the internet and computer communication (Council of Europe, 2005).

Article 8 – Right to respect for private and family life

1. Everyone has the right to respect for his private and family life, his home and his correspondence.

2. There shall be no interference by a public authority with the exercise of this right except such as is in accordance with the law and is necessary in a democratic society in the interests of national security, public safety or the economic well being of the country, for the prevention of disorder or crime, for the protection of health or morals or for the protection of the rights and freedoms of others.

Article 10 – Freedom of expression

1. Everyone has the right to freedom of expression. This right shall include freedom to hold opinions and to receive and impart information and ideas without interference by public authority and regardless of frontiers....

2. The exercise of these freedoms, since it carries with it duties and responsibilities, may be subject to such formalities, conditions, restrictions or penalties as are pre-scribed by law and are necessary, in a democratic society, in the interests of national security, territorial integrity or public safety, for the prevention of disorder, or crime, for the protection of health and morals, for the protection of the reputation or rights of others, for preventing the disclosure of information received in confidence,

---

Figure 11.1 *Articles 8 and 10 of the ECHR*

The declaration represents the first international attempt to draw up a framework on the issue and it brings the principles set out in the ECHR up to date for the cyber-age. It considers how stakeholders such as ISPs, hardware and software manufacturers, governments and civil society can co-operate at both a national and also an international level.

The declaration covers issues such as state and private censorship, protection of private information such as content and traffic data, education to help people evaluate and assess the quality of information, media ethics, the use of information technology for democracy and freedom of assembly in cyberspace.

In 2009 the UK's Equality and Human Rights Commission carried out an inquiry under section 16 of the Equality Act 2006 into human rights. The inquiry assessed how well and effectively human rights are respected and enjoyed in Britain. It demonstrated that 81% of people asked think human rights are important for creating a fairer society, and 84% agree that it is important to have a law that protects human rights in Britain.

11.1.1 Fundamental Rights Agency

A European Union Agency for Fundamental Rights (FRA) was established in 2007. The FRA is an advisory body of the EU. It was created by a legal act of the EU and is based in Vienna, Austria. It helps to ensure that the fundamental rights of people living in the EU are protected. It does this by collecting evidence about the situation of fundamental rights across the European Union and providing advice, based on evidence, about how to improve the situation. The FRA also informs people about their fundamental rights.

The Agency focuses on the situation of fundamental rights in the EU and its 27 Member States. Candidate countries and countries which have concluded a stabilization and association agreement with the EU can also be invited to participate following a special procedure.

The FRA liaises on a regular basis with the Council of Europe in order to ensure that there is no unnecessary duplication between the work of the Agency and that of the Council. Both institutions may at times work on either the same or similar issues. The Agency's data collection and evidence-based analyses may complement the work undertaken by the Council of Europe's monitoring bodies. The Council of Europe remains the major point of reference as regards human rights.

↠ Useful resource

The FRA maintains a case law database, www.fra.europa.eu/fraWebsite/research/case-law/case-law_en.htm, which provides a comprehensive compilation of leading case law on discrimination on grounds of racial and ethnic origin and on grounds of sexual orientation in the EU Member States. It contains 'landmark court decisions' as well as decisions of Special Bodies or similar institutions.

11.2   Online human rights code

A couple of years ago a number of companies – including Google, Microsoft and Yahoo! – promised to 'produce a set of principles guiding company behaviour when faced with laws, regulations and policies that interfere with the achievement of human rights'; in effect to write an online human rights code for internet users. The code has still not been completed, but the initiative consists of three core components:

- Principles on freedom of expression and privacy.
- Implementation guidelines (providing guidance on how participating companies will put the code into practice).
- A governance, accountability and learning framework.

Areas covered by the code are:

- freedom of expression
- privacy

- responsible company decision-making
- multi-stakeholder collaboration
- governance, accountability and transparency.

The code contains a focus on the issue of censorship of internet content, and considers how to address the practice of the jailing of bloggers and political dissidents by governments.

11.3 Guiding principles for library and information professionals

All actions of library and information professionals should take place in a framework where human rights are respected. Directly relevant to the work of librarians is the right to freedom of expression, which includes the freedom to hold opinions and to receive and impart information and ideas without interference by public authorities.

CILIP's *Ethical Principles and Code of Professional Practice for Library and Information Professionals* (2009) state that:

> The conduct of information professionals should be characterized by concern for the public good in all professional matters, including an acknowledgement and respect for diversity within society, and the promoting of equal opportunities and human rights.

This commitment should be demonstrated by information professionals regardless of whether we are referring to the hard copy or the electronic environment. The declaration of the Committee of Ministers (of the Council of Europe) on human rights and the rule of law in the information society (CM(2005)56 final 13 May 2005) states that:

> Freedom of expression, information and communication should be respected in a digital as well as in a non-digital environment, and should not be subject to restrictions other than those provided for in Article 10 of the ECHR, simply because communication is carried in digital form.

11.3.1 Human rights and the information society

Independent experts from around the world met in Geneva in early November 2003 for a preparatory conference ahead of the World Summit on the Information Society in order to discuss fundamental human rights in the information society. A statement on human rights, human dignity and the information society was produced and distributed, calling on governments to protect all human rights related to the information society, ranging from freedom of expression and information to privacy to intellectual property rights, and from bridging the digital divide to good governance (PDHRE, 2003). Paragraphs 22–27 deal with The Public Domain and Intellectual Property Rights:

> Intellectual property regimes and national and international agreements on patents, copyright and trade marks should not prevail over the right to education and knowledge. This right must indeed be exercised through the concept of fair use, that is, use for non-commercial purposes, especially education, and research.   (Para 26)
>
> The information and communication society will not contribute to human development and human rights unless and until access to information is considered a public good to be protected and promoted by the state. Information in the public domain should be easily accessible to support the information society. Intellectual property rights should not be protected as an end in itself, but rather as a means to an end that promotes a rich public domain, shared knowledge, scientific and technical advances, cultural and linguistic diversity and the free flow of information. Public institutions such as libraries and archives, museums, cultural collections and other community-based access points should be strengthened so as to promote the preservation of documentary records and free and equitable access to information.   (Para 27)

Four in five adults (79%) regard internet access as their fundamental right, according to a global poll conducted across 26 countries for BBC World Service (worldpublicopinion.org , 2010).

11.4   Human rights and data protection

Article 8 of the ECHR says that everyone has the right to respect for his private and family life, his home and his correspondence. But the Convention makes clear that this has to be balanced against issues of national security, public safety, the prevention of disorder or crime, and so on. One area where human rights and data protection issues converge is the use of thumbprints in place of library cards (see Figure 11.2).

It is not illegal for an employer to monitor its employees. Such monitoring encompasses their use of the internet and e-mail as well as CCTV monitoring. However, any such monitoring has to be carried out in a way that is consistent with the DPA. It also has to be consistent with the right of each worker (under the ECHR) to respect for their private and family life and correspondence. Broadly speaking, what this means is that, in deciding whether or not to carry out monitoring (and in actually carrying it out) an employer has to balance any potential adverse impact on the workers against the benefits likely to be obtained

School libraries throughout the UK have implemented technology enabling pupils to take out books by scanning their thumb prints instead of using a card. Such systems are intended to replace library cards and save time and money in managing the libraries. However, the use of electronic fingerprinting systems in this way to manage loans of library books has raised a number of privacy concerns.

The Department for Education and Skills and the Information Commissioner said that parents could not prevent schools from taking their children's fingerprints (The Register, 2006).

However, the pressure group Privacy International expressed the view that the practice breached both the DPA and the human rights of the individual children concerned.

The Protection of Freedoms Bill (HL Bill 99 [2010–2011]) envisages parental consent before processing of children's biometric information can be permitted. Under clause 26(4) of the Bill, even if the parent has consented, a school must not process or continue to process the data if the child objects. Where a child does object, they must be provided with a reasonable alternative to the biometric system.

Figure 11.2 *School libraries' use of thumbprints in place of library cards*

from carrying out the monitoring. The extent of the benefit has to justify any relevant adverse impact. So, the greater the potential adverse impact on workers for a particular type of monitoring, the more an employer has to do to justify carrying out that monitoring in the first place.

Over the years there have been a number of calls for a global data protection law. On 19 September 2005, Out-law.com published an article that reported that privacy chiefs from 40 countries had called upon the United Nations to prepare a legally binding instrument which clearly sets out the rights to data protection and privacy as enforceable human rights (Out-law.com, 2005). More recently, in March 2010, European leaders called for a worldwide agreement on data protection to address the data security weaknesses of cloud computing (Computer Weekly, 2010).

Thirteen privacy agencies around the world joined forces in September 2010 to launch the Global Privacy Enforcement Network (www.privacyenforcement.net), which is designed to facilitate cross-border co-operation in the enforcement of privacy laws.

11.5   Human rights and breach of confidence

The HRA has had a significant impact on the English law of confidentiality. When deciding whether information is confidential or not, the courts have to take into account the right to respect for private and family life under Article 8 of the ECHR. However, they have to balance this with the importance of freedom of expression under Article 10, particularly where it is the media that is trying to exercise this freedom. Freedom of the media is very important in a democratic society and this is recognized by both the ECHR and the HRA.

11.6   Human rights and copyright

Article 27 of the Universal Declaration of Human Rights 1948 says:

(1) Everyone has the right freely to participate in the cultural life of the community, to enjoy the arts and to share in scientific advancement and its benefits.
(2) Everyone has the right to the protection of the moral and material interests resulting from any scientific, literary or artistic production of which he is the author.

This Article demonstrates the difficulty of trying to balance the competing interests of the various stakeholders in copyright law.

On the one hand there is the need to respect the IPRs of others, including their right to deploy technical protection measures; whilst on the other hand, there is the fundamental right to freedom of expression and free flow of information, access to knowledge and education, and the promotion of scientific research and development.

The information society has brought with it a dramatic increase in the possibilities for people to create, view, use and reuse copyrighted materials online. As a result copyright is no longer the preserve of a few creators and publishers. In the wake of user-generated content, copyright is now an area of law which affects everyone who actively participates in the information society. Blogging software such as Blogger, WordPress or Typepad, and microblogging sites such as Twitter or Facebook, are worthy of note as they have opened up the possibility for everyone to become a publisher, enabling them to exercise their freedom of expression, and widening the possibilities for democratic participation.

An interesting legal case, which explored the boundaries between human rights legislation and copyright law, was Ashdown v. Telegraph Group Ltd (see below).

Ashdown v. Telegraph Group Ltd [2001] EWCA Civ 1142 (18 July 2001)

Background: Paddy (now Lord) Ashdown, the former leader of the Liberal Democrats, made a confidential record of a meeting held at 10 Downing Street on 21 October 1997 concerning plans for formal co-operation between the Labour Party and the Liberal Democrats. When Lord Ashdown was standing down from leadership of the Liberal Democrats it became known that he was considering publishing the diaries that he had been keeping of his life and political career. At this time he showed some material to representatives of various newspapers and publishers in strictest confidence. On 28 November 1999, *The Sunday Telegraph* published three separate items based on the minutes of that meeting. Indeed, roughly a fifth of the minutes was reproduced verbatim. *The Sunday Telegraph* revealed that Tony Blair had offered to replace two members of his Cabinet with Liberal Democrat MPs, less than six months after the 1997 election. Lord Ashdown sued the newspaper for breach of confidence and copyright infringement.

Outcome: It was found that, in rare circumstances, the situation could arise where the right of freedom of expression in the HRA came into conflict with the protection in the CDPA, despite the Act's express exceptions.

The court was obliged to apply the Act so as to give effect to the right of freedom of expression in Article 10 of the ECHR, which required the court to look closely at the facts of individual cases.

The Court of Appeal dismissed the appeal of the Telegraph Group Ltd against the decision of Sir Andrew Morrit, Vice Chancellor, in that it infringed the copyright of Lord Ashdown by publishing substantial extracts from his political diaries in *The Sunday Telegraph* on 28 November 1999. Lord Phillips said that restriction of the right of freedom of expression in Article 10 of the ECHR could be justified where necessary in a democratic society in order to protect copyright. However, copyright did not normally prevent the publication of information conveyed by a literary work. It was only the freedom to express information using the verbal formula devised by another that was prevented by copyright. That would not normally constitute a significant encroachment on the freedom of expression.

If a newspaper considered it necessary to copy the exact words created by another, there was no reason in principle why the newspaper should not indemnify the author for any loss caused to him, or account to him for any profit made as a result of copying his work. Freedom of expression should not normally carry with it the right to make free use of another's work.

The Telegraph Group's use of Lord Ashdown's work was done to further their own commercial interests; and one could not argue that the right to freedom of expression as set out in Article 10 of the ECHR permitted them to profit from the

11.7 Human rights and freedom of expression

The case of von Hannover v. Germany explored the issues relating to freedom of expression (Article 10) and the need to balance this with the right to privacy (Article 8). This is summarized below.

Von Hannover v. Germany (ECHR judgment 24 June 2004)

Background: Princess Caroline of Monaco does not hold any official position, although she does sometimes attend public events on behalf of her family. The Federal Constitutional Court in Germany refused to restrain the further publication of photographs which showed Princess Caroline in a variety of public places on the

> basis that there was a legitimate public interest in how a 'public figure par excellance' behaved generally in public. The Princess applied to the European Court of Human Rights on the ground that the decision of the German court infringed her right to respect for her private and family life under Article 8 of the Convention. Under German law she had protection for her privacy if she was in a 'secluded place' but the way that this was defined was too narrow to give her any assistance. Photographs that the Princess complained about showed her going about activities such as shopping, skiing, playing tennis or riding a horse.
>
> The court made a distinction between reporting facts which are capable of contributing to a public or political debate which is of general interest, and reporting the details of the private life of an individual who does not exercise official functions.
>
> Outcome: The ECHR considered the need to balance the competing interests of the freedom of expression guaranteed by Article 10 with the right of privacy in Article 8 of the Convention, and they decided that there had been a violation of Princess Caroline's right to privacy under article 8 of the ECHR.

The Parliamentary Assembly of the Council of Europe issued a recommendation (1950 [2011]) stating that the free exercise of journalism is enshrined in the right to freedom of expression and information, which is guaranteed by Article 10 of the ECHR (ETS No. 5) ('the Convention'). This right constitutes the foundation of a democratic society and an indispensable requirement for its progress and the development of every individual.

11.8   Further information

BBC News (2008) Tech Giants in Human Rights Deal, 28 October,
    http://news.bbc.co.uk/1/hi/7696356.stm.
Darkreading.com (2008) Google, Microsoft, Yahoo! & Others Nearing
    Completion of Online Human Rights Code, 20 August,
    www.darkreading.com/document.asp?doc_id=162064.
Global network initiative:
    www.globalnetworkinitiative.org.
Out-law News (2008) Tech Giants Near Agreement on Human Rights Code, 20
    August,
    www.out-law.com/page-9362.
Yahoo.com, Google, Microsoft, Yahoo! & Others Nearing Completion of Online
    Human Rights Code: document is designed to set IT standards for users'
    rights to privacy, freedom of speech,
    http://ycorpblog.com/files/yahoocodeletter.pdf.

References

CILIP (2009) *Ethical Principles and Code of Professional Practice for Library and Information Professionals*,
www.cilip.org.uk/get-involved/policy/ethics/pages/principles.aspx.

Computer Weekly (2010) Could Security Weaknesses Prompt Call for Global Data Protection Law? 26 March,
www.computerweekly.com/Articles/2010/03/26/240731/Cloud-security-weaknesses-prompt-call-for-global-data-protection.htm.

Council of Europe (2005) Declaration of the Council of Ministers on human rights and the rule of law in the information society, 56 final, 13 May.

Out-law News (2005) Global Data Protection Law Needed, Say Regulators, 19 September,
www.out-law.com/page-6132.

PDHRE (2003) Statement on Human Rights, Human Dignity and the Information Society, International Symposium on the Information Society, Human Dignity and Human Rights, Palais des Nations, Geneva, 3-4 November 2003,
www.pdhre.org/wsis/statement.doc.

The Register (2006) Schools Can Fingerprint Children Without Parental Consent, 7 September,
www.theregister.co.uk/2006/09/07/kiddyprinting_allowed.

worldpublicopinion.org (2010) *Four in Five Regard Internet Access as a Fundamental Right: Global Poll*,
www.worldpublicopinion.org/pipa/articles/btjusticehuman_rightsra/661.php.

CHAPTER 12

The reuse of public sector information

Contents

12.1   General principles

Public data that is reused (whether for free or for a fee) generates an estimated market turnover of at least 27 billion EUR in the EU every year, according to a study by Mark Dekkers et al. for the European Commission, *Measuring European Public Sector Information Resources* (Dekkers et al, 2006). In 2000, a report by PIRA entitled *Commercial Exploitation of Europe's Public Sector Information: final report* (PIRA, 2000) estimated the size of the European information industry to be 68 billion EUR whereas, by way of contrast, the United States' information industry is approximately five times that size. The European Commission and other commentators attribute this to the fact that in the United States Federal Government information is not subject to copyright, and therefore most information, certainly at Federal Government level, can be reused with virtually no restrictions. The European Commission judged that there is enormous scope for growth in this area, especially in terms of developing pan-European products and services.

This led to the European Directive on the Re-Use of Public Sector Information (2003/98/EC) which was implemented in the United Kingdom through The Re-use of Public Sector Information Regulations 2005: SI 2005/1515. These regulations came into force on 1 July 2005 and established a framework for making reuse easier and more transparent.

The UK government recognizes the importance of public sector information and its social and economic value beyond the purpose for which it was originally created. The public sector therefore needs to ensure that simple licensing processes are in place to enable and encourage civil society, social entrepreneurs and the private sector to reuse this information (see the UK Government Licensing Framework (The National Archives, 2011)) in order to:

- promote creative and innovative activities, which will deliver social and economic benefits for the UK
- make government more transparent and open in its activities, ensuring that the public are better informed about the work of the government and the public sector
- enable more civic and democratic engagement through social enterprise and voluntary and community activities.

The main obligations under the Re-Use of Public Sector Information Regulations 2005 are:

- public sector documents that are available for reuse should be readily identifiable
- documents should generally be available for reuse at marginal cost
- public sector bodies should deal with applications to reuse information in a timely, open and transparent manner
- the process should be fair, consistent and non-discriminatory
- the sharing of best practice should be encouraged across the public sector.

The scheme to help make the reuse of public sector information both easy and transparent is overseen by The National Archives. The key elements of the scheme are shown in Figure 12.1.

- **Licence terms:** public sector bodies have an obligation to publish licence terms whether in the form of a standard licence or a copyright notice on the material.
- **Details of charges:** where applicable these must be published and must be fair and consistent.
- **Responses to be within set time limits:** the time limit is 20 working days in line with FOIA.
- **Asset lists:** an obligation on public sector bodies to produce a list of material, both published and unpublished, which is available for reuse.
- **Robust complaints procedures:** public sector bodies are required to publish details of their complaints process. In addition, APPSI considers complaints about non-

---

Figure 12.1 *Main elements of the scheme for reusing public sector information*

The scope of the Re-Use of Public Sector Information Regulations 2005 differs from the freedom of information regime. Whilst both FOIA and the Re-Use Regulations relate to the public sector, nevertheless the range of public sector bodies covered by the two regimes does differ. This isn't surprising if one bears in mind that the RPSI regulations implement a European directive; whereas the FOIA was initiated by the Westminster Parliament.

The Regulations cover most of the public sector including:

- central government, including government trading funds and executive agencies
- local government
- the health service
- Parliament.

There are, however, some notable exemptions:

- public sector broadcasters, such as the BBC
- educational and research establishments, including universities
- cultural organizations, such as museums, libraries and archives.

The directive is regularly reviewed by the European Commission. An online consultation on the existing directive was undertaken in the autumn of 2010, and the review of the directive is one of the key actions of the 'Digital Agenda for Europe'. The Commission has considered whether or not these organizations should continue to be exempt from the directive.

The FOIA is all about *access* to information. The Re-Use Regulations go beyond access by dealing with the *reuse* of that information, for example, by publishing and making the information available to a wider audience. A key point to note is that any information that is exempt under the FOIA is not available for reuse.

Even before Member States of the European Union were required to implement the directive on reuse of public sector information, the United Kingdom already had in place a number of practical measures to make reuse of information easier. Much of this results from initiatives launched by The National Archives (an executive agency of the Ministry of Justice). These initiatives are:

1 The Click-Use Licence, which was replaced in September 2010 by the Open Government Licence (12.1.1).
2 The Information Asset Register (12.1.2), which provides detailed information on what material is available for reuse.
3 The Information Fair Trader Scheme (12.1.3), which sets out a framework for the verification of public sector bodies' licensing and information trading activities.

12.1.1 UK Open Government Licence (which replaces the Click-Use Licence)

On 30 September 2010, The National Archives launched the first UK Open Government Licence, making it faster and easier than ever before to freely reuse public sector information. It is a key element of the government's commitment to greater transparency. Key features are shown in Figure 12.2.

The data must have been expressly made available under the Open Government Licence. The licence is:

- worldwide
- royalty free
- perpetual
- non-exclusive.

It lets you:

- copy, publish, distribute or transmit the information
- adapt the information
- exploit the information commercially.

What you must do:

- acknowledge the source of the information by including any attribution statement specified by the Information Provider and where possible provide a link to this licence.

What you must not do:

- use the information in any way that suggests any official status or that the Information Provider endorses your use of the information
- mislead others or misrepresent the information or its source
- use the information in a way which would breach the DPA or The Privacy & Electronic Communications (EC Directive) Regulations 2003.

The terms of the licence have been aligned to be interoperable with:

- any Creative Commons Attribution Licence which covers copyright
- Open Data Commons Attribution Licence, which covers database rights and applicable copyright.

This licence does not cover the use of:

- personal data in the information
- information that has neither been published nor disclosed under information access legislation (including the Freedom of Information Acts for the UK and Scotland) by or with the consent of the Information Provider
- departmental or public sector organization logos, crests and the Royal Arms except where they form an integral part of a document or dataset
- military insignia

Figure 12.2 *Key features of the Open Government Licence*

- third party rights the Information Provider is not authorized to license
- information subject to other intellectual property rights, including patents, trade marks, and design rights

Figure 12.2 *Continued*

This licence removes the existing barriers to reusing information – it is simple, streamlined and a single set of terms and conditions provides assurance to anyone wishing to use or license government information at a glance. The licence is completely flexible and works in parallel with other internationally recognized licensing models such as Creative Commons.

The licence is applicable across the entire public sector both in terms of geography – because its coverage includes Scotland, Wales and Northern Ireland – as well as by type of public body, whether central government department, local authority or another public body that wishes to make their data more accessible to taxpayers.

The Open Government Licence replaced the Click-Use Licence and enables free reuse of a much broader range of public sector information, including Crown Copyright, databases and source codes. In addition, the licence does not require users to register or formally apply for permission to reuse data, unlike the old Click-Use Licence.

To support the UK Open Government Licence, The National Archives has developed the UK Government Licensing Framework, covering a wide spectrum of official information including copyrighted images and text, data, software and source codes for both commercial and non-commercial purposes.

The Open Government Licence is available in machine-readable format on The National Archives' website: www.nationalarchives.gov.uk/doc/open-government-licence. It provides a single set of terms and conditions for anyone wishing to use or license government information and removes some of the existing barriers to reuse.

Check whether the content is governed by the Open Government Licence. Developers and entrepreneurs wishing to use content covered by the licence in order to create new websites and applications will no longer need to register or formally apply for permission to reuse the data. The licence covers a broad range of public sector information, including Crown Copyright, databases and source codes and can be used across the entire public sector.

12.1.2 Information Asset Register

Government departments have information asset registers. These are a key part of the government's agenda for freeing up access to official information. The IAR lists information resources held by the UK government, concentrating on unpublished resources. In doing so it enables users to identify, from one single source, the information held in a wide variety of government departments, agencies and other organizations. HMSO previously had a central site known as 'Inforoute' which acted as a portal to the range of government information asset registers available, but at the time of writing the Inforoute website (www.hmso.gov.uk/inforoute/) no longer appears to be active.

The IAR aims to cover the vast quantities of information held by all government departments and agencies. This includes databases, old sets of files, recent electronic files, collections of statistics, research, and so on. The IAR concentrates on information resources that have not yet been, or will not be, formally published.

Individual departments have primary responsibility for putting in place their own IARs, which they maintain on their own websites. The National Archives has overall responsibility for IAR formats.

12.1.3 Information Fair Trader Scheme

The Information Fair Trader Scheme sets and assesses standards for public sector bodies. It requires them to encourage the reuse of information and to reach a standard of both fairness and transparency.

There are two levels to the scheme:

1 Full IFTS accreditation, which is The National Archives' gold standard accreditation scheme. It involves an on-site verification and is aimed at major information traders who wish to meet a very high standard of compliance with IFTS principles and the Re-use of Public Sector Information Regulations 2005.
2 IFTS Online assessment, which is an online assessment tool aimed at all public sector bodies who wish to demonstrate basic compliance with IFTS principles and the Re-Use of Public Sector Information Regulations 2005.

In 2003–4 it was estimated that the turnover of the larger public sector information holders (PSIHs) was in the region of £1 billion. The total value of public sector information in the UK economy is much higher than other European countries as the information is often reused as inputs for other products which may be supplied by the PSIHs themselves or by private companies. Examples of PSIHs include HM Land Registry, which holds a property database with access to 20 million registered properties in England and Wales, and the UK Hydrographic Office which holds navigational products and related information.

As well as making much information freely available, some PSIHs sell on information either in its raw data form or as 'value-added' information products involving further refinement of the raw data. Some PSIHs compete with private sector companies in the sale of value-added information. These competing companies have to buy the raw data on which their value-added products are based from the PSIH.

In December 2006, the Office of Fair Trading (OFT) published a market study into *The Commercial Use of Public Information* (OFT, 2006) to check whether public sector information holders were providing information to users fairly and reasonably. Many public bodies have a statutory obligation to collect information or do so as part of carrying out their functions. Often they may be the only body collecting and storing such information.

The study looked at whether or not the way in which PSIHs supply information works well for businesses. It examined whether PSIHs have an unfair advantage selling on information in competition with companies who are reliant on the PSIH for that raw data in the first place. To address this question the study looked at:

- how the raw data that PSIHs collect is turned into value-added information
- how pricing of raw data and access to it affects competition between PSIHs and private companies selling value-added information
- what situations benefit from vertical integration in the provision of value-added information
- the effectiveness of existing guidance and laws.

The study considered a number of areas relating to public bodies:

- the nature of the body
- the nature and scope of the public sector information held by the body
- the definition of the body's 'public task' (i.e. the work that it exists as a public body to do)
- whether the body exploits its public sector information by selling it, and if so how it does so, including pricing
- the body's financial arrangements, including publicity about costs and income
- the body's own commercial activities using its public sector information, and whether and to what extent these are in competition with the private sector.

OFT's study was not restricted to public authorities already covered by the Regulations, but it also looked at a range of other public bodies holding data.

In 2002 there were challenges to Companies House and to Ordnance Survey. The OFT had received complaints alleging that Companies House was abusing its dominant position by subsidizing prices for its products, and thereby unfairly taking business from its competitors. In October 2002, the OFT published a decision of the Director General of Fair Trading about Companies House, the Registrar for Companies for England and Wales. This concluded that there was no evidence that Companies House cross-subsidized its commercial activities (Companies House Direct and WebCHeck), and that it had not infringed the prohibition imposed on it by section 18 of the Competition Act 1998 by cross-subsidizing so as to allow it to engage in predatory pricing, or impose a margin squeeze on its competitors.

Meanwhile, in February 2002, Gettmapping plc, a provider of aerial digital colour imagery and the UK's largest independent aerial mapping company, commenced legal proceedings in the High Court against Ordnance Survey, the government-owned cartographic business. They sought an injunction to restrain Ordnance Survey from breaching section 18 of the Competition Act 1998 and from breaching its obligations under the written Resellers Agreement between the two parties which was dated September 2000.

12.2 Advisory Panel on Public Sector Information (APPSI)

There is an Advisory Panel on Public Sector Information (APPSI) which was formed in April 2003. The panel has three key roles:

1 To advise Ministers on how to encourage and create opportunities in the information industry for greater re-use of public sector information.
2 To advise the Director of the Office of Public Sector Information and Controller of Her Majesty's Stationery Office (HMSO) about changes and opportunities in the information industry, so that the licensing of Crown Copyright and public sector information is aligned with current and emerging developments.
3 To review and consider complaints under the Re-Use of Public Sector Information Regulations 2005 and advise on the impact of the complaints procedures under those regulations.

APPSI is charged with advising ministers strategically on how to open up opportunities for greater reuse of government information by the private and voluntary sectors of the economy, and advising the Controller of HMSO about changes and opportunities in the information industry.

12.3 Right to data

The Coalition: our programme for government (Cabinet Office, 2010) said: 'We will create a new "right to data" so that government-held datasets can be requested and used by the public, and then published on a regular basis'.

As part of that commitment, the Cabinet Office asked all government departments to develop a plan to give access to datasets on request, and to identify key datasets that they will proactively disclose.

In February 2011 the government published 'The Protection of Freedoms Bill' and clause 100 of the Bill relates to the 'Release and publication of datasets held by public authorities'.

The Coalition: our programme for government (Section 3: Civil Liberties and Section 16: Government Transparency) states that the Government will: 'extend the scope of the Freedom of Information Act to provide greater transparency'; 'create a new "right to data" so that government-held datasets can be requested and used by the public, and then published on a regular basis'; and 'ensure that all data published by public bodies is published in an open and standardized format, so that it can be used easily and with minimal cost by third parties'.

12.4   Public Data Corporation

The coalition government also announced their intention to set up a Public Data Corporation, which aims to free up public data and drive innovation as well as support the government's growth agenda. The Public Data Corporation will be governed by a consistent set of principles around data collection, maintenance, production and charging.

The 2006 OFT study on the commercial use of public information estimated that the then current value of PSI to the UK economy was approximately £590 million and that this could double to generate around £1.1 billion per year (OFT, 2006). This was because the existing situation was characterized by a failure to exploit PSI, distortion of competition, and unduly high prices.

The intention is for the Corporation to release 'high value' 'core reference data for free re-use'. This is seen by some as a revolutionary step towards the recommendations of the so-called 'Cambridge Study' on economic models for the provision of public sector information by trading funds (Pollock, 2008).

A Cabinet Office press release from January 2011 (Cabinet Office, 2011) says that:

A Public Data Corporation will bring benefits in three areas:

- Firstly and most importantly it will allow us to make data freely available, and where charging for data is appropriate to do so on a consistent basis. It will be a centre where developers, businesses and members of the public can access data and use it to develop internet applications, inform their business decisions or identify ways to run public services more efficiently. Some of this work is already taking place but there is huge potential to do more.
- Secondly, it will be a centre of excellence where expertise in collecting,

managing, storing and distributing data can be brought together. This will enable substantial operational synergies.

- Thirdly, it can be a vehicle which will attract private investment.

Source: Cabinet Office (2011).

The press release also sets out examples of the benefits that the Public Data Corporation could provide:

- a more consistent approach towards access to and accessibility of public sector information;
- make more data free at the point of use, where this is appropriate and consistent with ensuring value for taxpayers' money. This would create more opportunities for citizens, social enterprises and businesses to use public sector data in new and innovative ways;
- create a centre of excellence for collecting, holding and managing public data, driving further efficiencies and improving productivity across the public sector;
- identifying how data Government already holds can be used more effectively to provide better and cheaper public services; and
- create more certainty and predictability – encouraging businesses to invest in and develop new and innovative products and applications based on data. It will also provide opportunities for private investment in the Corporation.

Source: Cabinet Office (2011).

In 2011 The Public Data Corporation Project Team issued a set of Consultation Questions (http://pdcengagement.cabinetoffice.gov.uk/pdc/):

- Which public sector datasets do you currently make use of?
- How easy is it to find out what datasets are held by public sector organizations?
- How do you, or would you, decide whether a dataset has value for you or for your organization?
- Which datasets are of most value to you or your organization? Why?
- What methods of access to datasets would most benefit you or your organization?
- What gets in the way of you or your organization accessing datasets or data products?
- What are the most exciting applications of datasets or data products you are aware of – here or internationally?
- Are there any datasets or products you'd like to see generated? How would you or your organization use them, and what social or economic benefits do you think they would deliver?

- From your perspective, what would success look like for the Public Data Corporation?
- Have we got the name for this organization right? Do you have any suggestions on naming that might better convey our aims?

The philosophy behind making datasets of raw public sector information readily available in formats which make it as easy as possible for them to be reused is that people will then be able to add value to that data designing all manner of ingenious and innovative applications and that this process will be worth many millions of pounds to the economy, far more than the amount that the government would be able to make from selling licences to reuse that data. Tim Berners Lee said: 'the thing people are amazed about with the web is that, when you put something online, you don't know who is going to use it – but it does get used' (Crabtree and Chatfield, 2010).

This can be achieved through mashups – websites or applications that make use of content from several sources in order to create a completely new service. They are possible as a result of simple Application Programming Interfaces (APIs). For example, if raw data on bicycle accidents is combined with mapping data, people could then look up their journey's start and end points to see if there are any accident hotspots they need to be aware of.

12.5   Further information

12.5.1 Organizations

Advisory Panel on Public Sector Information (APPSI)
Information Policy and Services Directorate
The National Archives, Kew, Richmond, Surrey TW9 4DU
Tel.: 0208 392 5330 x2252
E-mail: secretariat@appsi.gsi.gov.uk
Website: www.appsi.gov.uk.

National Archives
Kew, Richmond, Surrey TW9 4DU
E-mail: opsilicensing@cabinet-office.x.gsi.gov.uk
Website: www.nationalarchives.gov.uk.

12.5.2 Publications

Cabinet Office (2010) *The Programme for Government*,
www.cabinetoffice.gov.uk/sites/default/files/resources/coalition_
programme_for_government.pdf.

OPSI (2004) *Information Fair Trader Scheme*, 21p,
  www.nationalarchives.gov.uk/information-management/ifts.htm.
OPSI (2005) *The Re-Use Of Public Sector Information: a guide to the regulations and
  best practice*, 34p.
OPSI (2005) *Procedures for Investigating Complaints Arising under the Re-Use of Public
  Sector Information Regulations*.
*Regulatory Impact Assessment: regulations implementing in England, Wales, Scotland and
  Northern Ireland a directive of the European Parliament and of the Council on the re-
  use of public sector information*, December 2004, HMSO.
*Summary of Responses to the Consultation Document on Implementation of European
  Directive on the Re-Use of Public Sector Information*, DTI/HMSO, 2004.
UK Government Licensing Framework, www.nationalarchives.gov.uk/
  information-management/uk-gov-licensing-framework.htm.
Uhlir, P. F. (2004) *Policy Guidelines for the Development and Promotion of
  Governmental Public Domain Information*, UNESCO.

References

Cabinet Office (2010) *The Coalition: our programme for government*,
  www.cabinetoffice.gov.uk/sites/default/files/resources/coalition_
  programme_for_government.pdf.
Cabinet Office (2011) Public Data Corporation to Free up Public Data and
  Drive Innovation, Cabinet Office press notice, 12th January 2011,
  www.cabinetoffice.gov.uk/news/public-data-corporation-free-public-
  data-and-drive-innovation.
Crabtree, J. and Chatfield, T. (2010) Mash the State, *Prospect*, February, 42-6.
Dekkers, M. et al (2006) *Measuring European Public Sector Information Resources*,
  European Commission,
  http://ec.europa.eu/information_society/policy/psi/docs/pdfs/mepsir/
  final_report.pdf.
The National Archives (2011)UK Government Licensing Framework, July 2011,
  www.nationalarchives.gov.uk/documents/information-management/
  uk-government-licensing-framework.pdf.
OFT (2006) Commercial Use of Public Information, Office of Fair Trading,
  December 2006, Annexe G, Economic value and detriment analysis,
  www.oft.gov.uk/OFTwork/publications/publication-categories/
  reports/consumer-protection/oft861.
PIRA (2000), *Commercial Exploitation of Europe's Public Sector Information: final report*,
  www.epsiplus.net/psi_library/reports/commercial_exploitation_of_europe_
  s_public_sector_information_pira_study).
Pollock, R. (2008) Models of Public Sector Information Provision via Trading
  Funds, www.berr.gov.uk/files/file45136.pdf.

CHAPTER 13

Defamation

Contents

13.1   Introduction

Defamation law attempts to strike a balance between society's interest in freedom of speech and the individual's interest in maintaining their reputation. It is relevant to information professionals, whether they be responsible for intranets, extranets, publicly available websites or online databases; users of their organization's internet e-mail system; members of internet e-mail discussion groups; or authors of books or articles in their own right.

13.2   General principles

English law distinguishes between libel (written) and slander (spoken). An item is defamatory if one of the following tests is satisfied:

1 The matter complained of tends to lower the plaintiff in the estimation of society.
2 It tends to bring them into hatred, ridicule, contempt, dislike or disesteem in society.
3 It tends to make them shunned, avoided or cut off from society.

In Scottish law, libel and slander are virtually indistinguishable with regard to both the nature of the wrongs and their consequences. The terminology of Scottish defamation law differs from that of English law. Where individual English litigants enjoy absolute privilege for what they say in court, their Scottish counterparts have only qualified privilege. 'Exemplary', or 'punitive', damages are not awarded by the Scottish courts. According to D.M. Walker: 'Absolute privilege protects all statements made in judicial proceedings, whatever the rank of the court or the position of the person sued, so long as it is not a gratuitous observation' (Walker, 1988). However, Walker confirms that, in Scotland, a party only has qualified privilege in his pleadings. This also extends to tribunals if the procedures are similar in essence to a court.

13.3 Slander

Slander is oral defamation – the use of the spoken word to injure another person's reputation. To be the basis of a legal action, a publication of the words complained of must demonstrably have taken place – that is, they must have been uttered within the hearing of a third party. It should be noted that the Scottish position is different, as Scots law does not require that a defamatory statement be communicated to third parties before it is actionable. Among statements considered slanderous per se are those that:

- impute the commission of a felony, such as calling someone a murderer
- impute an individual to be suffering from a communicable disease, such as leprosy
- are injurious to an individual in their trade or profession – for example, saying that an accountant fiddles the figures.

The party charged with the slander may hold, as a defence, that the words spoken were in fact true, inasmuch as true statements result in no injury to reputation. Defining slanderous language is sometimes difficult. The disputed words themselves need not be slanderous but may hold a hidden meaning, or innuendo, that the hearer understands, and that may therefore result in damage to the reputation of the slandered party. A defendant in a slander action cannot claim as a defence that another party had made the slanderous statement and that they were merely repeating the statement; nor can the defendant claim that they gave the name of the informant and expressed no opinion as to the truth. In some cases, words that would otherwise be considered actionable, or subject to laws of slander, may be uttered as a privileged communication. Privileged communications are words uttered for a purpose or in a context which is protected by law. Words uttered with qualified privilege for example, when giving an oral reference, are protected as long as the speaker is not motivated by malice. Words uttered with absolute privilege – for example, in Parliament – can never be slander.

McManus v. Beckham (2003)

Background: On 26 March 2001, Victoria Beckham visited a memorabilia and autograph business (GT's Recollections) owned by the McManus family based in the Bluewater Shopping Centre in Kent. On seeing a signed photograph of David Beckham in a display cabinet at the entrance, Mrs Beckham said that the signature that they were selling was not that of her husband. She did so in front of other customers, proclaiming loudly that the store was ripping off customers by selling the autograph.

The shop owners said this had damaged their reputation and sued Mrs Beckham for slander and malicious falsehood.

Outcome: Victoria Beckham paid £155,000 in damages and costs (consisting of £55,000 in damages and £100,000 in legal costs). She issued a statement apologizing for the hurt and damage her comments caused to the shop's owners; and she also donated several items of merchandise, which had been signed by David Beckham.

13.4 Libel

Defamation published in permanent form (such as writing, printing, drawings, photographs, radio and television broadcasts) is known as libel. You libel someone if you publish a defamatory statement about them, which you cannot defend. 'Published' in the legal sense means communicated to a person other than the plaintiff. So, for example, if a manuscript is sent to a publisher it would be deemed to have been published in the legal sense. A 'defamatory statement' is one that damages a person's reputation. For example, it is defamatory to say that someone has committed a criminal offence.

The courts will evaluate matters from the perspective of the ordinary person, so a statement would not be regarded as defamatory unless it would make ordinary readers think worse of the person concerned. An ordinary person,[1] in this context would be someone with the following characteristics:

- not naïve
- not unduly suspicious
- able to read between the lines
- capable of reading in an implication more readily than a lawyer
- capable of indulging in a certain amount of loose thinking
- not avid for scandal.

You can libel individuals, companies, partnerships and businesses. You cannot libel the dead and you cannot libel local authorities or other government bodies, although you can libel the individuals employed by those organizations. It is possible to libel someone even if you do not name them. Only people who are identified by the offending material can sue, but it is important to bear in mind that you might be identifying someone inadvertently. If, for example, there is only one 27-year-old male librarian living in a particular village, then describing him as such could identify him whether you name him or not. Small groups may also be identifiable and all its members may be able to sue. For example, if you were to write that 'one of the members of the ethics committee has been convicted of murder', and the ethics committee only consisted of five people, this casts suspicion on all five people as it could be referring to any of them. As such the statement would be actionable.

In an action for damages for libel, the plaintiff is required to establish that the matter they complain of:

- has been published by the defendant (publication)
- refers to the plaintiff (identification)
- is defamatory (defamatory words or gestures).

If the plaintiff does this, they establish a prima facie case – that is, they provide sufficient evidence for proof of the case. However, the defendant could still escape liability if they can show they had a good defence.

13.5   Defences to libel

The defences to a libel action are:

- justification (veritas in Scotland – see Section 13.5.1) – being able to prove that what you wrote was substantially true
- honest comment – showing it was an honest expression of opinion
- privilege – special protection to which the law determines that certain kinds of report are entitled
- offer to make amends (ss2–4 of the Defamation Act 1996).

13.5.1 Justification/veritas

The law of defamation exists to protect individuals who suffer damage to their reputation. It follows, therefore, that the law does not protect the reputation that a person does not possess. If you can prove that what you have written is true both in substance and in fact, then you have a defence against an action for damages. The key point is that you have to be able to prove that what you have written is true. Ultimately, it is not what you know or believe that matters, but rather whether your evidence will stand up in court, to the satisfaction of the jury. So if you will be relying on witness evidence:

1 Make sure your witnesses are likely to be available at trial. Relying solely on written statements from overseas witnesses will have far less impact in front of a jury.
2 Do not rely on witnesses who have spoken to you only off the record.
3 Only rely on witnesses who
  • are credible
  • are independent
  • have first-hand knowledge of what they are telling you.

It is important to keep safely any supporting documentation such as a notebook, tapes or documents, which might be used in evidence, because you might have to produce this material in court.

Like justification, the defence of veritas in Scotland is a complete defence. It is governed by section 5 of the Defamation Act 1952.

13.5.2 Honest comment (previously known as fair comment)

The defence of honest comment provides for the right of freedom of speech for individuals. For the defence to succeed, you must show that:

• the comment was made honestly and in good faith, based on true facts or on privileged material, as opposed to being inspired by malice
• it was on a matter of public interest
• if the claimant alleges malice, that you were not motivated by malice.

The distinction between the defences of justification and honest comment is that justification/veritas protects the publication of facts whereas honest comment protects the expression of opinion. In some cases it can be particularly difficult to distinguish between whether a statement is fact or opinion. If you can prove a statement, it is a fact. If you are drawing an inference from the facts, or if there are at least two possible views on the matter, then it is an opinion.

The Supreme Court case of Spiller and another v. Joseph and others [2010] UKSC 53 looked at the defence of fair comment. The judge said that the defence should be renamed from 'fair comment' to 'honest comment' (paragraph 117) and felt that the whole area merited consideration by the Law Commission or an expert committee (paragraph 117).

13.5.3 Privilege

Privilege affords a defence for certain types of report whether or not they are true. Many of these are specified by statute, and include fair and accurate reports of court proceedings, Parliamentary proceedings, reports in Hansard, public inquiries and international organizations; also a range of public meetings and the findings of governing bodies and associations.

'Absolute privilege' means that the statement can in no circumstances be the subject of libel proceedings. It covers contemporary, fair and accurate reports of court proceedings, communications within the government, and communications between solicitor and client about legal cases. Proceedings in Parliament are similarly protected, because the courts refuse jurisdiction over Parliamentary affairs.

'Qualified privilege' is available where the defendant acts without malice – that is, acts for the reasons for which the privilege exists, and not principally to harm the plaintiff. It applies generally to all communications that the defendant has a legal or moral duty to make, or makes, in protecting his or her own legitimate interests. Such a defence is wide-ranging and includes reports on most public proceedings and references on employees.

13.5.3.1 Qualified privilege for general media reports

Reynolds v. Times Newspapers Limited [1999] UKHL 453 was a case that arose as a result of a newspaper article that implied that Albert Reynolds, the former prime minister of Eire, had lied. In its judgment (28 October 1999) the House of Lords developed the common law defence of qualified privilege to general media reports on matters of public interest. The defence applies when the circumstances are such that a 'duty to publish' and a 'right to know' test is satisfied. Lord Nicholls set out ten factors to be taken into account (the tests have an emphasis on responsible journalism):

1   The seriousness of the allegation. The more serious the charge, the more the public is misinformed, and the individual harmed, if the allegation is not true.
2   The nature of the information, and the extent to which the subject matter is a matter of public concern.
3   The source of the information. Some informants have no direct knowledge of the events. Some have their own axes to grind, or are being paid for their stories.
4   The steps taken to verify the information.
5   The status of the information. The allegation may have already been the subject of an investigation which commands respect.
6   The urgency of the matter. News is often a perishable commodity.
7   Whether comment was sought from the plaintiff. He may have information that others do not possess or have not disclosed. An approach to the plaintiff will not always be necessary.
8   Whether the article contained the gist of the plaintiff's side of the story.

9   The tone of the article. A newspaper can raise queries or call for an investigation. It need not adopt allegations as statements of fact.
10   The circumstances of the publication, including the timing.

13.5.4 The offer to make amends

The procedure for the offer to make amends is set out in sections 2–4 of the Defamation Act 1996. The defendant must make an offer in writing to publish a suitable correction and apology and to pay damages and costs. When an offer of amends is made, a claimant must decide whether to accept or reject it. If they accept it, no further proceedings can be taken, except to decide disputes over apologies and the amount of any compensation payable. If they reject it, then the defendant may rely on the offer as a defence to an action of defamation where the maker did not know nor had reason to believe that the statement complained of referred to the pursuer and was false and defamatory.

It is no defence to libel to say that you were just reporting what someone else said. Therefore you cannot avoid liability by the use of words such as 'alleged' or 'claimed'. Nor is it a defence to show that someone has published the allegations before. Newspapers and magazines are liable for the contents of whatever they publish, including material not written by them such as readers' letters and advertisements.

It isn't sufficient for newspapers and magazines to ensure that the articles they publish are libelproof. They also have to pay careful attention to headlines and picture captions, because these can be a lucrative source of damages. In the case of picture captions, the words and the pictures should match.

13.6   Remedies

The remedies available are a civil action for damages, the awarding of costs, an injunction (known as interdict in Scotland) to prevent repetition, or a criminal prosecution to punish the wrongdoer by means of a fine or imprisonment. It is far more common for cases of libel to result in a civil action for damages or an injunction/interdict to prevent repetition.

13.6.1 Civil action for damages

Damages can be colossal, even though the Court of Appeal can now reduce libel awards. The main aim of a libel claim is in order to compensate the plaintiff for the injury to their reputation. A jury can give additional sums either as 'aggravated' damages, if it appears a defendant has behaved malevolently or spitefully, or as 'exemplary' or 'punitive' damages where a defendant hopes the economic advantages of publication will outweigh any sum awarded. Damages can also be nominal if the libel complained of is trivial (see Walker, 1981, on Delict, as awards are assessed on very different principles in Scotland from England).

Malice is irrelevant in awards for damages, although the award may be mitigated where it is shown that there was no malice involved in the defamatory statement. There is also a principle in Scots law that provocation may mitigate.

However, under the ECHR, damages must be necessary and there are controls on excess – as seen in Tolstoy v. UK (1995) 20 EHRR 442(13 July 1995).

13.6.2 Costs

Costs go up all the time. If you were to lose a libel case, then you would have to pay the claimant's expenses as well as your own, which would be likely to add at least a six-figure sum to the bill for damages. Indeed, in many of the high-profile libel cases of the past decade, the costs have often exceeded the damages.

13.6.3 An injunction/interdict to prevent repetition

Any individual or organization can seek an injunction either to stop initial publication of an article or to prevent any further publication. Injunctions/interdicts may be granted, temporarily and for a short while, *ex parte*, meaning that only the claimant is represented before the judge. If both parties appear before the judge, the defendant would have to argue on grounds of public interest or, for potential libels, be ready to declare on affidavit that they could justify the story.

Injunctions/interdicts against any publication bind all other publications that are aware of the injunction. To breach an injunction is a severe contempt of court that could lead to an offender's imprisonment.

13.6.4 Criminal prosecution to punish the wrongdoer by fine or imprisonment

Criminal prosecutions for libel were rare. There have been a number of changes in recent years which have removed criminal libel offences from the statute book. Section 79 of the Criminal Justice and Immigration Act 2008 abolished the common law offences of blasphemy and blasphemous libel; while section 73 of the Coroners and Justice Act 2009 abolished the common law offences of seditious libel, obscene libel and defamatory libel.

Section 8 of the Defamation Act 1996 introduced a summary procedure under which a judge may dismiss a plaintiff's claim if it has no realistic prospect of success, or give judgment for the claimant and grant summary relief, which means ordering the defendant to publish a suitable correction and apology and pay damages.

13.7 Defamation and the internet

The Law Commission has investigated the application of libel laws to the internet (Law Commission, 2002). In February 2002 they sent out a questionnaire to a number of interested parties, including online publishers, ISPs, barristers and solicitors. The responses highlighted four areas of concern:

- the liability of internet service providers for other people's material (13.7.1)
- the application of the limitation period to online archives 13.7.2)
- the exposure of internet publishers to liability in other jurisdictions (13.7.3)
- the risk of prosecution for contempt of court (13.7.4).

13.7.1 The liability of internet service providers for other people's material

ISPs offer services such as website hosting and newsgroups where they do not exert editorial control over the material. Where a defamatory statement appears on a website, the ISP is considered to be a 'secondary publisher' – they are involved in disseminating the defamatory statement even though they are not the author, editor or commercial publisher. They can be held liable if they exercise discretion over how long material is stored or if they have the power to remove the material.

Under section 1(1) of the Defamation Act 1996, an innocent disseminator such as a printer, distributor, broadcaster or ISP who is considered by the law to be a secondary publisher has a defence if they:

- were not the author, editor or publisher of the statement complained of
- took reasonable care in relation to its publication
- did not know, and had no reason to believe, that what they did caused or contributed to the publication of a defamatory statement.

The section builds upon the common law defence of 'innocent dissemination'. It does not apply to the author, editor or publisher of a defamatory statement but is intended for distributors. It is of particular relevance to ISPs. However, as soon as a secondary publisher such as an ISP has been told that something on a newsgroup or a web page is defamatory, if they do not promptly take down the disputed content they cannot use the section 1(1) defence.

ISPs are seen as tactical targets and regularly receive complaints that material on websites and newsgroups is defamatory. In such instances, the safest option for them is to remove the material immediately, even if it appears to be true; and often they remove not just the page in question but the entire website, even though this seems at odds with freedom of speech.

In view of the amount of e-mail messages, newsgroup postings or web pages that are uploaded daily, it is doubtful whether it would be practical for ISPs to pre-screen all content; and even if it were possible, whether they could do so in a cost-effective manner. It is, however, more reasonable for ISPs to undertake post-screening. If an ISP is told that material is defamatory, they should act promptly and responsibly by:

- removing the defamatory statements once they have been notified
- posting a retraction
- making a reasonable effort to track down the originator of the defamatory remarks in order to prevent future postings.

Failure to do so would suggest that the ISP had not acted responsibly and that they should be held accountable for the consequences. ISPs are well placed to block or remove obscene, illegal, infringing or defamatory content.

In their response to the Law Commission consultation process, the industry made three criticisms of the current position:

1 Receiving and reacting to defamation complaints was 'costly and burdensome'.
2 The industry felt uncomfortable about censoring material that may not in fact be libellous.
3 It was suggested that customers might be attracted to US ISPs, who had greater protection against being held liable for defamation, and who could therefore offer their customers more attractive terms.

ISPs should certainly take complaints seriously. In order to protect themselves, they should obtain warranties and indemnities from content providers, and post notices such as acceptable use policies on their services.

The Electronic Commerce (EC Directive) Regulations 2002: SI 2002/2013 implement the Electronic Commerce Directive 2000/31/EC.[2] The Regulations provide that intermediaries such as ISPs and telecommunications carriers are not liable for damages or criminal sanctions for unlawful material provided by third parties where the intermediary:

- is a mere conduit (the intermediary does not initiate the transmission, does not select the receiver of the transmission, and does not modify the information it contains)
- simply caches the information as part of automatic, intermediate, temporary storage, without modifying it

- simply hosts the information (such as a newsgroup or website) so long as the intermediary:
  — does not have actual knowledge or awareness of the unlawful activity
  — upon obtaining such knowledge or awareness acts expeditiously to remove or disable access.

Godfrey v. Demon Internet Ltd [2001] QB 201

This case concerns a posting to a newsgroup which was distributed to Usenet subscribers. An unnamed USA resident posted a contribution on another ISP purporting to come from Laurence Godfrey, which the judge described as 'squalid, obscene and defamatory'. When Dr Godfrey heard of the posting, he informed Demon Internet that the posting was a forgery and asked them to remove it from their Usenet server. They failed to do so and the posting was left on the site for a further ten days until it was automatically removed. Demon Internet argued that they had a purely passive role similar to that of a telephone company. However, it was held that as the defendants had chosen whether to store the material and for how long they could not be said to have played only a passive role.

Following the decision in Godfrey v. Demon Internet [2001] QB 201, ISPs are often seen as tactical targets. They are regularly put on notice of defamatory material and they find themselves facing a difficult choice – whether to surrender in the face of a claim which may be without merit, or continue to publish on the basis of indemnities and assurances from primary publishers that the material, although defamatory, is not libellous.

The defence of innocent dissemination also applies to booksellers, libraries and newsagents. The case of Weldon v. Times Book Co Ltd [1911] 28 TLR 143 indicates that while a library is not expected to review the contents of every book it possesses, some works may call for a more searching examination, taking account of the type of book in question, the reputation of the author, and the standing of the publisher.

The Law Commission (2002) report on defamation and the internet quotes from a response to their consultation on aspects of defamation procedure by the Booksellers Association of Great Britain and Ireland, which says that the provisions of section 1 of the Defamation Act 1996 […]

have encouraged plaintiffs or prospective plaintiffs with dubious claims who are unwilling to commence proceedings against the author or publisher of the allegedly defamatory publications to take or threaten action against booksellers to force them to remove such publications from their shelves. As those plaintiffs and their legal advisers clearly realize, booksellers are not in a position to put forward a substantive defence of justification because they have no direct knowledge of the subject matter of the alleged libel.

Bookshop Libel Fund

Two independent bookshops – Housmans Bookshop and Bookmarks Bookshop – faced potentially ruinous legal proceedings for stocking the anti-fascist magazine *Searchlight*; and the Bookshop Libel Fund was originally set up in 1996 to support small shops such as these who were caught up in libel cases.

The case is relevant here because of the innocent disseminator defence in section 1(1) of the Defamation Act 1996.

The case was first brought in 1996 and six years later the bookshops had to relaunch their appeal for funds as the case was still continuing. British law allows anyone who claims they have been libelled to sue any shop, distributor or library handling the allegedly libellous publication, as well as or instead of suing the author, editor and publisher. Housmans and Bookmarks fought the case with a defence of 'innocent dissemination' in effect arguing that it is impossible for bookshops, particularly small independents, to check – and take responsibility for – the content of the thousands of publications in stock at any one time. They felt it was important to try to take a stand, otherwise there might be no end to this sort of 'legal intimidation'.

The litigant had been referred to as a plagiarist in one sentence in a 136-page pamphlet stocked in the shop. He had chosen to sue only the shop, not the author or publisher concerned.

Although he had at one stage demanded that the shop pay him £50,000 to drop the case, the jury awarded him just £14. Because he had already rejected a settlement offer higher than that, he was also ordered to pay most of the shop's legal costs; however, it was not anticipated that he has the resources to do so.

Where tactical targeting of this kind does occur, it is open to secondary publishers to protect themselves by seeking indemnities from the primary publisher. The primary publisher could also apply to be joined in the action as a defendant in order to provide the necessary evidence for a defence of justification.

In March 2011, the Ministry of Justice published a *Draft Defamation Bill Consultation* on reforming the defamation legislation. The consultation paper contains a draft defamation Bill. The Ministry of Justice are proposing that measures could be taken to change the law to provide greater protection against liability to ISPs and other secondary publishers (which in an offline context could include booksellers or libraries), especially with regard to online publishers who are responsible for 'hosting' third-party content. Whilst this isn't included in the draft Bill, it is nevertheless included in the consultation paper. The consultation paper seeks evidence on the problems that are currently faced and suggestions as to how the law could best be clarified so that appropriate provisions could be included in the substantive Defamation Bill.

13.7.2 The application of the limitation period to online archives

The Defamation Act 1996 reduced the limitation period for defamation actions from three years to one year, although courts have discretion to extend that period. However, the application of this limitation to online archives has proved to be extremely contentious. For, while the limitation period is one year, in the case of Loutchansky v. Times Newspapers Limited [2001] EWCA Civ 1805, the Court of Appeal held that this limitation period commenced every time someone accessed a defamatory internet page. In other words every 'hit' on an online article could be regarded as a fresh publication of that article. The judgment means that a piece put on the internet five years ago could still be the subject of legal action today so long as the relevant pages are accessible. The effect of this is that the limitation period is potentially indefinite.

Similarly, in the Scottish case of Her Majesty's Advocate v. William Frederick Ian Beggs (High Court of Justiciary, 2001) the judge ruled that information held on the internet archives of newspapers was published anew each time someone accessed it. This potentially lays newspaper publishers and editors open to charges of contempt of court unless they remove material relating to the previous convictions and other relevant background material of anyone facing criminal proceedings (see Section 13.7.4). The judge did not take the same view of the paper archives held by public libraries, and this distinction takes into account the ease with which material on the internet can be accessed.

One also has to bear in mind the way in which certain search engines and websites automatically cache and/or archive the content of a vast number of websites, thus making web pages available even after the site owner has removed the content from their website.

A number of people have suggested that we should adopt the US single publication rule in which the limitation period starts running on the date of the first publication of the defamatory article, even if it continued to be sold or 'webcast' for months or years afterwards. This matter is of direct relevance to library and information professionals, who make regular use of online archives in order to carry out their research and enquiry roles, and for whom any reduction in the availability of online archives would hamper their work. The Law Commission's report *Defamation and the Internet: a preliminary investigation* (2002) says that 'online archives have a social utility and it would not be desirable to hinder their development'.

In the *Draft Defamation Bill Consultation* (www.justice.gov.uk/downloads/consultations/draft-defamation-bill-consultation.pdf), the Ministry of Justice said: 'We do not believe that the current position where each communication of defamatory matter is a separate publication giving rise to a separate cause of action is suitable for the modern internet age.' (paragraph 72, page 30).

Clause 6 of the draft Bill contained in the consultation paper makes provision for a single publication rule. As a result, if enacted, claimants would be prevented from bringing an action in relation to publication of the same material by the same publisher after a one-year limitation period from the date of the first publication of that material to the public or a section of the public has passed. If the claimant had not brought an action within that one-year period the court would have discretion to allow him or her to bring an action at a later date in respect of that article. However, the claimant would still be allowed to bring a new claim if the original material was republished by a new publisher, or if the manner of publication was otherwise materially different from the first publication.

13.7.3 Exposure of internet publishers to liability in other jurisdictions

England's libel laws are regarded as being 'plaintiff-friendly'. British courts, for example, do not have the First Amendment protections to consider and apply that United States courts do.[3] The nightmare scenario for online and internet publishers is for potential litigants to be able to undertake 'foreign shopping' or 'forum shopping', whereby they can launch an action in a country of their choosing, where the defamation laws are the most stringent. Foreign individuals or companies may, for that reason, be particularly interested in pursuing a British-based publication.

If pursued by overseas claimants, British publications face tricky issues in mounting a defence because subpoenaing foreign witnesses is impossible, although there is a procedure for taking written evidence abroad through foreign courts. Even if the claimant is not particularly well known here, the compensation that could be awarded for damage suffered elsewhere in the world can still be substantial.

In Dow Jones v. Gutnick, the Australian High Court justified their position, in part, by reference to the International Covenant on Civil and Political Rights (1966), which provides, among other things, that everyone shall be protected from 'unlawful attacks on his honour and reputation'. However, the covenant also provides that everyone shall have the right to:

- hold opinions without interference
- to freedom of expression; this right shall include freedom to seek, receive and impart information and ideas of all kinds, regardless of frontiers, either orally,

Dow Jones v. Gutnick [2002] HCA 56

In the Australian case Dow Jones & Company Inc v Gutnick [2002] HCA 56, the Australian High Court agreed that a person in Victoria was entitled to bring an action for defamation in Victoria in respect of the publication on the internet of an article in Barron's magazine in October 2000 about the tax affairs of Joseph Gutnick even though the article was uploaded to the web by Dow Jones in America.

The court said potential litigants needed to consider practical issues, such as whether they had assets or reputations in the jurisdiction where the material was published. Otherwise, the court would rule that it was not the appropriate place to hear the case. In Australia, the tort of defamation depends on publication and therefore the fundamental question to be decided was to determine the place of publication of the alleged damaging article. However, the High Court clearly distinguished between jurisdiction and applicable law. It was said that a court may have jurisdiction but it may equally be bound by the applicable rules of a foreign jurisdiction.

In 2004, following out-of-court mediation, lawyers acting on behalf of the publishers Dow Jones & Co issued a statement in Victoria Supreme Court and also agreed to pay Gutnick US$137,500 (180,000 Australian dollars) and a further US$306,000 (AUS$400,000) to cover his legal costs.

in writing or in print, in the form of art, or through any other media of his choice.

As an article in *The Australian* (2002) points out, the Gutnick decision would seem to put all of this in peril. There have been cases in the USA which have taken the opposite view to the Gutnick decision, but of course US libel law is not as plaintiff-friendly as is the case in the UK.

Traditional publishers are able to restrict sales of their publications by geography, but internet publishers do not seem to have that option. By choosing to publish on the internet they are in theory subjecting themselves to the laws of every nation from which the internet can be accessed. The court dismissed Dow Jones' contention that it would have to consider the defamation laws from 'Afghanistan to Zimbabwe' in every article published on the internet. 'In all except the most unusual of cases, identifying the person about whom material is to be published will readily identify the defamation law to which that person may resort,' the court said (paragraph 54, www.austlii.edu.au/au/cases/cth/HCA/2002/56.html). Online publishers are concerned that by publishing content on the internet they have to contend with a significant burden of legal risk. What they want are greater levels of certainty and clarity over which laws should be applied to them and their intermediaries. These publishers might feel it necessary to turn to technology for a solution. They might, for example, seek out the development of software that could let sites identify where visitors come from and then block them if they are deemed to expose the publishers to a high risk of potential lawsuits.

In an unprecedented move, the reporter who wrote the piece to which Joe Gutnick objected, responded by filing a writ at the United Nations Human Rights Commission, claiming that he was denied the right of free speech and that Australia is in breach of Article 19 of the United Nations International Covenant on Civil and Political Rights (*The Sydney Morning Herald*, 2003).

On 15 November 2004, Dow Jones settled the case, agreeing to pay Mr Gutnick about US$440,000 in fees and damages.

Some people argue that the UK should follow the US example and exempt ISPs from liability for material published. However, the Law Commission found that this would not prevent legal action against UK-based ISPs in foreign courts. An international treaty would be required in order to solve the problem of unlimited global risks.

The Ministry of Justice consultation paper on reforming the defamation legislation, which was published in March 2011, includes proposals to take action to address libel tourism by ensuring that a court will not accept jurisdiction, unless satisfied that England and Wales is clearly the most appropriate place to bring an action against someone who is not domiciled in the UK or an EU Member State.

13.7.4 The risk of prosecution for contempt of court

Material is held to be in contempt of court if it poses a substantial risk of serious prejudice to the administration of justice. Serious prejudice is likely to arise from publication of the following matters:

- a defendant's previous convictions
- details of a defendant's bad character
- suggestions that a witness's (particularly a defendant's) testimony is likely to be unreliable
- details of evidence that is likely to be contested at trial.

The law of contempt does not stop you writing about a case; it simply places certain limits on what you may say. For the purposes of contempt, criminal proceedings become active from the time of arrest or charge, or from the time a warrant for arrest is issued, and civil proceedings are active from the time arrangements are made for trial. The closer the case is to trial, the greater the risk of prejudice.

The rulings in Loutchansky v. Times Newspapers Limited [2001] EWCA Civ 1805 and Her Majesty's Advocate v. William Frederick Ian Beggs, High Court of Judiciary (2001) (see Section 13.7.2) that a web page is published each time a user accesses that page, in effect means that the limitation period is indefinite. The UK does not have the single publication rule that applies in the USA. Consequently, online publishers are concerned over the risk of being held to be in contempt of court because their websites and online archives may well contain records of a defendant's previous convictions or acquittals, which jurors could research during a trial. In order to eliminate those risks, newspapers would either have to monitor every criminal case throughout the country and to remove any offending material from their online archive for cases that were active – which would be impractical – or they could opt for the more cost-effective option of taking down the online archives of their publications in their entirety, which would clearly be to the detriment of historians and researchers.

The Ministry of Justice's *Draft Defamation Bill Consultation* (March 2011) acknowledges that at present publishers are potentially liable for any defamatory material published by them and accessed via their online archive, however long after the initial publication the material is accessed, and whether or not proceedings have already been brought in relation to the initial publication. Indeed, the consultation paper goes further and says that 'this is also the case with offline archive material (for example a library archive)'.

13.7.5 Social networking sites

Social networking and microblogging websites such as Facebook or Twitter, as well as weblogs, have completely changed the way in which content is 'published'. The means of publishing information are now effectively available to many millions of people. Anyone who is able to access the internet and participate in activities such as social networking or blogging can be viewed as a publisher. As a result there has been an exponential increase in the number of people who lay themselves open to the possibility of being sued for publishing a defamatory statement.

In the case of Twitter, for example, users of the service post 'Tweets' consisting of no more than 140 characters. Such online postings are unlikely to be subjected to the level of editorial checking and scrutiny that is characteristic of members of the editorial staff at newspaper publishers. The ease and speed with which people can publish content online can lead them to rush to make an online posting before thinking through the potential consequences of their actions.

There are a number of examples of people having to pay damages for something they published on a social networking site. They include:

1 Matthew Firsht was awarded damages of £22,000 following a successful claim of invasion of privacy and defamation on the social networking website Facebook. Grant Raphael, a former friend of Mr Firsht, was found to have set up a Facebook profile in Mr Firsht's name, which contained false details about his personal life.

2 A Welsh councillor was ordered to pay damages of £3,000 for a claim he posted on Twitter about a political rival.

3 In an out-of-court settlement, musician and actress Courtney Love agreed to pay US$430,000 dollars to settle a lawsuit over a series of Tweets in which she was alleged to have made a number of defamatory statements about the fashion designer Dawn Simorangkir.

The Press Complaints Commission ruled in February 2011 that information posted on Twitter should be considered public and publishable by newspapers. In addition, the Press Complaints Commission have said that they are intending to regulate reporter and newspaper Twitter feeds.

The best advice is to think very carefully before you publish items to the web, however short they may be. If they contain critical comments about an individual, ask yourself how you would feel if someone had made the same comments about you!

13.7.6 E-mail libel

The use of e-mail is fraught with danger. The informal nature of the internet increases the likelihood that people will make defamatory statements in e-mails, on discussion groups or in chat rooms. These defamatory statements can reach the far corners of the world in a matter of seconds, whether through e-mails being directed to a large number of recipients, or through the forwarding or copying of e-mail correspondence that typically happens.

It is extremely easy and indeed quite common for people to send e-mail to unintended recipients. Some discussion groups, for example, have as a default setting that when you reply to a message from an individual, the response goes to all members of the group. Many times has the author seen people apologizing for sending out a rather candid e-mail to an entire discussion group, when they had only intended to send the message to one person. Another common mistake is that of including the wrong file attachment in a message. The user may have published an item, which they had never intended to publish, and thereby perpetrated an accidental defamation. Similarly, it is all too easy to forward a long e-mail without reading the whole message. If the end of the e-mail contains a defamatory statement, the act of forwarding the e-mail would mean that the user had unwittingly repeated the defamatory statement and could be held liable for their actions.

Make use of e-mail disclaimers, as this can limit legal liability. The use of e-mail disclaimers is becoming more common. Whilst the disclaimer may be of dubious legal validity in the absence of any contractual relationship between the sender and the recipient, the sender will be in a better position if the unintended recipient has notice of the potentially confidential nature of the e-mail and is advised what to do with it. Therefore disclaimers may help to limit certain legal liability, but they will not of themselves be a defence to an action for defamation.

Norwich Union v. Western Provident Association

In 1997, Western Provident started an action against Norwich Union, a rival private healthcare insurance provider, when it was discovered that Norwich Union were circulating messages on their internal e-mail system which contained damaging and untrue rumours about their competitor to the effect that they were in financial difficulties and being investigated by the DTI. Western Provident sued for libel and slander. Norwich Union publicly apologized to Western Provident and paid £450,000 in compensation for damages and costs.

The Norwich Union case showed that the courts are willing to step in to order employers to preserve the evidence. The High Court in an interlocutory hearing ordered Norwich Union to preserve all the offending messages and to hand over hard copies of them to its rival. The fact that e-mail creates a discoverable document means that employees should be aware that apparently deleted e-mail may be held on the system for some time or be accessible from back-ups.

If an employee makes a defamatory statement using their company's internal e-mail system, or posts a defamatory comment on the company intranet, then it is possible for a legal action to be brought against the organization as employer by way of 'vicarious liability' for acts of their employees.

It is important for employers to issue guidelines such as an e-mail and internet policy with the employee's contract of employment, prohibiting defamatory statements so as to be able to prove that employees or other categories of e-mail, intranet and extranet users have acted contrary to guidelines. It is also good practice to have employees click on an 'I accept' button of the e-mail and internet policy before they are able to gain access to the computer system. You need to ensure that users are aware of such guidelines by making them accessible from the intranet home page and elsewhere, as appropriate. However, such action is not a guarantee of immunity from legal actions.

13.8   Checklist

In order to minimize the legal risk of being held liable for a defamatory statement it is worth considering the following points:

1 Does your organization have a guide to acceptable use of e-mail, the intranet, and the internet?
2 Does this mention anything about offensive, defamatory or derogatory material?
3 Is this covered in the staff handbook?
4 Is the policy mentioned as part of the induction process?
5 Emphasize disciplinary action for breaches of e-mail and internet policy.
6 Treat e-mails with the same care that you would show when composing a letter or a fax.
7 Educate and train employees as to the legal implications of sending messages which may be read by tens of thousands of users, and on the acceptable use of internet/e-mail.
8 Bear in mind that there is likely to be a back-up of the correspondence.
9 Use a disclaimer on e-mail correspondence.
10 Consider insurance cover for liability in defamation.

References

The Australian (2002) High Court Throws a Spanner in the Global Networks, *The Australian*, 11 December.

Independent (2003) 'Posh Spice' Pays £155,000 to Settle Autograph Dispute, 12 March.

Law Commission (2002) *Defamation and the Internet: a preliminary investigation*, Scoping Study no. 2, December, www.justice.gov.uk/lawcommission/docs/Defamation_and_the_Internet_Scoping.pdf.

Mirror (2003) £155,000: what Beckham's autograph will cost his wife in court loss, 12 March.

The Sydney Morning Herald (2003) Australian Laws Challenged at UN, 18 April, www.smh.com.au/articles/2003/04/18/1050172745955.html.

Walker, D. M. (1981) *The Law of Delict in Scotland*, 2nd rev. edn, W. Green.

Walker, D.M.(1988) *Principles of Scottish Private Law*, vol. 2, 4th edn, 637–8.

Notes

1 See Skuse v. Granada Television Ltd [1996] EMLR 278 and Gillick v. British Broadcasting Corporation [1996] EMLR 267.
2 EC directive 2000/31/EC of 8 June 2000 on certain legal aspects of information society services, in particular electronic commerce, in the Internal Market, Official Journal L178/1, 17 June 2000.
3 The first amendment of the US constitution says that Congress shall make no law respecting an establishment of religion, or prohibiting the free

exercise thereof; or abridging the freedom of speech, or of the press; or the right of the people peaceably to assemble, and to petition the government for a redress of grievances.

CHAPTER 14

Professional liability

Contents

14.1 General principles

This chapter considers professional liability from the perspective of library and information professionals. Although there hasn't been an instance of a UK librarian being successfully sued for negligence, that is no reason to become complacent.

Liability means having legal responsibility for one's acts, errors or omissions. It is the duty of care that one individual or organization owes to another, and it gives rise to the risk of being sued for damages if the individual or organization fails in that duty. A librarian owes the user of an information service (the client) a duty to exercise reasonable care; and this duty of care basically means that s/he should do the things that a prudent person would do in the circumstances and refrain from those things which they would not do.

Whilst there is no UK legislation which deals specifically with liability for information provision, librarians do need to be aware of the potential risk of facing a professional liability claim because they could potentially be held liable for their work either under contract law or the law of tort/delict.

Any organization whose professional employees provide advice, expertise, information or a consultancy service may be legally liable for a claim of malpractice where a breach of professional duty occurs. If you work for an employer, your employer is vicariously liable for the torts/delicts of their employees, if they are committed in the course of employment. This only applies if the act was of the type that the employee might have been expected to carry out as part of their normal duties. The employer is likely to have insurance cover against any actions brought against the company – although it is well worth checking that this is the case. Self-employed information consultants and brokers should consider taking out professional indemnity insurance (see Section 14.7).

Even if you work for an employer, there are potential dangers involved in assuming that your firm's professional indemnity insurance will protect you if liability is established, as the case of Merrett v. Babb demonstrates.

Merrett v. Babb [2001] EWCA Civ 214 (15 February 2001)

In this case the Court of Appeal held that a surveyor employed by a firm of valuers who negligently prepared a mortgage valuation report for a lender owed a duty of care to the purchasers who relied on the surveyor's report when buying the property, and that the surveyor was personally liable for the purchasers' loss. Permission to appeal was refused.

In the mortgage valuation report prepared by Mr Babb on the property that Miss Merrett was about to purchase it was noted that the property contained certain cracks but the report failed to point out that settlement had taken place. Miss Merrett said that the property was worth £14,500 less than the valuation and she sued Babb in his personal capacity.

The surveyor was employed as branch manager of a firm of surveyors and valuers from February 1992 to January 1993. On 1 June 1992 he signed the relevant mortgage valuation report. A bankruptcy order was made against the sole principal of the firm on 30 August 1994. The principal's trustee in bankruptcy cancelled the firm's professional indemnity insurance without run off cover in September 1994. The purchasers therefore brought an action in negligence against the surveyor personally rather than against the firm. The surveyor was not insured.

The implications of this case are that professional employees may be open to claims for negligent advice in situations where their firm has become insolvent or is otherwise under-insured. The case shows that there may be instances where individuals might need to take out personal insurance even after their employment

Taking the general principles of liability into account, it is necessary to consider how they relate to the information professional. You are expected to use reasonable skill and care when providing library and information services, and the key issue to establish is what is meant by 'reasonable'. 'Reasonable' would mean that which an information professional would be expected to do in the circumstances. 'Reasonable' constitutes good professional practice, and could be established by testimony from other information professionals acting as expert witnesses.

If you are called upon to be an expert witness, you will need to take great care with the evidence you give – the Supreme Court has removed the immunity that used to protect expert witnesses from being sued over the evidence that they give to courts (see the ruling in Jones v. Kaney [2011] UKSC 13). The Court took the view that where claims were made against expert witnesses on the grounds of them failing in their professional duty they should be open to suits for negligence.

The components of good practice include professional knowledge, core competencies and professional values. There are a number of documents that try to encapsulate some of these values.

⊷ Useful resources

- The American Association of Law Libraries Competencies of Law Librarianship:
  www.aallnet.org/main-menu/Publications/spectrum/Archives/Vol-5/pub_sp0106/pub-sp0106-comp.pdf.
- CILIP's Body of Professional Knowledge:
  www.cilip.org.uk/jobs-careers/qualifications/accreditation/bpk/pages/default.aspx.
- The Special Library Association's Competencies for Information Professionals of the 21st century:
  www.sla.org/content/learn/members/competencies/index.cfm.

And there are a number of sets of standards and guidelines including:

- CILIP guidelines for colleges:
  www.facetpublishing.co.uk/title.php?id=551-3.
- DCMS Public Library Service Standards 2007 (although these have now been abolished):
  www.culture.gov.uk/reference_library/publications/3662.aspx.

The American Library Association has a set of *Core Values of Librarianship* (2004) which define, inform and guide professional practice. These cover topics such as:

- access
- confidentiality/privacy
- democracy
- diversity
- education and lifelong learning

- intellectual freedom
- the public good
- preservation
- professionalism
- service
- social responsibility.

Only when we can say what a quality product or service consists of can we be clear about what wouldn't be a quality service; and therefore be able to speak of liability for low-quality work. Is the service performed to the standard of an average professional? Ultimately your own reputation with colleagues and clients is the best guide.

Information professionals should seek to do their job with due care and attention. Did they fail to search an appropriate source and thereby miss something vital? Did they try to verify the accuracy of the information? Information professionals should also act ethically. Indeed, they have a set of ethical principles and code of professional practice to follow (CILIP, 2009).

The CILIP *Ethical Principles* set out a number of personal responsibilities of information professionals, which include that they should:

1 Strive to attain the highest personal standard of professional knowledge and competence.
2 Ensure they are competent in those branches of professional practice in which qualifications and/or experience entitle them to engage by keeping abreast of developments in their areas of expertise.
3 Claim expertise in areas of library and information work or in other disciplines only where their skills and knowledge are adequate.

According to the CILIP leaflet *Working for Yourself* (2002): 'As yet there is no record of a library or information professional being sued on the grounds that their work caused loss or damage to their client.' However, this should not lure people into a false sense of security. It begs the question of whether you want to be the first information professional in the UK to be sued because your advice caused a client loss or damage.

It may seem hard to think of a situation where provision of information could lead to a client suffering loss or damage, but information professionals need to think about the nature of the information they are dealing with and the levels of risk attached to different types of information. For example, if an enquirer were to ask you to find a set of instructions on how to make your own parachute, you would need to make it absolutely clear that you had not tested the validity of the instructions and give the enquirer a disclaimer along the lines that you could not take any responsibility for any damage caused to the enquirer if they were to follow the instructions that you had given them. Where you are dealing with legal, financial, patent or medical information, you would need to be particularly careful.

 Librarians who claim subject expertise must use their expertise in ways that are appropriate to their role as a library and information professional. In a law library, for example, librarians (many of whom hold law degrees) must not offer legal advice or interpretations of legal materials. Similarly, a librarian working in a health library, such as the library of an NHS Trust, must not diagnose illnesses.

If you obtain a credit rating on a company for a user, care must be taken because it is quite feasible that, if the credit rating was either out of date or inaccurate, the user could end up experiencing financial loss if they were to do business with the company based largely on a healthy credit rating.

14.2   Contract

Contract law can also be relevant to the liability of information professionals where the service is chargeable. If, for example, an enquirer contacts the information centre and asks a member of staff to find some information for him, the researcher provides the requested information and the user accepts it in exchange for a fee, this whole transaction will be subject to contract law. This is the case even if there is nothing written down. It has to be said that where money does change hands clients have a higher expectation of the quality of service that is being provided; that is, they have higher customer expectations of the duty of care that is applied in delivering the service. In any question of liability, the courts too may well expect a higher level of duty of care for a priced service than is required for a free service.

A contract is a legally binding agreement between two or more parties, which is enforceable in a court of law. One party offers to do something for the other party and the other party accepts this offer. The essential elements of a contract are:

1 Offer: the proposal to make a deal. This offer must be communicated clearly to the other party and remain open until it is either accepted, rejected, withdrawn or has expired.
2 Acceptance: this is the acknowledgement by the other party that they have accepted the offer, except where a qualified acceptance is made, as this amounts to a rejection of the offer and is instead regarded as a counter-offer, which also requires acceptance.
3 Consideration: this is what supports the promises made. It is the legal benefit that one person receives and the legal detriment on the other person. This could, for example, take the form of money, property, or services.

Consideration is not necessary for a contract in Scots law. Contracts arise where the parties reach agreement as to the fundamental features of the transaction; this is often referred to as *'consensus in idem'* (meeting of the minds). To determine whether agreement has been reached, contracts in Scotland are analysed in terms of offer and acceptance.

The contract doesn't have to be a signed document. It could be entered into orally, although this does make it more difficult to establish whether or not there is a contract. A written contract sets out what has been agreed and can be used in any dispute, although the very fact that someone has a carefully worded written contract can help prevent a dispute occurring because it sets out clearly the rights and obligations of the parties.

 If you are a self-employed information professional, make sure that you have a carefully drafted set of terms and conditions in order to minimize the risk of being held liable for information you provide to a client.

Self-employed information professionals who charge for their expertise run the risk that they could be held liable for their expertise and advice. In order to minimize any such risk it is advisable to have a set of terms and conditions that the client is asked to sign before work on any assignment commences. The terms and conditions will set out what the client can expect from the information professional.

Any contracts entered into with users should include a formal disclaimer or exclusion clause limiting liability. However, this must be carefully worded, because if it is too general it could be deemed to be invalid. The exclusion clause should, therefore, be specific. It could put a limit on the extent of any potential liabilities, such as specifying the maximum amount that will be paid out in damages.

14.3   Tort (delict in Scotland)

Library and information services who provide their services free of charge cannot ignore professional liability issues, because they could become the subject of an action under the law of tort. Tort/delict refers to behaviour causing loss or harm to other people where no contract exists. It would cover the concept of negligence or carelessness, such as where a librarian carelessly provides inaccurate information to a user who suffers loss as a result. It would be necessary for the user to satisfy a court that the librarian owed the user a duty of care. If you cause your fellow citizens loss by your negligence, you potentially lay yourself open to claims for compensation.

Tort/delict does not require any contractual relationship between the parties involved, and it therefore follows that third parties who suffer loss because of your actions can sue for compensation. However, for such an action to succeed, the injured party would need to establish that:

- the other party owed him a duty of care
- this duty had been breached
- there had been damage
- the damage had been a direct result of the breach
- the damage could have been reasonably foreseen.

There are a number of key legal cases that set important precedents in the law of tort.

Donoghue v. Stevenson [1932] UKHL 100

The case of Donoghue v. Stevenson is important because it established the 'neighbourhood principle', which defines classes of persons to whom a duty of care is owed. The judgment concluded that one owes a duty of care to one's neighbour. Lord Atkin said 'Who then in law is my neighbour? The answer seems to be persons who are so closely and directly affected by my act that I ought reasonably to have them in contemplation as being so affected when I am directing my mind to the acts or omissions which are called in question' (www.bailii.org/uk/cases/UKHL/1932/100.html). This duty of care extends to financial loss where an expert is consulted, as illustrated by Hedley Byrne v. Heller.

Hedley Byrne & Co v. Heller and Partners [1964] AC 465

A bank advised that a certain business would be a good investment; it was not and the investor lost a lot of money. The case dealt with the question of whether someone who provides advice to another person without a contract being in place could be held liable for negligence. The House of Lords found that if the advice was being sought in circumstances in which a reasonable man would know that he was being trusted or that his skill or judgement was being relied upon, then if the person doesn't clearly qualify their answer so as to show that they do not accept responsibility, then they accept as a legal duty such care as the circumstances require. The case established that a duty of care could arise to give careful advice and that a failure to do so could give rise to liability for economic loss caused by negligent advice. Liability arose because the individual consulted had claimed expertise in business investments, his advice would be relied upon and was intended to be definitive. Financial harm can be compensated only in such cases where specific expertise is consulted.

Caparo Industries plc v. Dickman [1990] 2 AC 605

This case is important in defining the duty of care in the field of information provision, and dealt with the liability of auditors to potential investors. It established that the concept of 'duty of care' existed when a number of factors were present:

- the information is for a specific purpose
- the purpose is made known at the time that the advice is given or that the advice is sought
- the advisor knows that his or her advice will be communicated to the advisee or recipient.

Anns v. London Borough of Merton [1978] AC 728

The case of Anns v. London Borough of Merton developed the 'neighbourhood principle' further. In this case Lord Wilberforce said that first the court should establish proximity, using the 'neighbourhood test'; and then, if proximity is established, the court must take account of any 'consideration which ought to negate, reduce or limit the scope of the duty or the class of persons to whom it is owed or the damages to which breach of it may give rise'. For example, in the case of a public library providing a free enquiry service, a court might decide in any claim for liability that it would not be in the public interest to set a precedent that allows users to sue public libraries providing their services free of charge.

14.4   Liability and electronic information

In the late 1980s and early 1990s there was a lot of interest in the question of information quality and liability in relation to electronic information, as evidenced by the number of articles written on the topic at that time. Unlike the situation with hard-copy material, it isn't always possible with electronic information to browse the data or examine the indexes in detail, and then there are the added restrictions on time and cost. Users of online databases may find errors when they search for information, ranging from simple spelling errors, inconsistent use of controlled vocabulary through to factual errors. In the case of incorrect spellings, these can mean the difference between retrieving a record and not being able to retrieve that record.

To address such concerns, the Centre for Information Quality Management (CIQM)[1] was established in 1993 under the auspices of the Library Association (now CILIP) and UKOLUG, the UK Online User Group (now UKeIG, the UK eInformation Group) with the aim of providing a clearing house through which database users could report quality problems. In a 1995 CIQM survey on the effects of poor data on workflow, a surprisingly high figure (31.11%) was returned for retrieval of unusable records (either missing data, badly formatted tables or erroneous data). The questionnaire was addressed to professional intermediaries and it was noted that end-user searchers might be affected more seriously.

If information professionals obtain data from an online service, the information provider is likely to have a liability exclusion clause in their contract making it more difficult to take action against them. Library and information professionals need to take steps to protect them from potential claims for liability. CILIP's *Ethical Principles* (2009) sets out a number of responsibilities of information professionals, and as far as responsibilities to their users are concerned the first two that are listed in the code are particularly relevant:

1 Ensure that information users are aware of the scope and remit of the service being provided.
2 Indicate to information users the reliability of the information being provided.

Information professionals need to warn their users that output from the online service doesn't necessarily carry a guarantee of accuracy. You are not in a position to promise that all of the information retrieved from an online database is correct, complete and accurate because the database provider is responsible for that, and it is outside your control.

Librarians should watch out for signs of how reliable an online database is:

- How frequently is the database updated?
- Does it contain typographical errors?
- Are there any gaps in coverage?
- Are there any inconsistencies or errors in the indexing?

 Where information workers have reservations about the accuracy, reliability or trustworthiness of an information source, they should convey these to the user and make the user aware that there is no guarantee of accuracy. Where the service is chargeable, your terms and conditions of service should make clear that you cannot accept responsibility for errors or omissions in the databases or other sources that you use in your search.

 Whenever possible, the information professional should seek to double-check and verify the accuracy of the data.

 Information staff should maintain good records of the sources used to answer an enquiry. This is particularly important in cases where a fee is charged. The record that is kept can be used as a checklist to ensure that the key sources have all been consulted, and can also be referred back to in the event that a user of the service challenges you about not doing a thorough job.

14.5   Liability for copyright infringement

There are a number of instances where an information professional could potentially be held liable for copyright infringement. In the case of the library regulations (SI 1989/1212), library staff working in 'prescribed libraries' (which are limited to libraries in not-for-profit organizations) are given an indemnity to do copying on behalf of their users that users would themselves be entitled to make under the fair dealing provisions in s29 of the CDPA. The copyright declaration is the librarian's indemnity and if this is false the onus is on the signatory and not the librarian. However, if a user is unsure as to whether or not a particular instance of copying is permitted, they may understandably turn to the librarian for advice before signing the declaration form. The librarian should be careful not to decide for people whether or not a commercial purpose applies, because if they do so they could be held jointly liable for a false declaration.

Library staff also need to be particularly careful to ensure that in answering a user enquiry they are not infringing someone's copyright. As the CILIP *Ethical Principles* (2009) say: 'Information professionals should defend the legitimate needs and interests of information users, while respecting the moral and legal rights of the creators and distributors of intellectual property.'

If a library were to provide internet access to its users, then the library as the subscriber to the internet access service would be liable under the terms of the DEA to:

- receive Copyright Infringement Reports relating to infringements that have taken place on its premises/using IP addresses allocated through its premises.
- be placed on a 'copyright infringement list' if the number of infringements that take place exceed a certain limit - and this may result in private civil or criminal action being taken against the institution by copyright holders.

If the copyright infringement provisions of the DEA are implemented in their entirety, then a library which subscribes to an internet access service could potentially be subject to technical measures, such as limiting the speed of connection or temporary removal of their internet connection if that were deemed to be an appropriate measure.

The library would have the right of appeal. It would be able to say that the act which constituted the apparent infringement was not something done by the library or its staff, and it would have an opportunity to show that it had taken 'reasonable steps' to prevent other people from infringing copyright; but it would need to show precisely what those steps consisted of.

14.6   Risk management

It is important for librarians to be aware of how liability arises, in order to be aware of the risks involved and to be able to take steps to minimize the possibility of legal action. Jonathan Tryon (in *Premises Liability for Librarians, Library and Archival Security*, **10** (2), 1991) says: 'In a litigious society every library administrator must take care to institute procedures which will minimise the likelihood of law suits based on harm caused by the library's negligence.' However, whilst effective risk management can help reduce exposure to allegations of neglect, error or omission it can never completely eradicate that risk. A simple error, omission or misquote could potentially trigger a claim. The best defence against such claims is to:

- pay attention to your own professional development
- keep yourself up to date
- be aware of the range and content of the available sources
- be aware of the accuracy, timeliness and reliability of the sources.

Indeed, the CILIP *Ethical Principles* (2009) say that information professionals should 'ensure they are competent in those branches of professional practice in which qualifications and/or experience entitle them to engage', and also that they should 'undertake continuing professional development to ensure that they keep abreast of developments in their areas of expertise'.

In any promotional material about your information service, you might wish to note that you follow the code of ethics of the professional organization to which you belong – such as CILIP or the Strategic and Competitive Intelligence Professionals (SCIP).

The *ASIST Professional Guidelines* (ASIST stands for the American Society for Information Science and Technology) state that, as part of their responsibility to the profession, members are required to truthfully represent themselves and the information which they utilize or which they represent. ASIST sets out a number of key ways in which this is achieved. These include:

- not knowingly making false statements or providing erroneous or misleading information
- undertaking their research conscientiously, in gathering, tabulating or interpreting data; in following proper approval procedures for subjects; and in producing or disseminating their research results
- pursuing ongoing professional development and encouraging and assisting colleagues and others to do the same.

The Business Reference and Services Section of the Reference and User Services Association (RUSA) has produced the *Guidelines for Medical, Legal, and Business Responses* (RUSA, 2001), in which they state that:

Libraries should develop written disclaimers stating a policy on providing specialized information service denoting variations in types and levels of service. The level of assistance and interpretation provided to users should reflect differing degrees of subject expertise between specialists and non-specialists. When asked legal, medical, or business questions, information services staff should make clear their roles as stated in their library's specialized information services policies.   (paragraphs 1.0.3 and 1.0.4)

In a case of professional liability, the courts would take into account a number of key factors:

1 The nature of the information service being provided. Was the information service, for example, a general service providing information about a wide range of subjects where it would be unreasonable to expect an information professional to be an expert in all of the areas covered by the information service? Or was it a specialist information service covering a narrowly defined subject area, where the information service had built up an international reputation and in which the information staff had specialist knowledge and which had made claims of having expertise in that field?
2 The level of knowledge of the user of the information service. If the topic that enquirers are asking about is one in which they themselves have considerable expertise, then they can be expected to use their own judgement on the validity of the information received. Or was it a member of the general public who could not be expected to use professional judgement on the quality of information?

The EIRENE *Code of Practice for Information Brokers* (EIRENE, 1993) has a section relating to liability, in which it says that a broker shall:

- clearly state the accuracy limits of the information provided, within their professional competence and available sources
- state clearly their liability and will not use total disclaimers
- abide by the existing local laws regarding liability, arbitration procedures or professional negligence, when providing information services
- accept limited liability up to the value of the contract between broker and client, and
- indicate their arbitration procedures in their terms of business.

14.7   Indemnity and insurance

Indemnity is protection or insurance against future loss or damage. Professional indemnity insurance is an insurance against a claim from a client or any other independent third party who suffers financial loss as a result of alleged neglect, error or omission.

Any organization whose employees provide advice, information or a consultancy service may be legally liable for a claim of malpractice where a breach of professional duty occurs. If you give professional advice, your clients will regard you as an expert. Nowadays, clients are often very aware of their legal rights and are ready to assert those rights, so you could find yourself facing a claim from a client who feels that they have received substandard advice.

 Self-employed information consultants should consider taking out professional indemnity insurance.

CILIP recommends professional indemnity insurance for self-employed information consultants and brokers, particularly if they are giving advice that could result in financial loss to their clients. This is because if they work as a sole practitioner, they would be personally liable for negligence, if proven, whatever the legal form of their company. The insurance provides them with financial protection. In *Working for Yourself* (2002), CILIP says that: 'clear and reasonable disclaimers are also helpful, for example stating that you have no liability for errors in published sources. Pay attention to deadlines and keep records – ideally for six years.' Professional indemnity insurance is not compulsory for the library and information profession. Some information professionals may not be keen on taking out professional indemnity insurance because of a perception that the premiums are quite high and that they don't always provide the desired protection. In the case of freelance workers it makes sound business sense and should not be regarded as an expensive or unnecessary business overhead. Furthermore, for freelance workers the premiums are tax-deductible.

In June 2005, CILIP announced a partnership with insurance intermediary Endsleigh who will provide insurance and personal financial services for CILIP members, including independent financial advice. The range of insurance products includes professional indemnity insurance cover (CILIP, 2005).

References

CILIP (2002) *Working for Yourself* (no longer available).

CILIP (2005) CILIP Acts to Meet Demands for Professional Indemnity Insurance and Agrees New Insurance Package for Members, 22 June, www.highbeam.com/doc/1G1-133467024.html.

CILIP (2009) *Ethical Principles and Code of Professional Practice for Library and Information Professionals*, www.cilip.org.uk/get-involved/policy/ethics/pages/principles.aspx.

EIRENE (1993) *Code of Practice for Information Brokers* (no longer available).

RUSA (2001) *Guidelines for Medical, Legal, and Business Responses*, The Business Reference and Services Section of the Reference and User Services Association (RUSA), www.ala.org/ala/mgrps/divs/rusa/resources/guidelines/ALA_print_layout_1_ 512065_512065.cfm.

Notes

1   www.i-a-l.co.uk/ciqm_index.html.

CHAPTER 15

Cybercrime and computer misuse

Contents

15.1   General principles

Cybercrime and computer misuse covers activities such as hacking, viruses, fraud, theft and copyright abuse.

Cybercrime is defined by the British police as the use of any computer network for crime; and in the Council of Europe's Convention on Cybercrime it is defined as 'criminal offences committed against or with the help of computer networks'.

The phrase 'computer misuse' could be used to refer to a wide range of activities including accessing inappropriate material on the internet such as pornographic material; inappropriate use of e-mail; hacking; spreading viruses; fraud; theft; copyright abuse; or the use of a computer to harass others, whether that be sexual harassment, racial harassment, or some other form of harassment.

According to a report by Detica published by the UK Cabinet Office (2011), UK cybercrime costs £27 billion a year including:

- £9.2 billion on intellectual property theft
- £7.6 billion on industrial espionage
- £2.2 billion on extortion
- £1.3 billion on direct online theft

- £1 billion on theft of customer data
- £1.7 billion on identity theft
- £1.4 billion for online scams
- £30 million for scareware and fake anti-virus software
- £2.2 billion cost to government.

Of the £27 billion cost, the economic cost is £3.1 billion per annum to UK citizens, £2.2 billion to the government (including tax and benefits fraud, NHS fraud and pension fraud), and £21 billion to business.

Cyberspace has provided new opportunities for criminals. They are attracted by the anonymity factor and the ability to communicate simultaneously with an unlimited number of users around the world. Hackers find a thrill in penetrating networks and destroying data, while terrorists could purposely disrupt the critical infrastructures that are dependent upon networked computers. Meanwhile, consumers hesitate from disclosing personal and credit card data on the internet, with security and privacy being their number-one concern, and businesses face the potential loss of proprietary data, intellectual property, and online access to customers and suppliers through breaches of security and intentional service disruptions.

With regard to cybercrime, the computer can play a number of different roles:

1 Firstly, a computer can be the target of crime, for example when someone is intent on stealing information from, or causing damage to, a computer or computer network.
2 Secondly, a computer can be the tool that is used in order to commit an offence such as fraud, or the distribution of child pornography.
3 Thirdly, a computer stores evidence, and can be of great value to criminal investigators.

15.2   Council of Europe Convention on Cybercrime

The Council of Europe Convention on Cybercrime was adopted by the Council of Europe in 2001. Cybercrime is a major global challenge, which requires a co-ordinated international response; and the Convention tries to achieve its aims by having legislation at an international level and by fostering international co-operation.

The Convention places the onus on internet service providers as regards encryption and provides for the use of 'coercive powers' such as electronic surveillance, interception, search and seizure in dealing with offences.

The Convention covers three key sets of issues:

- substantive computer crimes
- government access to communications and computer data
- trans-border co-operation.

The offences covered by the Convention on Cybercrime are listed in Figure 15.1. They are not all 'pure' cybercrimes in the sense that some of the crimes can exist whether or not a computer is involved – such as copyright infringement.

Illegal access	Article 2
Illegal interception	Article 3
Data interference	Article 4
System interference	Article 5
Misuse of devices	Article 6
Computer-related forgery	Article 7
Computer-related fraud	Article 8
Offences related to child pornography	Article 9
Offences related to infringement of copyright and related rights	Article 10

Figure 15.1 *Offences covered by the Council of Europe Convention on Cybercrime*

Each of the offences uses a form of words along the lines 'when committed intentionally and without right'. In other words, to qualify as an offence the action must have been committed intentionally, and in circumstances where the person committing the offence did not have the right to do what they did.

The Convention is the first international treaty on crimes committed via the internet and other computer networks, dealing particularly with infringements of copyright, computer-related fraud, child pornography and violations of network security. It also contains a series of powers and procedures such as the search of computer networks and interception.

Its main objective, set out in the preamble, is to pursue a common criminal policy aimed at the protection of society against cybercrime, especially by adopting appropriate legislation and fostering international co-operation. There is also an additional protocol from 28 January 2003 making any publication of racist and xenophobic propaganda via computer networks a criminal offence (http://conventions.coe.int/Treaty/en/Treaties/Html/189.htm).

15.3 The Computer Misuse Act 1990

The Computer Misuse Act (CMA) was published in the wake of Law Commission Working Paper No. 186, on Criminal Law: Computer Misuse (Cm 819), published in October 1989 in order to create specific offences to secure computers against unauthorized access or modification. Whilst the Act was originally intended mainly to address the problems caused by computer hacking, it is also being used effectively to deal with the deliberate release of computer viruses.

The CMA creates three offences:

- unauthorized access to computer material (s1)
- unauthorized access with intent to commit or facilitate commission of further offences (s2)
- unauthorized modification of computer material (s3).

And a fourth was added by the Police and Justice Act 2006 as CMA s3A: Making supplying or obtaining articles.

Under section 1 of the CMA, it is an offence to cause a computer to perform any function with intent to gain unauthorized access to any program or data held in any computer, knowing at the time that it is unauthorized. The section specifically provides that the intent of the person need not be directed at any particular program or data, a program or data of any particular kind, or a program or data held in any particular computer. This means that the Act is suitable for use against activities carried out across networks.

Under section 17(5) a person's access is unauthorized if the person is not himself entitled to control access of the kind in question to the program or data, and he does not have consent to access by him of the kind in question to the program or data from any person who is so entitled.

Under section 2 of the CMA, it is an offence to commit an offence under s1 with intent to commit or facilitate a further offence, whether or not both offences occur on the same occasion.

Under section 3 of the CMA, it is an offence to do anything intentionally and knowingly to cause an unauthorized modification of the contents of any computer which will impair its operation, prevent or hinder access to any program or data, or which will impair the operation of the program or the reliability of the data.

The requisite knowledge is knowledge that any modification he intends to cause is unauthorized. The section provides that intent need not be directed to any particular computer, any particular program or data, or a program or data of any particular kind, or any particular modification or modification of any particular kind. A case study is shown in Figure 15.2.

Under section 3A of the CMA a further offence came into force in 2008 through SI 2008/2503 on making, supplying or obtaining articles for use in offence under section 1 or 3 (which defines 'article' as any program or data held in electronic form). This criminalizes making, supplying or obtaining 'hacking tools': a person is guilty of an offence if that person 'supplies [...] any article intending it to be used to commit, or assist in the commission of [a computer misuse offence]' or 'believing that is likely to be used to commit, or assist in the commission of [any such offence]'.

The penalty for the first offence could be up to two years in prison or a fine (up to level 5 on the standard scale) or both; whereas the second and third offences are considered to be much more serious. The second offence carries a maximum

A 17-year-old clerk was sacked from an insurance company. He decided to get his own back on his former employer. He downloaded a 'useful' piece of software from the internet – which is often referred to as a 'bomber' – and proceeded to use the software in order to send 5 million e-mails to his former employer over a period of three days. This resulted in the ex-employer's website becoming overloaded, and the site having to be taken down for a period of time, with a consequent loss of revenue.

Actions of this kind are likely to cause an unauthorized modification of the contents of the computer to which the e-mails are directed and as such this would be a potential breach of the CMA. If the perpetrator's actions were intended to impair the operation of, or hinder access to, the computer or any program held on it, this would constitute a criminal offence under section 3 of the CMA. If the consequences of their actions could be said to be reasonably foreseeable, then they would be likely to be treated as having such intent.

As a result of his actions, the ex-clerk was interviewed by the Metropolitan Police.

Figure 15.2 *Case study: sacked employee wreaks revenge on former employer*

penalty of up to five years in prison or an unlimited fine or both; whereas for the third offence the maximum penalty could be up to ten years in prison.

The penalty for the offence under section 3A is two years in prison and/or a fine. Figure 15.3 shows an example of a prison sentence for offences under the Act.

Simon Vallor, a web designer, created viruses on his home computer in Llandudno which he then distributed over the internet in September and October 2001. The viruses were designed to e-mail themselves to everyone in the recipient's address book. One virus was designed to delete all the data on a hard drive on 11 November. At least 29,000 computers were infected in 42 countries, while another 300,000 copies of the virus were stopped by anti-virus software. The cost of the episode ran to millions of pounds for businesses and computer users. Mr Vallor was sentenced to two years imprisonment for offences under the CMA. At the time this was the harshest sentence that there had been for this type of offence.

Figure 15.3 *Prison sentence for offences under the Computer Misuse Act*

According to section 17 of the Act, a person secures access to any computer program or data held in a computer if by causing a computer to perform any function they:

- alter or erase the program or data
- copy or move it to any storage medium other than that in which it is held or to a different location in the storage medium in which it is held
- use it
- have it output from the computer in which it is held (whether by having it displayed or in any other manner).

Computer Misuse Act 1990 – section 3 offence

In a legal case from 2002 a manufacturing business decided to update its computer system. They employed an IT contractor to do the work for them. Unfortunately, they felt that he had not done a very good job and went to a second contractor to get the job completed. When it came to payment, they clearly had to pay for the services of the new contractor and decided that they would not pay the original contractor.

Access to the IT system had been set up for the original contractor to work from home, and this access was still available at the time of the dispute. When the company refused to pay the original contractor he was upset about this and decided to take matters into his own hands. He accessed the system and deleted all of the files on it. These files included three years' worth of fairly complicated design drawings. The company assessed the amount of damage it had suffered as a result at around £50,000.

It is a criminal offence under section 3 of the CMA to carry out an unauthorized modification of material held on computer, when your intention is to prevent or hinder access to the data or impair its operational reliability. The contractor was prosecuted and convicted and was jailed for 18 months.

There are a number of lessons from this case, even if some of them may seem rather obvious:

* take regular backups
* keep the backups in a separate place
* be careful about who can access the computer system
* be prompt at disabling access for employees and contractors as soon as they cease working for you
* be very careful about who you give remote access to
* for contractors – don't damage or disable a computer system, no matter what the provocation might be, as it is surely not worth a prison sentence.

Computer crime can raise a number of issues relating to jurisdiction, since it is obviously possible for someone anywhere in the world to access a computer located in the UK. Sections 4–9 of the Act deal with jurisdictional issues. Provided that either the accused or the computer was within the jurisdiction at the time of the offence, then a prosecution is permitted.

15.4 Hacking

Hacking is the act of deliberately gaining unauthorized access to an information system. Many instances of hacking might be classed as nuisance attacks, but far more serious are instances where the hacker had malicious intent.

Section 1 of the CMA makes hacking per se a criminal offence, regardless of whether or not any harm is intended. If, for example, a hacker broke into a computer simply out of curiosity, they would have committed an offence so long as they were aware that their access was unauthorized.

Hackers can be deterred through the use of well-configured firewall protection, intrusion detection software and filtering software.

15.5   Viruses, worms and Trojans

Computer viruses, in the same way as biological viruses, make copies of themselves and cannot exist without a host. They may infect program files, programs in disk sectors, or files that use a macro.

Worms are similar to viruses. Like viruses, they make copies of themselves, but do so without the need to modify a host. By repeatedly making copies of itself, a worm tries to drain system resources.

Trojans are named after the Trojan Horse – a giant wooden horse that concealed Greek soldiers who used it in order to invade the ancient city of Troy – because Trojan horse programs conceal hidden programming which can cause significant damage to your computer.

It is no longer the case that a computer user has to click on a file attachment in order to trigger a virus infection. It may be sufficient merely for the user simply to read an infected e-mail in order for the virus to be launched.

The CMA applies to those who release damaging viruses into the wild, even if the person doing so does not have the intent to damage a particular computer. Some e-mails aren't intended to destroy data or prevent programs from operating, but might simply use directories to propagate themselves around e-mail systems. Nevertheless, there could still be the possibility of a criminal conviction. Under section 1 of the Act, the use of the recipient's e-mail program to cause the incoming e-mail virus to propagate onwards by means of the e-mail system could be said to be access of an unauthorized nature and would therefore be liable to prosecution under section 1.

Section 3 of the CMA can be used to prosecute people who introduce viruses, worms or Trojans to computer systems. Under s3(2), an offence occurs if damage to a computer impairs the operation of any computer.

15.6   Intellectual property infringement

There are a number of cybercrimes that represent various different aspects of intellectual property infringement. These include cybersquatting (see Section 5.3.4), plagiarism, software piracy, making illegal downloads of music files, or other examples of copyright abuse.

Plagiarism means to use or to pass off as one's own the ideas or writings of someone else. Electronic detection tools such as Turnitin software are increasingly being used to detect student plagiarism electronically.

Software piracy is the copying of software without permission. This is a crime that can potentially be punished by imprisonment and a fine. Ongoing auditing and tracking of software use is essential to ensure compliance with software licensing agreements.

According to the seventh annual BSA/IDC global software 09 piracy study (2010), the commercial value of unlicensed software put into the market in 2009 totalled $51.4 billion; and the worldwide piracy rate increased from 41% in 2008 to 43% in 2009, largely a result of exponential growth in the PC and software markets in higher piracy, particularly in fast-growing markets such as Brazil, India and China.

A number of peer-to-peer file-sharing networks have been used by internet users in order to make illegal music downloads. Organizations representing the music industry such as IFPI and the British Phonogram Industry have taken out legal actions in order to protect the interests of their members. Indeed, they have taken court action, to force ISPs to disclose the details of people alleged to have used peer-to-peer file-sharing services to copy or to share unlawfully copied files.

According to a story which appeared in Out-law News (2005) a Hong Kong man received what was reported to be the world's first jail sentence for making movies available online on a file-sharing website. The 38-year-old man was given a three-month custodial sentence. The Motion Picture Association of America (MPAA) said that the man faced a maximum of four years in prison and a possible US$6,400 fine for every copy distributed without permission. The MPAA has filed a considerable number of lawsuits. These have been targeted both at users themselves; and also at website operators, who stand accused of helping online pirates to make millions of illegal copies of movies and television programmes.

15.7 Pornography

The computer has made it much easier for people to store and disseminate offensive material than was the case in the paper-based world. There have been instances where employees have used company servers as a repository for pornographic material. From the point of view of an employer, the key issue is that such material may already be stored on their company's systems without their knowledge. Pornography can be split up into two main types, according to whether it is legal or not. Firstly, there is pornography directed at adults, which it is illegal for adults to read or view according to the rules of a particular legal system. The material most universally accepted as falling into this category would be child pornography. Secondly, there is pornography or other sexual material which is not illegal for adults to access, but which may nevertheless be considered to be harmful or upsetting for others including children to see. The traditional approach of UK legislation has been that it is acceptable to possess obscene material in private as long as there is no attempt to publish, distribute or show it to others – particularly for gain. With regard to child pornography – which by its very nature features the sexual abuse of children – the UK Parliament has taken the view that possession as well as circulation of such material should be criminalized. In 2005, the UK government also sought views on tightening the law with regard to extreme pornography – that is, pornography that contains actual scenes or realistic depictions of serious violence, bestiality or necrophilia.

There have been proposals (COM(2010)0094) for a European directive on combating sexual abuse, sexual exploitation of children and child pornography, repealing framework decision 2004/68/JHA. The proposals include blocking access to internet pages, and getting ISPs to develop codes of conduct and guidelines for blocking access.

R v. Perrin [2002] All ER 359

In R v. Perrin, a Frenchman was convicted under the Obscene Publications Act 1959 in relation to a website hosted in France. The only occurrence of downloading in the UK from the website that the prosecution relied upon was undertaken by a police officer at New Scotland Yard who accessed the site and downloaded material from it. When the defendant happened to be passing through the UK, the opportunity was taken to arrest, charge and convict him on the basis of that download by the police officer. Mr Perrin was given a 30-month prison sentence.

This case would seem to suggest that issues such as where the website was developed and hosted, where the website owner lives or which countries the site is aimed

Storage and transmission of obscene material is a criminal offence under the Obscene Publications Acts 1959 and 1964. It is also an offence under The Obscene Publications Act 1959 to publish an obscene article, whether or not for gain; and this is further extended in the Criminal Justice and Public Order Act 1994 which deals specifically with 'obscene publications and indecent photographs of children'.

Other relevant legislation includes the Protection of Children Act 1978. There is also the Criminal Justice Act 1988, which makes it an offence for a person to have any indecent photograph of a child in his possession. A 'child' in this context is defined as a person under the age of 16. The test for 'obscenity' is set out in The Obscene Publications Acts 1959 and 1964 as being material which tends to 'deprave and corrupt' those who are likely, having regard to all relevant circumstances, to read, see or hear it.

The European Commission has called for increased efforts to protect minors in the context of new media services. The Community's Safer Internet Action Plan also encourages initiatives such as the development of rating and filtering systems and the establishment of 'walled gardens' (portals where the operators guarantee the quality of sites which can be accessed through them).

University of Central England's library investigated under Obscene Publications Act

In October 1997 the University of Central England's library was 'raided' by West Midlands Police Paedophile and Pornography Squad who confiscated a copy of *Mapplethorpe* published by Jonathan Cape in 1992, a book about Robert Mapplethorpe and his work.

A final year undergraduate student at UCE's Birmingham Institute of Art and Design was writing a paper on the work of Robert Mapplethorpe and intended to use images from the book for a major piece of coursework on 'Fine Art Versus Pornography'. She took the photographs to the local chemist to be developed and the chemist informed West Midlands Police because of the unusual nature of the images. The police confiscated the library book from the student and informed the university that as two photographs in the book were obscene they would have to be excised. If the university agreed to the excision, no further action would be taken.

The police interviewed University Vice Chancellor Dr Peter Knight under caution with a view to prosecution under the terms of the Obscene Publications Act 1959, which defines obscenity as material that is likely to deprave or corrupt. The Vice Chancellor was under threat of imprisonment unless he agreed to the destruction of portions of the book. The Senate of UCE decided that 'principles are priceless' and fully supported the Vice Chancellor, Dr Knight, who took the view that the book was a legitimate book for the university library to hold and that the action of the police was a serious infringement of academic freedom.

After the interview with the Vice Chancellor a file was sent to the Crown Prosecution Service (CPS). The decision as to whether or not the matter should proceed to trial was down to the Director of Public Prosecutions (DPP). The DPP decided that no action would be taken as 'there was insufficient evidence to support a successful prosecution on this occasion'. The original book was returned, in a slightly tattered state, and restored to the university library.

The decision not to prosecute brought to an end a year of uncertainty for the university, during which time students had been denied access to vital materials which

↝ Useful resource

Europa Safer Internet Programme:
http://ec.europa.eu/information_society/activities/sip/index_en.htm.

In December 2010, Ed Vaizey (Minister for Culture, Communications and Creative Industries) indicated that he believed ISPs should block pornographic content at the network level, forcing people who want to look at it to opt in (see Guardian, 2010). The digital rights activist group the Open Rights Group labelled the proposal as censorship.

Porn protest librarian

Ceri Randall, a supervisor at the library in Pyle, South Wales, refused to serve a library user whom she caught sharing sexual fantasies on a library computer. Press reports at the time suggested that Ms Randall was facing disciplinary action as a result whilst the library user had been given an apology by the head of library services (*The Times*, 2005).

In order to clarify the situation, Bridgend County Borough Council issued a statement on 19 October 2005. It explained that:

> Over two years ago, a member of the public was banned from using library facilities due to the inappropriate use of internet facilities. There is no evidence of this being anything other than use of a chat room. This has been investigated by the authority and the police were informed. The use breached the council's own protocol, but was not unlawful. The authority has a significant investment in filtering technology and takes issues of the misuse of its facilities extremely seriously. The member of the public apologised immediately and accepted the ban [...] There has been, and is, no proposed disciplinary action against the member of staff concerned. The authority has offered every support to the member of staff, including enabling the member of staff not to serve the individual concerned.   (Source: Bridgend County Borough Council, 2005)

R v. Schofield [2003]

This case involved a Trojan virus, which, as its name suggests, is something that looks innocuous and does not do anything until it has installed itself on your computer. Once there, it can do all sorts of nasty things. In particular, someone else can use it to obtain remote access to, and control of, your computer.

Background:

- Mr Schofield was charged in relation to the making of indecent images of children, based on 14 'depraved images' that were found on his PC.
- Mr Schofield claimed that he didn't know how these images had got onto his computer.
- Vigilantes drove him out of his home and he had to spend a month in hiding.

- When an expert examined Mr Schofield's PC, a Trojan virus was discovered; and this had been installed on the machine a day before the offending images had been downloaded. The expert concluded that the Trojan could have downloaded the images from the internet without the knowledge of Mr Schofield; and the prosecution accepted that they were not able to show that Mr Schofield was the only person who could have downloaded these images onto the PC and he was consequently acquitted.

This case is interesting for a number of reasons:

- It is extremely worrying that Trojans might be used to download illegal material to an individual's PC without the individual knowing.
- There is a real risk of an innocent person being convicted (and subsequently having their life ruined, as nearly happened to Mr Schofield).
- There have been a number of reports of Trojans that, once installed on an individual's computer, allow that computer to be used as a sort of mini server to enable the downloading of pornography. The person actually responsible for the pornography can, in effect, conceal himself behind a number of other peoples' computers without that person even knowing that their computer is acting as a conduit.
- This is possibly the first time a defence has been used based on the suggestion that 'the computer did it'.
- It makes investigation of genuine offenders more difficult. Not only may law enforcement agencies have to be more cautious when they find images on a PC, but genuine offenders may also seek to use the 'Trojan' defence themselves. In the end, if this happens with any frequency it may reduce the chances of achieving a successful prosecution of genuine offenders.
- Unless there is clear evidence that there has been no third-party interference with a computer, using an argument about a computer virus may be enough to introduce a reasonable doubt into the minds of a judge or jury. The defence may well be a genuine one in some cases, but it may also prevent successful prosecutions being brought against genuine offenders and thus reduce the effectiveness of laws against hacking or the dissemination of offensive or

In August 2005 the Home Office issued a consultation paper on the possession of extreme pornographic material (Home Office, 2005), which sought views on a proposal to make illegal the possession of a limited range of extreme pornographic material featuring adults. The aim was to mirror the arrangements already in place in respect of indecent photographs of children, possession of which was already an offence. It set out options for creating a new offence of simple possession of extreme pornographic material which is graphic and sexually explicit and which contains actual scenes or realistic depictions of serious violence, bestiality or necrophilia. The material in question would be illegal to publish, sell or import under the Obscene Publications Acts 1959 and 1964, and, in Scotland, the Civic Government (Scotland) Act 1982. This led the government to introduce a new offence of possession of extreme pornographic images when it passed the Criminal Justice and Immigration Act 2008 section 63, which came into force in January 2009.

15.8 Fraud

Computers can be used as a tool to commit fraud. There is a wide range of different types of fraud which can be classed as cybercrimes. These would include securities and financial fraud, credit card fraud, and other types of computer-related fraud such as phishing or identity theft. Identity theft, said to be Britain's fastest growing fraud, is where a thief steals someone's identity, which could then potentially be used in order to open a bank account or set up a number of credit cards in that person's name. A new Fraud Act received Royal Assent in 2006. It came into force on 15 January 2007 and created a new offence of fraud that can be committed in three ways: by making a false representation (dishonestly, with intent to make a gain, cause loss or risk of loss to another), by failing to disclose information, and by abuse of position. Offences were also created of obtaining services dishonestly, possessing equipment to commit frauds, and making or supplying articles for use in frauds.

15.8.1 Phishing

Phishing is the fraudulent acquisition, through deception, of sensitive personal information such as passwords and credit card details, by masquerading as someone trustworthy with a genuine need for that information. The term was coined back in the 1990s by crackers attempting to steal AOL accounts. A fraudster would pose as an AOL staff member and send an instant message to a potential victim. The message would ask the victim to reveal his or her password, for instance to 'verify your account' or to 'confirm billing information'. Once the victim gave over the password, the fraudster could access the victim's account and use it for criminal purposes, such as spamming.

This has become very common using the websites of financial services companies, auction websites or internet payment services. Companies are trying to educate their customers not to give out personal data in response to an e-mail.

In the struggle against phishing there are tools available such as SpoofStick (www.spoofstick.com) which makes it easier to spot a spoofed website by prominently displaying only the most relevant domain information. Spoofed websites are ones which are deliberately designed in order to look like a legitimate website. In order to verify whether a website is genuine or not, it is best to verify the security certificate of the site. To do this, users should click onto the yellow lock icon on the status bar. This symbol signifies that the website uses encryption to help protect any sensitive personal information.

15.8.2 Pharming

Pharming is the ability to connect to your PC or laptop with the purpose of retrieving 'sensitive' information and even your keystrokes (these can be used to trap your log-in names and passwords). You do not necessarily know this is happening, and, generally, these attacks happen wirelessly.

 In order to minimize the risks posed by pharming, it is advisable to make sure you have up to date anti-virus protection – which means not only installing anti-virus software, but also making sure that you run regular updates; and also to install spyware removal software on your equipment and run regular scans.

15.9   Denial of service attacks

There may be occasions when accessing a website could be said to be an offence under the CMA. Accessing a publicly available website is not an offence in itself, as there is an implied authorization for people to access the website. Where it gets more tricky is in those instances when that access is abused. Is, for instance, a denial-of-service attack (DoS) an offence? Such an attack consists of sending massive quantities of otherwise normal messages or page requests to an internet host, with the result that the server is overloaded, is unable to deal with legitimate requests and in effect becomes unavailable.

The perpetrator of a DoS might wish to use the space on your hard drive and your central processing unit (CPU), combined with the computer power of many thousands of other machines, in order to take control of those PCs and to have them direct traffic on the web to one well-known internet site. This then overloads the web server, making the site unavailable.

The Police and Justice Act 2006 included a number of provisions which amended the CMA, although these didn't come into force until 2008 as a result of SI 2008/2503: The Police and Justice Act 2006 (Commencement No. 9) Order 2008. The amendments clarified that the launching of denial-of-service attacks is a criminal offence, whether it is done recklessly or with intent.

There is a Council framework decision 2005/222/JHA of 24 February 2005 on attacks against information systems IN L69/67, 16 March 2005, whose objective is to improve co-operation between judicial and other competent authorities responsible for law enforcement in the Member States, by approximating rules on criminal law in the Member States in the area of attacks against information systems and ensuring that such attacks are punishable by effective, proportional and dissuasive criminal penalties in all Member States.

The specific crimes covered are:

1 Unauthorized access to information systems (hacking).
2 Disruption of information systems (denial of service).
3 Execution of malicious software that modifies or destroys data.
4 Interception of communication.
5 Malicious misrepresentation.

Member States are required to take the necessary measures to ensure that illegal access to an information system and interference with the integrity of an information system or of its data are punishable as criminal offences. Given that information systems are the subject of attacks, particularly from organized crime, and the increasing potential for terrorist attacks against information systems which form part of the critical infrastructure of the Member States, a response at the level of the Member States is required to avoid compromising the achievement of a safer Information Society and an Area of Freedom, Security and Justice.

In 2010 a draft directive on attacks against information systems was published (COM(2010) 517) which is intended to eventually replace the council framework decision 2005/222/JHA. The new elements would require all Member States to criminalize:

• the intentional interception of non-public transmissions of computer data from an information system (Article 6)
• the production, sale, procurement, import, possession or distribution of any device or tool for the purpose of committing any of the offences contained in the draft Directive (Article 7).

In addition, the draft directive would require Member States to impose tougher criminal penalties if any of the following 'aggravating' circumstances apply:

• where a criminal organization is involved in the commission of an offence
• where the offence has been committed by means of a tool (such as a botnet) designed to attack a significant number of information systems or to cause considerable damage
• where the commission of the offence conceals the real identity of the perpetrator and causes prejudice to the rightful identity owner.

15.10 Acceptable use policies

Companies should set policies for employees to abide by, in order that they know what is expected of them. This can be in the form of a written policy statement on reasonable use of the internet, e-mail and the company's computer network. All employees should be given a copy, and this should include new members of staff when they join the firm. It could, for example, be covered as part of the induction process.

Well-drafted policy statements are of no use if they are not sent to all employees, or some employees are unaware that the policy exists.

It is also important that the principles enshrined in these policies are policed adequately and any breaches are dealt with in a consistent manner through the company's disciplinary policy. If companies fail to enforce these policies adequately, they cannot seek to rely on them indiscriminately when dealing with any breaches, as employees would be able to challenge the enforceability of the policy if it were not adequately policed and implemented. There has to be a consistency in their approach.

Examples of unacceptable content should be outlined. For example, in the case of publishing content to the company's intranet, you might want the list of unacceptable content to cover:

- offensive material (such as pornographic, abusive, indecent or profane items)
- items which insult or intimidate someone
- lewd comments, jokes or banter
- swear words and offensive language
- chain letters
- any purpose which is illegal or contrary to the employer's interest
- disclosing personal data without consent of the data controller, contrary to the DPA.

15.11 Communications Act 2003

Section 127 of the Communications Act 2003 says that 'a person is guilty of an offence if he sends by means of a public electronic communications network a message or other matter that is grossly offensive or of an indecent, obscene or menacing character' and 'public electronic communications network' is defined widely enough for it to be able to cover internet traffic which goes through telephone lines or other cables; and in section 151 there is a definition of 'public electronic communications network'. It means an electronic communications network provided wholly or mainly for the purpose of making electronic communications services available to members of the public.

References

Bridgend County Borough Council (2005) 19 10 05 Statement re: Internet Usage at Pyle Life Centre, www.bridgend.gov.uk/Web1/groups/public/documents/press_release/009323.hcsp#TopOfPage.

BSA (2010) *Seventh Annual BSA and IDC Global Software Piracy Study*, http://portal.bsa.org/globalpiracy2009/index.html.

Detica (2011) *The Cost of Cybercrime*, www.cabinetoffice.gov.uk/sites/default/files/resources/THE-COST-OF-CYBER-CRIME-SUMMARY-FINAL.pdf.

Guardian (2010) 19th December, www.guardian.co.uk/society/2010/dec/19/broadband-sex-safeguard-children-vaizey.

Home Office (2005) *Consultation on Possession of Extreme Pornographic Material*, www.homeoffice.gov.uk/documents/cons-extreme-porn-300805.

Out-law News (2005) First Jail Sentence for Movie File Sharing, 7 November, www.out-law.com/page-6310.

The Times (2005) Porn-Protest Librarian Faces Sack, 19 October.

CHAPTER 16

Disability discrimination

Contents

16.1   General principles

Disabled people are among the most excluded in society. They encounter many barriers to accessing the services of archives and libraries, including physical, sensory, attitudinal, cultural and intellectual ones. Library and information services need to ensure that they do not discriminate against those who are disabled. This is not solely a moral issue; the Equality Act 2010 makes the fair treatment of disabled people a legal requirement.

According to the definition of 'disability' under the Equality Act 2010 a person has a disability if they have a physical or mental impairment and if the impairment has a substantial and long-term adverse effect on their ability to perform normal day-to-day activities. For the purposes of the Act, 'substantial' means more than minor or trivial; 'long-term' means that the effect of the impairment has lasted or is likely to last for at least twelve months; and 'normal day-to-day activities' include everyday things such as eating, washing, walking and going shopping.

Discrimination against disabled people can take place in either of two ways, by:

- treating them less favourably than other people (EA 2010 s13(1))
- failing to make a reasonable adjustment (EA 2010 ss20–21) when they are placed at a 'substantial disadvantage' compared to other people for a reason relating to their disability.

A reasonable adjustment might be any action that helps to alleviate a substantial disadvantage. This could involve changing the organization's standard procedures; providing materials in Braille as an additional service; providing appropriate adjustments to the physical environment; or training staff to work with disabled people.

People with disability can include those with physical or mobility impairments; hearing impairments; dyslexia; medical conditions; mental health difficulties; visual impairment; or people with learning difficulties.

The Office for Disability Issues has published *Equality Act 2010: guidance on matters to be taken into account in determining questions relating to the definition of disability*. Whilst the guidance doesn't impose legal obligations in its own right, schedule 12 of the EA 2010 requires courts, tribunals and adjudicating bodies to take the guidance into account.

> In order to ensure that they do not discriminate on the grounds of disability, library services need to take account of disability issues when considering matters of service planning, delivery and quality; they need to be able to provide equality of access to their services; and they also need to assess, deliver and evaluate disability training.

Managers of library and information services can make use of a number of toolkits, checklists and best-practice standards (see Section 16.5 – although it is important to bear in mind the date of publication of the items, and the change to the law brought about by the passing of the Equality Act 2010) to help them identify and assess whether or not their existing policies and procedures result in disabled people receiving a level of service which is inferior to the one which is available to everyone else. They should think about the accessibility of their service to people with disabilities; both in terms of physical access and intellectual access.

↝ Useful resource

The RNIB has a document entitled *Information is Power: How Public Libraries can Empower Blind and Partially Sighted People* (www.rnib.org.uk/getinvolved/campaign/accesstoinformation/Documents/ infolibrariesw.doc), which sets out a number of practical ways in which libraries can make things better for visually impaired users.

Libraries can invest in a number of adaptations for people with disabilities. For example, adjustments made to the physical access can include:

* ramps
* colour-contrasting handrails
* swing-resistant automatic doors
* ensuring the appropriate widths needed for wheelchairs
* checking the rise of steps and the height of lift-call buttons

- signage and guiding, including international access symbols
- appropriate shelf heights
- access to catalogues and terminals
- access to library publications and websites
- fully adjustable tables and chairs.

 If the library is planning a refurbishment, staff should take account of best-practice guidance and any relevant British Standards.

For example, there is a British Standard covering the slip-resistance of different floor surfaces. Access requirements are often equated with wheelchair access when only around 8% of disabled people are wheelchair users. This lack of awareness can be a barrier to serving the majority of disabled people.

There are many adaptations to technology, which can greatly assist people with disabilities. These include:

- different-sized keyboards
- mouse alternatives
- lap trays
- wrist rests
- screen magnifiers
- dyslexia and literacy software
- document readers
- voice-recognition technology.

It is also important to ensure that staff are equipped with the knowledge that they need in order to serve disabled users effectively – for example, by being able to adjust a computer to an individual user's needs.

 Library and information services need to have appropriate policies, procedures and plans in place to serve the needs of their disabled users effectively; and staff training is a key part of ensuring that this isn't just a theoretical aim, but that the policies and procedures are put into practice.

 Library and information services need to be mindful about the needs of their disabled users when they prepare promotional literature about their services, and the literature must be accessible to those users (see Figure 16.1).

1	Is the information about library facilities accessible to disabled people?
2	Is promotional literature available in alternative formats such as Braille, audio tape or large print?
3	Is web-based material accessible to those using assistive technology, such as screen-reading software, or those not using a mouse?
4	Does information about services and facilities make clear the adjustments that are already in place? And does it also point out that additional adjustments can be made on an individual basis?

Figure 16.1 *Promotional material*

Institutions are expected to make 'anticipatory' adjustments, and not simply to wait until a disabled person requires a particular adaptation, although the Equality Act 2010 doesn't use the word 'anticipatory'. In considering what anticipatory adjustments should be made, it is important to ask a number of key questions. For example:

1 Are the library buildings accessible?
2 Do they have accessible toilets?
3 Are the fire and emergency procedures appropriate for the library's disabled users?
4 Are the catalogue and instructions on its use available in accessible formats?
5 Are aisles wide enough for wheelchairs?
6 Are there staff available to fetch books for those who cannot reach or see them?
7 Does the library provide materials in large print or online in order to cater for those who cannot use standard print?
8 Are longer loans periods available for those who need them?
9 Have staff been given the appropriate training? For example, could they support someone having an epileptic seizure?

It will ultimately be for the courts to decide what anticipatory adjustments it is reasonable to expect organizations to make.

It is essential to review services periodically in order to take into account any changes in best practice or technological advances. Figure 16.2 provides a checklist of areas to address in order to ensure compliance with current disability discrimination legislation.

16.2   Copyright (Visually Impaired Persons) Act 2002

Visually impaired people are those who are blind or partially sighted, and people who are physically unable to hold or manipulate a book, focus or move their eyes or are otherwise physically unable to use a standard print book. However, for the

1	Do you have an equal opportunities policy that makes specific reference to disabled people?
2	Has your organization carried out a disability access audit?
3	Does your organization carry out staff training to increase awareness of disability access?
4	How does your organization consult with its disabled users and non-users?
5	In what ways are your services accessible to disabled people?
6	How is technology used in order to improve access for disabled people?
7	How is publicity and promotion targeted towards disabled people?
8	How does your organization keep abreast of the growing body of best practice on

Figure 16.2 *Compliance checklist*

purposes of the Act, it does not cover people with dyslexia.

The Copyright (Visually Impaired Persons) Act 2002 is intended to give people with sight loss easier access to alternative formats of copyright material, such as large print, Braille and audio. The Act came into force in October 2003 and it introduces two exceptions to copyright to overcome problems of access to material by people with visual impairment:

1 **Part I: The 'one-for-one' exception (CDPA s31A)**. This entitles a visually impaired person to make a single accessible copy of a copyright work for their personal use, subject to a number of conditions. In order to be able to make an accessible copy under this exemption, you must be visually impaired, have or have access to a 'master copy' which is inaccessible because of your visual impairment and know that an accessible copy is not commercially available. Accessible copies made under s31A of the CDPA must be accompanied by a statement that they are made under this section and also by a sufficient acknowledgement.

2 **Part II: The 'multiple copy' exception (CDPA s31B)** (see Figure 16.3 overleaf). Educational establishments or not-for-profit organizations can make multiple accessible copies of a copyright work and supply them to visually impaired people for their personal use. The types of educational establishment who are able to benefit from this exception are set out in The Copyright (Educational Establishments) Order 2005. The exception is subject to a number of conditions. For example, accessible copies cannot be supplied to anyone who can access a commercially available copy. Within a reasonable time from making accessible copies, copyright owners must be notified of activity under the exception. Where copyright owners have established a licensing scheme covering the activity that would otherwise be permitted under the exception, licences under that scheme must be taken out.

Accessible copies made under s31B of the CDPA must be accompanied by a statement that they are made under this section and also by a sufficient

I	Only educational establishments and not-for-profit institutions can participate.
2	Most libraries will just be making one-to-one copies based on the user's legal access to the inaccessible copy.
3	The exception applies to non-print materials, including the internet, but excludes databases.
4	No institution has to implement this exception if they do not wish to.
5	No institution has to be a repository if it does not wish to.
6	Institutions can charge but only marginal costs.
7	If the master copy is in copy-protected electronic form, any accessible copy made under s31B should incorporate the same or an equally effective copy protection.

Figure 16.3 *The 'multiple copy' exception – salient points for libraries*

acknowledgement.

There are several licensing schemes in place. In May 2010 the CLA introduced a free Print Disability Licence for copying from books and journals. It covers both people who are visually impaired as well as other disabilities such as dyslexia. The licence gives people the right to reproduce items into formats such as Braille, audio and large print (www.cla.co.uk/licences/licences_available/visual_impaired). Meanwhile the Music Publishers Association (MPA) operates a licence for sheet music. The multiple copies exception does not apply for items covered by the CLA or MPA schemes.

⇢ Useful resource

In 2001 the PLS issued the *Joint Industry Guidelines on Copyright and Visual Impairment*:
www.publishers.org.uk/images/stories/AboutPA/Copyright_and_Visual_Impairment.pdf.

The guidelines were the result of a wide-ranging consultation among rights holders and organizations helping visually impaired people in an effort to strike a balance between the requirements of visually impaired people and the special problems surrounding uncontrolled copying, transcription and distribution.

There may be a number of scenarios where the guidelines will permit people to make accessible copies in more situations than those permitted by the exceptions in the Copyright (Visually Impaired Persons) Act 2002 – for example, the guidelines are not limited with regard to databases – and so long as the Joint Industry Guidelines continue to be promoted, visually impaired people may rely on the guidelines.

In September 2010, a Memorandum of Understanding was signed by the European Writers Congress, the Federation of European Publishers, the International Federation of Reproduction Rights Organisations and the International Association of Scientific, Technical & Medical publishers, in conjunction with the PA and the PLS on behalf of publishers. The Memorandum of Understanding's ultimate goal is to increase access to works for people with print disabilities, in particular by establishing a network of Trusted Intermediaries to enhance this access across Europe.

The PA, Society of Authors, Association of Authors' Agents and The Right to Read Alliance have released a joint 'recommendation to publishers' to encourage the use of accessibility functions on e-reading devices (PLS, 2011). The agreement recommends that text to speech is routinely enabled on all e-books across all platforms, at least where there is no audiobook edition commercially available. It goes some way to offering people with print disabilities the same rights to access e-readers as those without disabilities, and should provide a more equal footing as sales of these devices take off in the UK.

WIPO are considering a binding treaty on limitations and exceptions for the print-disabled community, which would create a harmonized set of minimum exceptions that all signatories must have for people who are blind or who have other disabilities. The World Blind Union and copyright experts have had an input into the drafting of the treaty.

16.3   The Right To Read

The Royal National Institute of Blind People (RNIB) have been running a 'Right to Read' campaign for over a decade. According to the RNIB's 2003 report, *Written Off*, three million people in the UK are being denied the right to read. They make the point that whilst government is pouring billions of pounds into literacy initiatives across the UK, people with sight problems or print reading disabilities are being forgotten. According to the RNIB, figures show that a staggering 96 per cent of books are never published in formats that people with sight problems can read like large print, audio or Braille (RNIB Press Release 15/11/04). See also the Right to Read Charter at www.rnib.org.uk/righttoread.

⚬ Useful resource

There is a report which documents the results of the 'Availability of accessible publications' project:
Lockyer, S., Creaser, C. and Davies, J. E. (2005) Availability of Accessible

Publications, LISU Occasional Paper no. 35,
www.lboro.ac.uk/departments/dis/lisu, which was undertaken for the RNIB
by LISU.

16.4   Website accessibility

The codes of practice produced by the Equality and Human Rights Commission
(which incorporates what was the Disability Rights Commission) make clear that
online services are subject to the anti-discrimination legislation. Indeed, the
EHRC worked with the British Standards Institution in order to produce guidance
website accessibility which resulted in the publication of BS8878: 2010 'Web
ssibility. Code of practice'.

Maguire v. Sydney Organising Committee for the Olympic Games [1999] HREOCA 26

The Australian case of Maguire v. Sydney Organising Committee for the Olympic
Games is useful in illustrating what adjustments might be considered reasonable in
the context of website accessibility.

This was an action brought in front of Australia's Human Rights and Equal Opportunities Commission (HREOC) by Maguire, who had been blind since birth. His action
was in respect of the defendant's website, which he alleged was inaccessible and thus
infringed the Commonwealth Disability Discrimination Act 1992.

Maguire was an experienced computer user who accessed the internet using a refre-
shable Braille display and a web browser. Despite a number of changes made by the
defendant, Maguire delivered a statement asserting that the website was still inaccessible as of 17 April 2000 and requested the HREOC to order certain changes to
the website. Maguire asked the HREOC to order that the defendant ensure access
from the Schedule page to the Index of Sports, among other things.

The defendant argued that access to the Index of Sports was possible by entering the URL for each sport directly into the browser. However, the Commission noted
that this went against the way the internet worked, i.e. by using links to avoid having to know the correct URL for every page. The HREOC held that discrimination
had taken place in that blind people were treated less favourably.

The HREOC looked at the defendant's claim that unjustified hardship would be
caused to it as a result of having to make changes to the website. It held that the detriment to the defendant would only be moderate, and had the issue been considered
at the planning stages, detriment would have been negligible.

Although this is an Australian case, the equivalent Australian legislation is very similar to the UK's disability discrimination legislation. The case suggests that it would
be a reasonable adjustment to make an inaccessible website accessible to disabled
people.

Blind people are the most disenfranchised, but partially sighted and dyslexic people also have problems accessing the web.

There are a number of tools available to test technical aspects of website accessibility such as W3C www.w3.org/WAI/ER/tools.

16.5   Further information

AbilityNet: www.abilitynet.org.uk.

Bookshare, a subscription service providing an online library of accessible reading materials to people with print disabilities who are visually impaired, learning disabled or physically disabled: www.bookshare.org.

CILIP has a set of web pages on disability: www.cilip.org.uk/get-involved/policy/equalopps/pages/disabilityintro.aspx.

Craven, J. (ed.) (2008) *Web Accessibility: practical advice for the library and information professional*, Facet Publishing. Also available as accessible PDF, ISBN 978-1-85604-660-2.

Directgov: www.direct.gov.uk/en/DisabledPeople/index.htm.

Equality and Human Rights Commission: www.equalityhumanrights.com.

Equality and Human Rights Commission, Code of Practice Post-16 Accessibility of websites guidance: www.equalityhumanrights.com/uploaded_files/code_of_practice_revised_for_providers_of_post-16_education_and_related_services_dda_.pdf.

Hopkins, L. (ed.) (2000) Library Service Provision for Blind and Visually-impaired People: a manual of best practice, *Library and Information Commission Research Report* 76.

JISC Techdis: www.jisctechdis.ac.uk.

MLA Disability Portfolio is a collection of 12 guides on how best to meet the needs of disabled people as users and staff in museums, archives and libraries, www.mla.gov.uk/what/support/toolkits/libraries_disability/find_out_about_disability.

MLA (2001) *The Disability Directory*, www.mla.gov.uk/what/support/toolkits/libraries_disability/choose_a_module/~/media/Files/pdf/2003/disdir.ashx.

My Web, My Way: www.bbc.co.uk/accessibility.

This BBC Accessibility website is designed to help people with disability get the most out of the web. The site equips anyone using their computer with the tools and understanding to enable them to make the most of the internet, whatever their ability or disability, and regardless of the operating system they use.

Office for Disability Issues: http://odi.dwp.gov.uk.

Owen, J. (2003) Making Your Website Accessible, *CILIP Update*, January 2003.

Publishers Licensing Society (2001) *Copyright and Visual Impairment: access to books, magazines and journals by visually impaired people*, Joint industry guidelines.

Publishers Licensing Society (2001) *Permission Requests for Visually Impaired Persons: guidelines for publisher rights owners*.

Raschen, B. (2004) Web Accessibility: ensuring access for all, http://web.freepint.com/go/newsletter/169.

Resource (2002) *Resource Disability Action Plan: achieving equality of opportunity for disabled people in museums, archives and libraries*.

Resource (2002) *Access to Museums, Archives and Libraries for Disabled Users*, toolkit to help libraries measure how accessible they are to disabled users and identify areas where improvements can be made.

RNIB Library Catalogue: http://librarycatalogue.rnib.org.uk.

Robertson, L. (2007) *Access for Library Users with Disabilities*, SCONUL, www.sconul.ac.uk/publications/pubs/access_disabilities.pdf, p. 102.

Royal National Institute for Blind People, 105 Judd Street, London WC1H 9NE, Tel.: 020 7388 1266, Fax: 020 7388 2034.

World Wide Web Consortium (2010) *W3C Authoring Tool Accessibility Guidelines Working Draft*, 8 July, www.w3.org/TR/ATAG20.

World Wide Web Consortium (2008) *Web Content Accessibility Guidelines*, www.w3.org/TR/WCAG20.

References

PLS (2011) *Print Disabled Learners*, www.pls.org.uk/services/accessibility1/default.aspx?PageView=Shared.

CHAPTER 17

Other legal issues relevant to librarians

Contents

17.1   Introduction

This chapter draws together a number of legal issues relevant to information professionals which either don't fit neatly within existing chapters because they cover more than one area of law; or else are topics which a book of this kind ought to include but which don't warrant a chapter of their own.

17.2   Police, surveillance and libraries

In 2008 CILIP undertook a *Survey on Police, Surveillance and Libraries* (CILIP, 2008). The survey had been prompted as a result of CILIP receiving a number of reports concerning increased police or other security agency activity.

Forty-one of the 55 libraries who responded to the survey mentioned a total of 134 incidents in the previous 18 months and these covered criminal activity, terrorism and pornography.

The survey found that 38% of respondents didn't have a formal policy for dealing with police requests and 13% only had a formal policy covering data protection issues.

The survey also found evidence of five 'fishing expeditions'. A number of libraries responding to the survey did not have a formal policy in place for responding to police requests. As a result, former CILIP president Margaret Watson was asked to chair a CILIP 'Task and finish' group on the subject of privacy of library users and access to information which reported back with a document entitled *User Privacy in Libraries: guidelines for the reflective practitioner* (CILIP, 2011).

In February 2011 the BBC News website ran a story 'Snooping devices found in Cheshire library computers' (BBC News, 2011) in which it said that police were investigating the discovery of snooping devices which were attached to public computers in two Cheshire libraries.

⤙ Useful resource

In 2005 CILIP sought a legal opinion on 'Rights of Access to Confidential Information'. Written by James Eadie of Blackstone Chambers, the legal opinion looked at the rights of the police and other security and intelligence services to demand access to confidential client information (www.cilip.org.uk/get-involved/advocacy/information-society/Privacy/Pages/rightsofaccess.aspx). The information in question will normally comprise names, addresses, other contact details and records of borrowing or internet usage by individual library clients.

The police have had powers to apply to court for production and removal of, or access to, material held by private persons for a number of years. The relevant powers are contained in Part II of the Police and Criminal Evidence Act 1984 (PACE). The relevant features of that statutory regime are as follows.

A police constable can apply to a circuit judge or a Justice of the Peace/magistrate for access to material under section 9 and Schedule 1 of PACE. The material in question includes 'special procedure material' which is defined in section 14 of PACE as material in the possession of a person who acquired or created it in the course of any trade, business, profession or other occupation or for the purpose of any paid or unpaid office and holds it subject to an express or implied obligation of confidence.

There are essentially five 'access conditions' that need to be established by the police to trigger the court's discretion to order access to the material according to PACE 1984 (as amended by the Serious Organised Crime and Police Act 2005):

1 An indictable offence has been committed (that is, more serious cases which are tried in the Crown Court before judge and jury rather than a magistrates' court)
2 the material is likely to be of substantial value (whether by itself or together with other material) to the investigation
3 the material is likely to be relevant evidence
4 other methods of obtaining the material have been tried and failed (or appear to be bound to fail)

5 ordering access is in the public interest having regard to the benefit likely to accrue to the investigation and to the circumstances in which the person in possession holds the information (see Schedule 1, para 2).

The orders that can be made if the access conditions are met and the judge decides to make the order (as will almost inevitably be the case if the access conditions are satisfied) are an order that the person who appears to be in possession of the material (a) produces it to the police constable for him to take it away or (b) gives the police constable access to it (Schedule 1, para 4). Specific provision is made for material stored in electronic form to be ordered to be produced in visible and legible form (Schedule 1, para 5). A failure to comply with such an order is treated as if it was a contempt of court.

Such orders usually include provisions limiting the extent to which confidentiality is breached by requiring that the material is returned as soon as the investigation or criminal proceedings are finished or it becomes apparent that the material is not of any significant value to the investigation; and that the material is only used for the purposes of the criminal investigation and any subsequent criminal proceedings.

A person holding such material is entitled to notice of the application from the police. Once he has been given such notice, the material must not be concealed, destroyed, altered or disposed of until the application has been determined unless the leave of the court or written permission from the police has been obtained.

The critical feature in any such application is likely to be whether or not it is likely to be of value to a serious criminal investigation. If it is, the likelihood is that the order will be made.

A similar regime exists under the Terrorism Act 2000 section 37 and Schedule 5 (as amended by the Terrorism Act 2006).

In addition to the powers vested ultimately in the courts (through PACE and the Terrorism Act) there are the powers set out in the RIPA. This confers powers in relation to the interception of communications and communications data (Part I) and also in relation to surveillance (Part II).

Surveillance is defined in section 48(2) as including monitoring persons' activities or communications, recording anything so monitored and surveillance by or with the assistance of a surveillance device.

Part II of RIPA applies to various types of surveillance including 'directed' surveillance (section 26(1)). Directed surveillance is defined in section 26(2) as covert surveillance (that is surveillance carried out in a manner calculated to ensure that persons subject to it are unaware that it is or may be taking place) which is undertaken for the purpose of a specific investigation or operation, in such a manner as is likely to result in the obtaining of private information about a person.

Certain persons are designated as having power to grant authorizations for carrying out directed surveillance. They are set out in the Schedule to SI 2010/521 The Regulation of Investigatory Powers (Directed Surveillance and Covert Human Intelligence Sources) Order 2010 and include senior police officers (superintendent and above) and members of the security services.

The test to be applied by the person authorizing is whether he 'believes' that the authorization is necessary on grounds falling within section 28(3) (these include necessity in the interests of national security, for the purpose of preventing or detecting crime, and in the interests of public safety and that the authorized surveillance is proportionate).

Article 8 of the ECHR (private life), which was enacted through the HRA, must be complied with by public authorities. However, even if the provision of information is an interference with private life rights of the individual concerned, Article 8 does allow interferences where these are undertaken in order to prevent crime where these are necessary and proportionate.

Looking at the legal framework and trying to establish the rights of the police to access confidential information about a library user (and the books they have borrowed or the websites that they have visited, etc.) is not straightforward because of the number of relevant statutes (PACE, RIPA, Terrorism Act). The consequence of the various legal regimes is that there may be some activities by the police or security services that fall within more than one of the regimes. In that case, it is predictable that those bodies will use the least onerous regime to achieve their aim. That is likely to involve the system of self-authorization under RIPA rather than the more onerous applications either to the Secretary of State or to the courts.

The installation of spyware is not so clear-cut. However, in the legal opinion prepared for CILIP in 2005, James Eadie's view was that the powers under RIPA and under the Intelligence Services Act 1994 are broad enough to permit the agencies concerned to insist on the installation of such spyware in an appropriate (required and proportionate) case.

17.3 Cloud computing

Cloud computing incorporates software as a service (SaaS), of which Google Docs would be one example; and also infrastructure as a service (IaaS) or hardware as a service (HaaS), of which Amazon's Elastic Compute Cloud (EC2) is an example. The common theme in cloud computing is a reliance on the internet to meet the computing needs of users.

Many library and information service managers have considered whether or not there are compelling reasons for the adoption of cloud computing or software as a service in a library setting.

In cloud computing users are able to access data, software, applications or computer processing power from a 'cloud' of online resources. There are undoubtedly significant advantages with cloud computing. For example, users are no longer tied to one particular device in order to use their data and applications but can instead access them from any device. In cloud computing the customer delegates to the service provider responsibility for keeping software up to date, secure, undertaking regular backups and managing the hardware. Although it is important to ensure that the service level agreement includes these in a way that satisfies your requirements. Meanwhile, organizations are able to reduce their capital costs by purchasing software and hardware as a utility service.

There are, however, a number of important legal issues which should be factored into any plans to adopt cloud computing. What would happen, for example, if you encountered a series of service disruptions? Or what if your data was the subject of a malicious attack from an internet hacker? In the light of these concerns, organizations want assurances in the form of legal guarantees from SaaS or IaaS providers. These assurances are encapsulated within service level agreements which spell out the extent of any guarantees (in the form of warranties and indemnities) with regard to service availability, security, and privacy.

Problems can occur even with big-name companies offering cloud-computing services. For example in April 2011 Amazon had to apologize when its web hosting service EC2 suffered an outage which led to a number of well known websites going offline, some for a number of days.

It is important, therefore, to make sure that the service level agreement you have with a vendor covers the following points to your satisfaction:

- availability of the service
- service response times
- problem resolution times
- consequences of missing service level commitments.

In the traditional model for the purchase of software, the customer installs that software on locally held hardware. But in cloud computing, everything is held remotely. Both the software application and the firm's proprietary data are held outside the organization's firewall; and there are significant risks associated with such an arrangement. What would happen if the service provider goes into administration? Or what if the service provider is acquired by a larger company, which subsequently decides that it no longer wishes to support the SaaS solution that you use? These problems can be resolved by the customer taking out an escrow agreement.

17.3.1 Escrow agreements

A technology escrow agreement drafted for cloud computing would require the service provider to deposit their source code and related materials with a neutral third party. Then, if release conditions are triggered – such as the service provider going into administration – the customer would be able to gain access to the application, to their own proprietary data, and also to the intellectual property which supports the SaaS solution.

17.3.2 Data protection issues

Cloud computing raises a number of data protection issues. For example, the eighth data protection principle states that: 'Personal data shall not be transferred to a country or territory outside the European Economic Area, unless that country or territory ensures an adequate level of protection for the rights and freedoms of data subjects in relation to the processing of personal data.' Where a company makes use of cloud computing, does it make clear to everyone where the customer data is being held? Some contracts specify that the data will not be transferred to any countries or territories outside the EEA.

Then there is the question of data security. Is there any possibility, for example, that a competitor also using the service could see your data? The seventh data protection principle states that: 'Appropriate technical and organisational measures shall be taken against unauthorised or unlawful processing of personal data and against accidental loss or destruction of, or damage to, personal data.'

Before organizations decide to make use of cloud computing they need to ask whether it is right for them, or whether the risks outweigh the undoubted advantages. If people do ultimately decide to go ahead with cloud computing, they should only do so after undertaking a risk assessment, and where appropriate put in place strategies – such as the use of a technology escrow agreement – to minimize the risks that they have identified. They should also undertake vendor due diligence, visiting reference sites of existing customers and checking the financial history and strength of the company.

Key priorities when selecting a vendor include privacy and security, quality of service and performance, flexibility, scalability and resilience to failure. Cloud computing is a new area and as a result it will be a while before a body of case law has developed, which means that in the meantime the legal position is somewhat unclear. A checklist for cloud computing contracts and service level agreements is provided in Figure 17.1.

17.4   Stocking extremist/controversial literature

Stock selection is subject to a range of laws. Whilst individual librarians could use their personal judgement in deciding which law is applicable, this could lead to them minimizing risk by not stocking books which might be regarded as controversial, extremist or inflammatory.

> Is personal data being processed?
> Who is the data controller?
> Who is the data processor?
> Who can see my information?
> Is the data held securely?
> Where is customer data held?
> Is the data exported to a country which doesn't have adequate data protection laws?
> What happens if the supplier goes into administration?
> What if the supplier stops providing an SaaS solution?
> What if the data is subject to a malicious attack?
> What happens if there is a service disruption?
> Who is responsible if an illegality occurs (such as copyright infringement, defamation, race hate materials, incitement to terrorism)?
> What is the jurisdiction/applicable law specified in the contract?
> Who owns copyright/database right in the data in the cloud?
> Who is responsible if the data gets corrupted?

Figure 17.1 *Cloud computing contract and service level agreement checklist*

Indeed, Human Rights Watch warned in their 2007 report (Human Rights Watch, 2007) that the 'War on Terror' poses a growing threat to free expression: 'Counter terrorism has given new vigour to some old forms of censorship and created new ones.'

A report by the think tank the Centre for Social Cohesion entitled *Hate on the State: how British libraries encourage Islamic extremism* (Brandon and Murray, 2007) claimed that public libraries have been inundated by extremist Islamic literature, and that many of these books glorify acts of terrorism against followers of other religions, incite violence against anyone who rejects jihadist ideologies, and endorse violence and discrimination against women.

In November 2007 the government commissioned the MLA to produce guidance for public libraries on the management of extremist and inflammatory material. They subsequently developed guidance on the stocking of extremist material.

➼ Useful resource

Guidance on the management of controversial material in public libraries, 2009, MLA: www.mla.gov.uk/what/support/guidance/~/media/ B4414D2012F5437CAF13939D5C904BAE.ashx.

Section 1 of the Terrorism Act 2006 makes the encouragement of terrorism an offence. This section makes it an offence for a person to publish a statement to which the section applies, or causes another to publish such a statement. By providing library users with computers that have internet access, for example, they could be said to be 'publishing' statements; and, further, if they allowed library users access to 'terrorist' sites that could be construed as being 'reckless'.

Section 2 of the Terrorism Act 2006 makes the dissemination of terrorist publications an offence. Librarians could potentially be found guilty of providing access to terrorist material under section 2 if it was proved that they did so as the result of both a guilty act (such as loaning a terrorist publication, distributing or circulating it, providing a service which enables a person to obtain, read, listen to or look at such a publication or transmits the contents of such a publication electronically) and a guilty mind (the intention to encourage or induce an act of terrorism). The sentence for this offence is imprisonment for a maximum of seven years and/or a fine. Librarians run a greater risk of committing the section 2 offence (dissemination of terrorist publications) than they do the section 1 offence (encouragement of terrorism).

Offences under the Terrorism Act 2006 can be committed by the library authority as a 'body corporate' if the offence is committed with the consent or connivance of a director, manager, secretary or other similar officer of the body corporate. Both this individual and the body corporate would be guilty of the offence.

Library and information professionals who are involved in the decision-making process as to which publications to purchase could also be found guilty of an offence, whether or not the library authority as a body corporate is liable.

A librarian would have a defence against both the section 1 and the section 2 offences if the terrorist publication or statement did not express their views or have their endorsement, and it was clear in all the circumstances that it did not.

In the case of the section 2 offence, the defence is not available if the publication in question is of the type that might be useful in the commission or preparation of terrorist acts. So, for example, a book glorifying a historical act of terrorism might be covered by the defence whilst an instruction manual on how to make a device would not.

The definition of 'publication' in the Act includes matter to be read, listened to, looked at or watched. It isn't just books, and it includes matter that is likely either to be understood as a direct or indirect encouragement or inducement to commit, prepare or instigate terrorist acts; or else to be useful to those ends and to be understood as such.

The question of whether a publication is a terrorist publication would be determined based on the facts of the individual case which would be determined at the time and in the circumstances in which it is disseminated, and with regard to the contents of the publication as a whole. In order for a librarian to have committed the offence of disseminating terrorist publications, it would need to be shown that they intended the dissemination of the publication(s) to encourage, induce or assist in acts of terrorism or that they had been reckless as to whether it has such an effect.

In this context, 'recklessness' means taking an unreasonable risk of which the risk-taker is aware. It is not the same as carelessness or negligence.

Librarians could potentially be served with what is known as a 'section 3 notice'. It is a declaration by a police constable that the statement, article or record is unlawfully related to terrorism and, when the notice is issued, the person to whom it is addressed must stop making the matter available to the public within two working days (for example, block an offending website), or modify it so it complies with the Act.

> If served with a section 3 notice, it is imperative for librarians to comply within the two-working-day period otherwise they will be deemed to have endorsed the matter in question.

It is a criminal offence under section 58 of the Terrorism Act 2006 to collect or make a record of information of a kind likely to be useful to a person committing or preparing an act of terrorism; or even to possess such a document or record. This would include a photographic or electronic record.

An individual who does so will have a defence if they can show that there was a reasonable excuse for the action or possession insomuch as the information is possessed for a purpose other than to assist in the commission or preparation of an act of terrorism (see, for example, R v. K [2008] EWCA Crim 185) (www.bailii.org/ew/cases/EWCA/Crim/2008/185.html).

17.5   Theft or mutilation of rare books

There have been numerous examples of rare books being stolen or damaged by library users or even by members of library staff. In one instance the judge said that the thief was relying on the reluctance of library staff to challenge people when they were used to dealing with people whom they could trust.

> Libraries need to have a security policy in place so that staff can feel confident that their actions are in accordance with the official policy. The policy statement should include the appropriate actions that will be taken against borrowers who are caught attempting to steal books.

Checklist
Deterrance
- Libraries should implement regular checks of their library materials.
- Libraries should mark special collection titles with an indelible mark of ownership or accession.

What to do where theft has taken place

- referral to the police
- warning letters
- temporary bans
- permanent bans
- preventing the resale of stolen material (add to the Antiquarian Booksellers Association list of stolen books at www.abainternational.com and the Art Loss Register, on the request of insurers).

17.5.1 Examples of theft by library users

- Farhad Hakimzadeh was given a two-year sentence for cutting and stealing pages from antiquarian books in the British and Bodleian libraries over seven years (January 2009).
- William Simon Jacques was jailed for four years for stealing rare and ancient books worth £1 million from the British Library. Jacques was 'relying on the reluctance of library staff to challenge people' (see Telegraph, 2010) when they were used to dealing with members of the public whom they could trust, the judge said.
- Edward Forbes Smiley III admitted stealing 97 maps worth US$3 million from major institutions, including the British Library, and was sentenced to three-and-a-half years' imprisonment (September 2006).

17.5.2 Examples of theft by library staff

- Norman Buckley worked as a library assistant at Manchester Central Library. He stole rare books valued at £175,000, selling some of them on eBay. He was sentenced to 15 months in prison, suspended for two years (2006). A spokesman for Manchester City Council said that a thorough review of security measures at the central library had been carried out and further actions taken to ensure the security of the collections (see Times, 2006).

⊷ Useful resource

LIBER: the Association of European Research Libraries (www.libereurope.eu) has a security network which is a forum for advice to members on protection against theft and on confidential reporting of both actual theft and suspicious activity.

17.6   Public lending and e-books

In July 2009 the DCMS issued a *Consultation on the Extension of Public Lending Right to Rights Holders of Books in Non-Print Formats* which sought views on policy proposals to:

- extend eligibility for Public Lending Right (PLR) to non-print books, in particular audiobooks and e-books;
- extend PLR to the lending rights holders in respect of these non-print works where they are not currently eligible under the PLR Scheme.

Expanding the PLR Scheme to include new types of works and new types of rights holders would require a consequential expansion to the 'infringement exemption' under the 1988 CDPA and would thus remove the possibility of enforcement of lending rights by rights holders against lending libraries for newly eligible works; i.e. it would remove the need for libraries to obtain consent for lending of the newly eligible works. In exchange for this expanded 'exemption', the Scheme would remunerate rights holders who registered with the Scheme.

The proposals in the consultation paper would have extended the categories of publications eligible for PLR to include non-print books – i.e. works primarily based on an authored text – whether experienced aurally or visually. This includes:

- hard-copy audiobooks, primarily CDs
- soft-copy audiobooks, such as digital audio files (e.g. MP3) provided to a library user either as a download, for licensed short-term access or loaded on appropriate hardware (e.g. MP3 player)
- e-books – digital files as above, but to be read rather than heard. This may include image-based, as well as text-based, books such as graphic novels.

In November 2009, the DCMS published the government response to the consultation, in which it said that the government believe it is important to extend PLR to non-print formats, to:

- keep libraries relevant to users in the digital age
- reward authors and creators.

At the time the government expressed an intention to extend PLR to digital files but said that remote downloads (files downloaded outside library premises) won't be eligible for PLR payment. The policy was for PLR to be extended to all rights holders and for PLR to be paid on the basis of one loan to one reader at one time.

It led to the inclusion of section 43 in the Digital Economy Act 2010. If enacted, section 43 would mean the extension of PLR to cover books, audio books and e-books.

It does not look as though PLR will be extended to audio books and e-books in the short term. The provision in the Digital Economy Act 2010 can only come into force when the Secretary of State makes the relevant statutory instrument. Since the Act was passed there has been a change of government (in May 2010), and the extension of PLR was one of the early casualties of the Coalition Government's cost cutting measures.

A press notice from the DCMS of 17 June 2010 (DCMS, 2010) said:

> The Government has decided not to pursue the £2 million (per annum) spending commitments set out in the Public Library Modernisation Review Policy statement published in March 2010. These were free internet access in all libraries and to promote library membership as an entitlement from birth. It also included extending the Public Lending Right to non-print format books, estimated at £300,000.

The lending of e-books is currently governed by contract law. Many libraries use the e-book and audiobook distributor OverDrive (www.overdrive.com). In February 2011, Overdrive notified customers of a change in the licensing terms for one particular publisher which turned out to be HarperCollins who were planning to limit the purchase of their e-books to 26 checkouts, after which the e-book would expire unless libraries paid an additional fee in order to re-license the title.

In October 2010, the PA set out a position statement on library e-book lending which claimed that 'untrammelled' remote lending of digital books could pose a 'serious threat' to publishers' commercial activities. As a result they announced a clampdown, informing libraries they may have to stop allowing users to download e-books remotely and instead require them to come to the library premises, just as they do to get traditional print books – arguably defeating the object of the e-reading concept.

17.7   Statutory duty of local authorities to provide a comprehensive library service

The Public Libraries and Museums Act 1964 places a statutory duty on local authorities to provide comprehensive and efficient library services, and allows the Secretary of State to monitor and inspect library services:

> Section 7(1): 'It shall be the duty of every library authority to provide a comprehensive and efficient library service for all persons desiring to make use thereof'. Section 7(1) goes on to make clear that this duty only extends to people living, working or being educated within the area.

> Section 7(2)(a) sets out a specific duty to provide a sufficient number, range and quality of books (and other library materials) to meet the needs of adults and children 'by the keeping of adequate stocks, by arrangements with other library authorities, and by any other appropriate means, that facilities are available for

the borrowing of, or reference to, books and other printed matter, and pictures, gramophone records, films and other materials, sufficient in number, range and quality to meet the general requirements and any special requirements both of adults and children'.

If local residents want their library to stock particular literature, the library may be bound to do so in order to ensure a 'comprehensive' service.

R v. London Borough of Ealing and others *ex parte* Times Newspapers Ltd and others (1987) 85 LGR 316

The decision of several libraries to ban *The Times* on political grounds (specifically, in support of print workers in an industrial dispute) was held to be an unlawful abuse of the libraries' powers granted under the 1964 Act.

The actions of the three councils were successfully challenged in the courts. The ulterior political motive of the local authorities in refusing to stock News International titles was irrelevant to their statutory duty to provide 'a comprehensive and efficient library service'; and was deemed to be an abuse of their statutory powers.

In November 2011 the High Court ruled that proposed library closures in Somerset and Gloucestershire were unlawful. In the judicial review R. (Green) v. Gloucestershire County Council and R. (Rowe & Hird) v. Somerset County Council ([2011] EWHC 2687 (Admin)) the court held that both Gloucestershire and Somerset councils had failed to take account of their equalities duties towards vulnerable members of society such as the elderly, poor, or disabled.

In March 2011 the Department for Communities and Local Government (DCLG) launched a *Review of Statutory Duties Placed on Local Government* in which respondents were invited to comment on the duties and to challenge government on those which they felt were burdensome or no longer needed.

The consultation process ran until April 2011. In it the DCLG identified 1,294 statutory duties that central government places on local authorities, inviting people to comment on what duties are vital to keep, what duties should be repealed, and what burdens have been created through particular duties and associated regulations and guidance.

Three of the 1,294 statutory duties apply to public library services in England. All three of these duties are held by the DCMS under the Public Libraries and Museums Act 1964. The Act requires local authorities to provide a public library service which is comprehensive and efficient, and available to all who wish to use it; and it also gives the Secretary of State the right to gather information and inspect library services.

At an MPs' debate on the 28 February 2011, Minister for Culture, Communications and Creative Industries Ed Vaizey said that there were no plans to repeal the statutory provision of libraries under the Act: 'The statutory duty remains a very important safety net for the provision of libraries.' (Hansard, 2011).

The three duties under review that apply to public library services (under the 1964 Public Libraries and Museums Act) were:

1 Legislation: Public Libraries and Museums Act 1964 Section 1(2).
   Title: To provide information and facilities for the inspection of library premises, stocks, records, as the Secretary of State requires.
   Function: Necessary for Secretary of State to fulfil duty to superintend library service.
2 Legislation: Public Libraries and Museums Act 1964 Section 7.
   Title: To provide a comprehensive and efficient library service.
   Function: Secure provision of local library services.
3 Legislation: Public Libraries and Museums Act 1964 Section 11.
   Title: Supplemental provisions as to transfers of officers, assets and liabilities.
   Function: Provisions provide, for example, continuity of employment for transferring employees. This secures consistency across library transfers, etc. and in line with other local authority employment legislation.

In 'Summary of the review of statutory duties placed on local government' (2011) (www.communities.gov.uk/documents/localgovernment/pdf/l934356.pdf), DCLG said that the Review received over 6000 responses covering the breadth of interests from local authorities, individuals, groups and the private sector. In the summary of responses document, DCLG said that there was 'considerable interest in retaining those requirements around services for disabled children, libraries and the provision of allotments. The Government has made specific announcements on these areas of concern and confirmed that it is not the intention of the Government to remove the duties which protect such services'.

17.8   Further information
Police, surveillance and libraries
Hyams, E. (2007) Preserving Users' Privacy in Spite of Surveillance, *CILIP Update*, October, 26.

Cloud computing
Marchini, R. (2010) *Cloud Computing: a practical introduction to the legal issues*, BSi.

Stocking controversial literature

Brandon, J. and Murray, D. (2007) *Hate on the State: how British libraries encourage Islamic extremism*, Centre for Social Cohesion, www.socialcohesion.co.uk/files/1229624470_1.pdf.

CILIP Update (2006) A Very British Campaign: challenging the Terrorism Bill, July/August, 22–3.

Magi, T.J. (2006) *Protecting Library Patron Confidentiality: checklist of best practices*, www.aallnet.org/products/pub_sp0709/pub_sp0709_Handout.pdf.

MLA (2009) *Guidance on the Management of Controversial Material in Public Libraries*, www.mla.gov.uk/what/support/guidance/~/media/ B4414D2012F5437CAF13939D5C904BAE.ashx.

Theft or mutilation of rare books

Burrows, J. and Cooper, D. (1992) *Theft of Books and Manuscripts from Libraries: an advisory code of conduct for booksellers and librarians*, Home Office.

McCree, M. (2000) *Theft in the Public Library: an investigation into levels of theft and the impact it has on both services and staff*, http://dagda.shef.ac.uk/dissertations/1999-00/mccree.pdf.

The Times (2006) Thieving Library Staff Take a Love of Rare Books Too Far, 24 November.

Public lending and e-books

DCMS (2009) *Consultation on the Extension of Public Lending Right to Rights Holders of Books in Non-Print Formats*, www.dcms.gov.uk/reference_library/consultations/6283.aspx.

DCMS (2009) *Government Response to the Consultation on the Extension of Public Lending Right to Rights Holders of Books in Non-Print Formats*, http://webarchive.nationalarchives.gov.uk/+/ www.culture.gov.uk/images/publications/PLR_nonprint_books_government_ response.pdf.

References

BBC News (2011) Snooping Devices Found in Cheshire Library Computers, www.bbc.co.uk/news/uk-england-manchester-12396799.

Brandon, J. and Murray, D. (2007) *Hate on the State: how British libraries encourage Islamic extremism*, Centre for Social Cohesion, www.socialcohesion.co.uk/files/1229624470_1.pdf.

CILIP (2008) *Survey on Police, Surveillance and Libraries*, www.cilip.org.uk/sitecollectiondocuments/PDFs/policyadvocacy/ CILIPPSLSurveyresultspublicjul08.pdf.

CILIP (2011) *User Privacy in Libraries: guidelines for the reflective practitioner*,
www.cilip.org.uk/get-involved/advocacy/information-society/privacy/
pages/privacy-guidelines.aspx.

DCMS (2010) press release,
www.culture.gov.uk/news/media_releases/7191.aspx.

Hansard (2011) *Hansard*, 28 February 2011,
www.publications.parliament.uk/pa/cm201011/cmhansrd/cm110228/debtext/
110228-0004.htm#1103012000380.

Human Rights Watch (2007) Report,
www.hrw.org/sites/default/files/reports/wr2007master.pdf.

Telegraph (2010) Serial Book Thief William Jacques Jailed for Three Years, *The
Telegraph*, 20 July 2010,
www.telegraph.co.uk/culture/books/7900548/William-Jacques-Britains-most-
prolific-book-thief.html.

Times (2006) Librarian Sold Stolen Books on eBay, *The Times*, 26 October 2006,
www.timesonline.co.uk/tol/news/uk/crime/article613813.ece.

Further reading

Armstrong, C. and Bebbington, L. (eds) (2003) *Staying Legal: a guide to issues and practices affecting the library, information and publishing sectors*, 2nd edn, Facet Publishing, ISBN 978-1-85604-438-7.

Banks, D. and Hanna, M. (2009) *McNae's Essential Law for Journalists*, 20th edn, Oxford University Press.

Bayley, E. (2009) *The Clicks That Bind: ways users 'agree' to online terms of service*, Electronic Frontier Foundation, www.eff.org/wp/clicks-bind-ways-users-agree-online-terms-service.

Birkinshaw, P. (2010) *Freedom of Information: the law, the practice and the ideal*, 4th edn, Cambridge University Press.

BSI. *Guide to Freedom of Information*, ISBN 0-580-4476-2.

Carey, P. (2004) *Data Protection: a practical guide to UK and EU law*, Oxford University Press.

Carey, P. (2007) *Media Law*, 4th edn, Sweet & Maxwell.

Charlesworth, A. (2009) *Digital Lives: legal and ethical issues*, British Library.

Christie, A. and Gare, S. (2010) *Blackstone's Statutes on Intellectual Property*, 10th edn, Oxford University Press.

CILIP (2005) *A Safe Place for Children*, [accessible to members only], www.cilip.org.uk/get-involved/special-interest-groups/youth/publications/children/pages/safeplaceforchildren.aspx

CILIP (2009) *Ethical Principles and Code of Professional Practice for Library and Information Professionals*, www.cilip.org.uk/get-involved/policy/ethics/pages/principles.aspx.

Clark, C. (ed.) (1990) *Photocopying From Books and Journals: a guide for all users of copyright and literary works*, British Copyright Council.

Collins, M. (2005) *The Law of Defamation and the Internet*, 2nd edn, Oxford University Press.

Consumers International (2001) Privacy@net: international comparative study of consumer privacy on the internet, www.consumersinternational.org/news-and-media/publications/privacy@net-an-international-comparative-study-of-consumer-privacy-on-the-internet.

Cornish, G.P. (2009). *Copyright: interpreting the law for libraries, archives and information services*, 5th edn, Facet Publishing, ISBN 978-1-85604-664-0.

Department of Trade and Industry (2005) DTI consultation document on the Electronic Commerce Directive: the liability of hyperlinkers, location tool services and content aggregators, www.bis.gov.uk/files/file13986.pdf.

Durrant, F. (2006) *Negotiating Licences for Digital Resources*, Facet Publishing, ISBN 978-1-85604-586-5.

EIRENE (European Information Researchers Network) (1993) *Code of Practice for Information Brokers*, www.jiscmail.ac.uk/cgi-bin/webadmin?A2=LIS-UKEIG;df511604.99.

European Commission (2000) *Data Protection in the European Union* [PF-39-99-008-EN-V-C].

Experian (no date) *A Simplified Guide to the Data Protection Act 1998*, www.uk.experian.com/e-consumerview/samples/databk.pdf.

Hales, A. and Atwell, B. (2012) *The No-Nonsense Guide to Copyright in All Media*, Facet Publishing, ISBN 978-1-85604-764-7.

Healey, P. D. (2008) *Professional Liability Issues for Librarians and Information Professionals*, Neal-Schuman.

Korn, N. and Oppenheim, C. (2012) *The No-Nonsense Guide to Digital Content and Licensing*, Facet Publishing, ISBN 978-1-85604-805-7.

Law Commission (2001) *Electronic Commerce: formal requirements in commercial transactions*.

Law Commission (2002) *Defamation and the Internet: a preliminary investigation*, Scoping Study no. 2, www.justice.gov.uk/lawcommission/docs/Defamation_and_the_Internet_Scoping.pdf.

Library Association (1995) *The Library Association Code of Professional Conduct and Guidance Notes*, 2nd edn.

Lloyd, I. (2000) *Legal Aspects of the Information Society*, Butterworths.

Lloyd, I. (2004) *Information Technology Law*, 4th edn, LexisNexis.

Lloyd, I. J. and Simpson, M. (1995) *Law on the Electronic Frontier*, Hume Papers on Public Policy Volume 2 No. 4.

Marett, P. (2002) *Information Law in Practice*, Ashgate.

McLeod, T. and Cooling, P. (1990) *Law for Librarians: a handbook for librarians in England and Wales*, Library Association Publishing.

McKilligan, N. and Powell, N. (2009) *Data Protection Pocket Guide: essential facts at your fingertips*, BSI, 2nd edn.

Moore, A.D. (ed.) (2005). *Information Ethics: privacy, property and power*, University of Washington Press.

National Archives (2008) *Guidance – Freedom of Information Publication Schemes: Number 19*, rev. edn., www.nationalarchives.gov.uk/documents/information-management/freedom-of-information-publication-schemes.pdf.

Norman, S. (2004) *Practical Copyright for Information Professionals: the CILIP Handbook*, Facet Publishing, ISBN 978-1-85604-490-4.

Ofcom (2010) *Online infringement of copyright and the Digital Economy Act: draft initial obligations code*,
http://stakeholders.ofcom.org.uk/consultations/copyright-infringement.

Oppenheim, C. (2001), *The Legal and Regulatory Environment for Electronic Information*, 4th edn, Infonortics.

Oppenheim, C. and Korn, N. (2012) *The No-Nonsense Guide to Legal Issues in Web 2.0 and Cloud Computing*, Facet Publishing, ISBN 978-1-85604-0.

Oppenheim, C. and Muir, A. (2001) Report on Developments World-Wide on National Information Policy Prepared for Resource and The Library Association.

Padfield, T. (2010) *Copyright for Archivists and Users of Archives*, 4th edn, Facet Publishing, ISBN 978-1-85604-705-0.

Pedley, P. (ed.) (2005) *Managing Digital Rights: a practitioner's guide*, Facet Publishing, ISBN 978-1-85604-544-5.

Pedley, P. (2007) *Digital Copyright*, 2nd edn, Facet Publishing, ISBN 978-1-85604-608-4.

Pedley, P. (2008) *Copyright Compliance: practical steps to stay within the law*, Facet Publishing, ISBN 978-1-85604-640-4.

Schulz, C. and Baumgartner, J. (2001) *Don't Panic! Do E-commerce: a beginner's guide to European law affecting e-commerce*, European Commission Electronic Commerce Team.

Sherman, B. and Bently, L. (2008) *Intellectual Property Law*, 3rd edn, Oxford University Press.

Singleton, S. (2003) *eCommerce: a practical guide to the law*, rev. edn. Gower.

Smith, G. (2002) *Internet Law and Regulation*, 3rd edn, Sweet & Maxwell.

Society of Authors (1997) Copyright in Artistic Works, Including Photographs.

Society of Authors (1999) Your Copyrights After Your Death.

Society of Authors (2000) Libel, Privacy and Confidentiality.

Society of Authors (2009) Quick Guide to Copyright and Moral Rights.

Society of Authors (2009) Quick Guide to Permissions. (These are on the website but, as they are only available to members for free, I don't have the url for the place behind the paywall for them – see www.societyofauthors.org/guides-and-articles).

Tambini, D. (2002) *Ruled by Recluses? Privacy, journalism and the media after the Human Rights Act*, Institute for Public Policy Research.

Ticher, P. (2001) *Data Protection for Library and Information Services*, Aslib.

Torrans, L.A. (2004) *Law and Libraries: the public library*, Libraries Unlimited.

Upshall, Michael (2009) *Content Licensing: buying and selling digital resources*, Chandos.

Index

Copyright Compliance
Practical steps to stay within the law
Paul Pedley
This is something to disappoint the litigation lawyers: 'Copyright
Compliance: practical steps to stay within the law' is the title of a very
useful work...this book is certainly up-to-date and refreshingly
direct...Well done! – iPkAT
Quite frankly, the price of this book in comparison to the detriment to
an organisation for non-compliance of copyright law is minimal. –
legAl inForMATion MAnAgeMenT
This practical book aims to promote the understanding of copyright
compliance by users, and to simplify the task of library and information
professionals in advising on it. Fully supported by examples of case law, the
text is divided into two main parts. The first part considers what constitutes
an infringement of copyright, and what happens when things go wrong. The
second part deals with how to stay within the law, and what one can do
proactively to minimize the risks associated with copyright infringement.
2008; 176pp; hardback; 978-1-85604-640-4; £54.95